KNOWLEDGE IN ENGLISH

Focusing on a key area of debate within the world of secondary English, the 'knowledge-based curriculum', this book explores in detail the question of knowledge in the teaching of English in secondary schools, drawing on specific concrete cases and a range of academic theories. *Knowledge in English* also investigates how to teach both facts and skills through the required texts to produce a balanced educational experience.

Elliott brings together classic texts with contemporary knowledge and viewpoints to critically examine teaching in the English Literature classroom, and situates them within the broader cultural and political context. The book includes discussions on race and gender in texts, Shakespeare and his influence, facts and emotions in poetry, and reading experiences.

Knowledge in English is a foundational and accessible guide for researchers, practitioners, teacher educators and teachers around the world. It is a valuable resource for those involved in the English curriculum to keep the subject relevant and useful to students in the contemporary classroom.

Victoria Elliott is Associate Professor of English and Literacy Education at the University of Oxford, UK.

NATIONAL ASSOCIATION FOR THE TEACHING OF ENGLISH (NATE)

The National Association for the Teaching of English (NATE), founded in 1963, is the professional body for all teachers of English from primary to Post-16. Through its regions, committees and conferences, the association draws on the work of classroom practitioners, advisers, consultants, teacher trainers, academics and researchers to promote dynamic and progressive approaches to the subject by means of debate, training and publications. NATE is a charity reliant on membership subscriptions. If you teach English in any capacity, please visit **www.nate.org.uk** and consider joining NATE, so the association can continue its work and give teachers of English and the subject a strong voice nationally.

This series of books co-published with NATE reflects the organisation's dedication to promoting standards of excellence in the teaching of English, from early years through to university level. Titles in this series promote innovative and original ideas that have practical classroom outcomes and support teachers' own professional development.

Books in the NATE series include both pupil and classroom resources and academic research aimed at English teachers, students on PGCE/ITT courses and NQTs.

Titles in this series include:

Unlocking Poetry (CD-ROM)
An Inspirational Resource for Teaching GCSE Literature
Trevor Millum and Chris Warren

Teaching English Language
A comprehensive guide for teachers of AS/A2 level English Languages
Martin Illingworth and Nick Hall

Teaching English Literature 16–19
An essential guide
Carol Atherton, Andrew Green and Gary Snapper

International Perspectives on Teaching English in a Globalised World
Andrew Goodwyn, Louann Reid and Cal Durrant

Teaching Caribbean Poetry
Edited by Beverley Bryan and Morag Styles

Sharing not Staring, 2nd Edition
21 interactive whiteboard lessons for the English classroom
Trevor Millum and Chris Warren

Teaching Grammar Structure and Meaning
Exploring theory and practice for post-16 English Language teachers
Marcello Giovanelli

Researching and Teaching Reading
Developing pedagogy through critical enquiry
Gabrielle Cliff Hodges

Creative Approaches to Teaching Grammar
Developing your students as writers and readers
Martin Illingworth and Nick Hall

Introducing Teacher's Writing Groups
Exploring the theory and practice
Jenifer Smith and Simon Wrigley

Knowing about Language
Linguistics and the secondary English classroom
Edited by Marcello Giovanelli and Dan Clayton

English and its Teachers
A History of Policy, Pedagogy and Practice
Simon Gibbons

International Perspectives on the Teaching of Literature in Schools
Global Principles and Practices
Edited by Andrew Goodwyn, Cal Durrant, Louann Reid and Lisa Scherff

Students, Places, and Identities in English and the Arts
Creative Spaces in Education
Edited by David Stevens and Karen Lockney

The Future of English Teaching Worldwide
Celebrating 50 Years From the Dartmouth Conference
Andrew Goodwyn, Cal Durrant, Wayne Sawyer, Lisa Scherff, and Don Zancanella

Teaching English Language 16–19, 2nd edition
A Comprehensive Guide for Teachers of AS and A Level English Language
Martin Illingworth and Nick Hall

Teaching English Language and Literature 16–19
Edited by Furzeen Ahmed, Marcello Giovanelli, Megan Mansworth and Felicity Titjen

Knowledge in English
Canon, Curriculum and Cultural Literacy
Velda Elliott

For more information about this series, please visit: https://www.routledge.com/National-Association-for-the-Teaching-of-English-NATE/book-series/NATE

KNOWLEDGE IN ENGLISH

Canon, Curriculum and Cultural Literacy

Victoria Elliott

Routledge
Taylor & Francis Group

LONDON AND NEW YORK

First published 2021
by Routledge
2 Park Square, Milton Park, Abingdon, Oxon OX14 4RN

and by Routledge
52 Vanderbilt Avenue, New York, NY 10017

Routledge is an imprint of the Taylor & Francis Group, an informa business

© 2021 Victoria Elliott

The right of Victoria Elliott to be identified as author of this work has been
asserted by her in accordance with sections 77 and 78 of the Copyright, Designs
and Patents Act 1988.

First edition published 2021

British Library Cataloguing in Publication Data
A catalogue record for this book is available from the British Library

Library of Congress Cataloging-in-Publication Data
A catalog record has been requested for this book

ISBN: 978-0-367-35417-6 (hbk)
ISBN: 978-0-367-35420-6 (pbk)
ISBN: 978-0-429-33127-5 (ebk)

Typeset in Bembo
by Taylor & Francis Books

Dedication: This is for Mrs Gadd, without whom I would never have studied English Literature and never have become an English teacher; who, when I told her I wanted to write, told me not to write Mills & Boon; and who wrote on my Year 9 report, 'Victoria makes an excellent Sir Toby Belch.' Gutted.

CONTENTS

TABLES

ACKNOWLEDGEMENTS

There are many people who have supported and shaped my thinking and who have enabled me to rant at them. I would like to thank Chris Aspinall, my husband, who listens and argues, and reads (almost) without complaint, and also kept our son, Harry, occupied during the spring and summer of 2020 when I wrote most of this manuscript. My colleagues Nicole Dingwall, Lesley Nelson-Addy, Gary Snapper and Ian Thompson, and my DPhil student and friend Paul Riser have all contributed to the vibrant English atmosphere at Oxford Department of Education and had enthusiastic conversations about our mutual subject. All the English interns over the years have been influential on my thinking; I have particularly benefited from conversations with Joseph La Porte and Geraint Davies on reading, which is shown in Chapter 3. Beth Borne, SJ Cooper-Knock, Kat Howard, Stephanie Palmer, Nikki Fine, Paul Riser, Nicole Dingwall and Geraldine Hale all kindly read chapters and commented, which has made the book stronger. Ashmita Randhawa tracked down where I had read about the Implicit Association Test. Chris proofread the entire draft manuscript, which is beyond the requirements of spousal duty. All mistakes remain my own. I would also like to acknowledge the broader English community of the National Association for the Teaching of English and the English and Media Centre who have all been influential in one way or another: John Hodgson, Gary (again), Sue Dymoke, Marcello Giovanelli, Jess Mason and Barbara Bleiman, to name but a few.

1

INTRODUCTION

The 'knowledge turn' and 'facts' in English

In recent years the curriculum in England, and more broadly, has been undergoing a 'knowledge turn' (Lambert, 2011) – a shift towards a focus on knowledge over skills and preparing workers for the 'knowledge economy' (Lauder et al., 2012) – which has reached its peak in the reform of the English schools inspectorate's framework for inspection. Ofsted is now most interested in curriculum and in the provision of knowledge to students. 'The end result of a good, well-taught curriculum is that pupils know more and are able to do more' (Ofsted, 2019a, p. 3).

'Knowledge' is a difficult beast. It feels as if it should be simple, but in taking a simplistic route we may trip ourselves up over the difference between 'information' and 'knowledge', or dismiss as 'skills' things which are also forms of knowledge. Philosopher A. J. Ayer, in his book *The Problem of Knowledge*, starts by considering the meanings of the verb 'to know' in a familiar opening gambit from the sixth form essay – defining terms from the dictionary:

A glance at the dictionary will show that the verb 'to know' is used in a variety of ways. We can speak of knowing, in the sense of being familiar with, a person or a place, of knowing something in the sense of having had experience of it, as when someone says that he has known hunger or fear, of knowing in the sense of being able to recognize or distinguish, as when we claim to know an honest man when we see one or to know butter from margarine. I may be said to know my Dickens, if I have read, remember, and can perhaps also quote his writings, to know a subject such as trigonometry, if I have mastered it, to know how to swim or drive a car, to know how to behave myself. Most important of all, perhaps, are the uses for which the dictionary gives the definition of 'to be aware or apprised of', 'to apprehend or comprehend as fact or truth', the sense, or senses in which to have knowledge is to know that something or other is the case.

(Ayer, 1956/1990, p. 8)

The usage of 'knowledge' in the knowledge turn in education in recent years is primarily in the last form Ayer notes, to 'know that'. To 'know how' in particular has been denigrated as mere skill, although there has also been quite reasonable discussion that to exercise skill one must also have knowledge. The corollary, that to exercise knowledge one must also have skill, has not been widely considered. As far as I am concerned, it is a strawman to say that so-called 'progressives' only wish to teach skills without any knowledge; to write an essay takes skill and knowledge. To develop knowledge, particularly in English Literature, as I will argue in Chapter 2, takes skill – the skills of analysis, for example, and of argument.

The Platonic definition of knowledge is as 'justified true belief'; that is, that Mary knows ★a thing★ if ★a thing★ is *true*; Mary believes ★a thing★; and Mary is justified in believing ★a thing★. This has been somewhat challenged by 20th-century philosophers (see 'the Gettier problem', for example) by the production of a handful of counter examples, but the knottier problems of philosophy of knowledge are not entirely relevant to our general use of a rule of thumb about the nature of knowledge. The role of justification in the generation of knowledge in English Literature, and conversely the question of what is 'true', will also be further considered in Chapter 2.

One particular aspect of knowledge in English Literature which challenges the focus on factual knowledge is the fact that it is a discipline that prizes personal interpretation. To deliver 'knowledge that' in the form of information can cause problems:

> [I]f you are studying Charlotte Brontë's *Jane Eyre* (1847) and an authority figure bombards you with a catalogue of historical facts about the novel and its nineteenth-century context, this knowledge may drown out your own responses, ideas and interpretation and leave you feeling ignorant and, probably, a bit intimidated … [I]f you have been told that *Jane Eyre* is about the oppression of women in the Victorian period (it's how the catalogue presented it and it's not incorrect), then that's what you are expected to spot and talk about. In contrast, the moments in which the novel questions or subverts this idea or where it explores other aspects of the world falls out of focus or even becomes invisible because you are concentrating your gaze so intently on making the novel fit the data from the catalogue.
>
> (Eaglestone, 2019, pp. 36–7)

One of the consequences of this is that each person who reads a text creates their own particular schema – a mental map – of that text and their interpretation of it. Each additional piece of information, or knowledge, or meaning that we uncover becomes adopted into that mental map and affects how we then understand or adopt later input on that text. The impact of this on reading in class will be discussed in Chapter 3. Our schemas are also affected by the entirety of our previous reading and life experience – because reading occurs at what Louise Rosenblatt described as 'the coming together' 'of a reader and a text', not independently of the reader (Rosenblatt, 1978, p. 12). Narrative schemas accrete (Mason, 2014) from reading, re-reading, contextual knowledge, what we are told and our own experiences.

Validating knowledge in English Literature

There are four potential ways in which we might validate what constitutes knowledge in English Literature. First, we might look to school examinations and assessment: the knowledge required to pass those examinations is the true form of knowledge for school English Literature as far as many are concerned. In England, those examinations are governed by a mixture of factors: the subject experts who advise the Awarding Bodies on setting their specifications, which are composed in line with guidance issued from political sources, and modified in relation to requirements from Ofqual who validate the qualifications and employ their own subject experts.

Second, we might look to the field of English Literature more broadly, and specifically to progression after school into university-level study of English Literature. This is an area of anxiety for the discipline. As Carol Atherton has written:

> I get very twitchy about the issue of transition. I am uneasy with the deficit model that it seems to set up: the assumption that students are not adequately prepared for degree level study and that this is because teachers are not doing their jobs properly.
>
> *(Atherton, 2010, p. 56)*

Ten years later, this remains an area of concern (Stevens, 2018), but in the different light of reduced applications to study English at university. What counts as valid knowledge in English Literature, we might say, is closely linked to the discipline of literature outside school, and the needs of students who are going to progress in the subject. One particular issue raised by this type of validation is the question of literary critical approaches, and of the work of specific critics; the engagement with critical opinions of texts that is required varies wildly between specifications for study at GCSE and A level. The tension caused for our subject by the fact that it is both a foundational one studied by all students and also has the same desires to prepare a smaller subset for onward progression is one that is drawn on at points throughout this book, in the core question: What are we teaching English Literature for? It is evident that we cannot rely *only* on disciplinary knowledge for advanced study as the source of valid knowledge, because that ignores the other purposes of teaching English Literature in school, although it may echo some of those purposes. Equally, the questions over preparedness for university study in the discipline suggest that examination and assessment cannot provide complete validation either. (Both these types of validity are what is called, in assessment terms, consequential validity – the fitness for purpose of the study is based on the consequences of that study – that is, passing exams or being prepared for university.)

Third, the validity of knowledge in English Literature in particular has to pass the 'common sense' test for the general public: because it is a subject which everybody studies, it is a subject which everyone has an opinion on (much like education in general, as every teacher and education researcher can, I am sure, attest). This is felt through governmental commentary, media coverage and parental response. An example would be the periodic uproar to keep Shakespeare compulsory (usually not stimulated by any suggestion that he should not be); this level of validation tends to be at the level of text choice, rather than some of the more complex issues relating to knowledge that will also be discussed later in this book. This kind of validity might also reject critical approaches as unnecessary or irrelevant to the study of 'great literature', particularly if the approach chosen contradicts personal political beliefs of parents.

Finally, again on the level of text choice, we could appeal to a unified objective standard, something established over time. We might call this the canon, or the 'core knowledge' required for cultural literacy (Hirsch, 1987). The problems with the objectivity of both of these concepts is examined in Chapters 5 and 7 of this book, which broadly take the line that 'there is no neutral knowledge and every discipline is saturated with its cultural history' (Grumet, 2014, p. 15). This fourth approach to validity, as with the one above, leads to the second core question of this book: Whose knowledge is it anyway?

Whose knowledge is it anyway?

Too rarely do we acknowledge in the knowledge-driven curriculum that knowledge has come from somewhere: it is selected by someone and has originated in a particular paradigm. For English teachers, that brings up a number of questions: Who chooses? Whose values do we espouse, whose text choices do we follow, whose version of culture is the one we teach for?

It is almost axiomatic to quote Gradgrind from Dickens' *Hard Times* when discussing education and knowledge, and I cannot disappoint. Pupils are 'little vessels', 'arranged in order, ready to have imperial gallons of facts poured into them until them were full to the brim' (Dickens, 1854/2000, p. 3). The onomatopoeically and evocatively named head teacher declaims:

> Now, what I want is, Facts. Teach these boys and girls nothing but Facts. Facts alone are wanted in life. Plant nothing else, and root out everything else. You can only form the minds of reasoning animals upon Facts: nothing else will ever be of any service to them.
>
> *(Dickens, 1854/2000, p. 3)*

The capitalisation of 'Facts' suggests they are undebatable, objective, easily identifiable and easily transmitted. Later, Dickens uses the definition of the horse as graminivorous quadruped to demonstrate that facts are perhaps not everything there is to the story of knowledge, and raises the question: Whose facts? The dictionary's? Gradgrind's? Or those of Sissy Jupe, the poor girl whose intrinsic knowledge of horses learned at her father's side has no place in the formal classroom?

Eaglestone (2019) highlights the bias in Hirsch's cultural literacy model, which we will return to in Chapter 7: too often the culture is that of white men. But 'Whose facts?' is just as valid a question. Facts are not valueless, and the delineation of the fact which is to be learned reveals the values behind it. Many of us learned as children, for example, that 'In fourteen hundred and ninety-two, Columbus sailed the ocean blue'. In the USA, children know a far longer version, with another 13 couplets recounting the voyage, in which Columbus is 'brave' and 'bright', 'joyful' to have found America, where the 'Arkarawa natives were very nice'. The facts might be that Columbus left Spain with his three ships, seeking the Indies, and 'discovered' America; the names of his ships; the year. Few of us learned that Columbus was instrumental in the genocide of the Taíno people (referred to as Arkarawa natives in the poem), who were the indigenous population of the Caribbean. Columbus excitedly wrote in his diaries of trading even 'broken pottery' for their riches, and of the native population's suitability for being servants – he later sent thousands of Taínos back to Spain as slaves, many of whom died, and many of the rest were enslaved as forced labour in gold mines, meaning that there was no labour left to raise food. Within as little as 60 years, there were only a few hundred of an estimated quarter of a million left on the island on which Columbus had landed on his way to mainland America. Memorialisation and memorisation often demands a simple story, not a complex one.

More recently, this was demonstrated by the tearing down of a statue of Edward Colston, the Bristol slave trader, from its plinth in Bristol where it had been erected by the Victorians as a memorial to his philanthropy more than 150 years after his death. The plaque on the statue made no mention of his role in the slave trade; attempts to have a re-contextualising plaque put on the statue had been thwarted by vested interests in the four years leading up to the demolition of the statue. Whose facts?

On the day Colston's statue was pulled down, there was an instant link made on Twitter by English teachers to the widely taught poem *Ozymandias*, which brings us back to the other core question of this book: What are we teaching when we teach English Literature? Here is a vivid moment for a classical poem to be used to help students process and make sense of events in their own lives, rather than to use their own lives to make sense of literature. Jane Davis, writing of her practice in Continuing Education, talks of reading 'literature as myself, through my own eyes, trying to apply it to my own life and my own moral problems'; her classes were 'a community of regular readers attending, teaching and learning in these classes … to a greater or lesser degree using literature as a practical tool for life' (Davis, 2018, p. 211). In such a context, how can the 'facts' of literature be anything other than pliable?

Some of the concern, both in this section, and more widely in this book, is about the question of representation in knowledge: whose views are represented, who is seen? But as a tool to unpack our own lives, this question is transcended:

> Yes, representation matters, but there is more to transformation than looking into a book the way you would look into a mirror. Instead, at Spelman College I learned to understand literature as a means of unravelling the thorny questions of my life as a black woman. Literature wasn't just about inclusion, it was the springboard to intense questioning.
>
> *(Jones, 2019, p. 24)*

In the face of 'intense questioning', which facts stand?

There are some facts, some concrete knowledge, more or less objectively true, which do stand in English Literature. The year a text was published, the birthplace of the author, for whom it was written perhaps. These facts are easily graspable, as with some of the socio-historical contextual knowledge which is taught alongside literary texts and often forced into GCSE essays by students whether or not it is relevant and helpful to the argument. The things that are easily learnable, however, are not always the most valuable, either within the discipline of English Literature or more widely outside the classroom. Green (2018) asks: 'What knowledge is of most worth?' (p. 24), and the truth is that there is not one undebatable answer to that question, as the fierce debates that have raged over the knowledge turn in the curriculum have shown. This book is partly my answer to the question, and partly simply my consideration of the things that we need to take into account in order to reach an answer.

We may also ask 'Whose knowledge is it anyway?' in another context. Education has increasingly become a field of polarised debate, fed by the shortness and lack of nuance of EduTwitter. This, coupled with the rise of a number of 'Edu-Celebs' who have written popular books on education which have required the construction of strawmen, or whose rhetorical stance depends on hyperbole, has led to a situation where the 'progs' and the 'trads' are put at odds with one another. The strawman framing has progressives only interested in decontextualised skills, where the traditionalists have claimed the grounds of knowledge for themselves. (I concur with Robert Eaglestone, a university English specialist, on a principle that many of the 'tiger teachers' seem to have claimed for themselves: 'you can only learn skills in context' (2019, p. 81)). In truth, knowledge has always belonged to all teachers and none. In this book, I follow the habit of education researchers in insisting on the complexity of apparently simple concepts, and hope to provide a number of prompts to enable the reader to come to their own answer to 'What knowledge is of most worth?'

Powerful knowledge

Powerful knowledge was Michael Young's answer to this question, developed and expounded over 40 years. It is interesting to note that, counter to the way that his work has been drawn on in recent years, he initially distinguished between *the knowledge of the powerful* and *powerful knowledge* (Young, 2009); although he uses this distinction to denigrate 'sociological critiques of school knowledge' which have 'equated school knowledge and the curriculum with the "knowledge of the powerful"' (pp. 13–14). In contrast, he defined powerful knowledge as a concept which

> refers not to who has most access to the knowledge or who gives it legitimacy, although both are important issues; it refers to what the knowledge can do – for example, whether it provides reliable explanations or new ways of thinking about the world.
>
> *(Young, 2009, p. 14)*

In most cases, he suggests, this powerful knowledge is 'specialist knowledge', which is transmitted from expert teachers to learners, and this negates the role of 'learner choice' because they do not know what they do not know (echoes of Donald Rumsfeld's unknown unknowns). I would suggest in the case of English Literature there are certainly places where learners do know what they don't know and can ask for the specific disciplinary knowledge they need ('What's it called when?'; 'What does this mean?' etc.), but it is also true that deep subject knowledge is a crucial part of what enables teachers of English to expertly guide students through a text and to raise the relevant and interesting parts of contextual knowledge as they do so, as will be discussed throughout this book.

What Young does make clear is that his *powerful knowledge* is context-independent or theoretical knowledge, which enables the holder to make generalisations and to make judgements in wider fields. Context-dependent knowledge, on the other hand, 'deals with particulars' and 'tells the individual how to do specific things' (Young, 2009, p. 15). Powerful knowledge is thus the end of the schooling process, dependent on learning a great many other things first, and, he argues, may be particularly hard for students from disadvantaged backgrounds to gain, which puts the onus on schools to ensure they gain the fundamental knowledge on which powerful knowledge depends. This does echo the ways in which his concepts are used in England today, although 'powerful knowledge' has been expanded by its users, I feel, to refer to all the lesser knowledge also required, not just the deep disciplinary expertise which allows for generalisation and understanding of universals. Specifically, Young argues that the point of school is to make sure that students acquire knowledge and concepts which are not available to them in their home or everyday life. Despite his acknowledgement that some students will have more of the material support to enable this knowledge at home than others (access to the arts, museums, discussion of scientific questions over dinner, for example), he does not acknowledge that the 'knowledge of the powerful' and 'powerful knowledge' may have more overlap than he cares to admit. We will return to this concept in Chapter 7 in reference to cultural capital and cultural literacy.

Returning to his concept of powerful knowledge in 2014, Michael Young wrote that 'being social and historical doesn't just (as of course it can) make knowledge biased, it also makes it true' (p. 66), drawing on the examples of Newton's law of gravity and the continuing relevance of Shakespeare's plays. There should surely be another 'can' in that sentence: it *can* also make it true. Otherwise, the biased knowledge is also true. We all 'knew' in my childhood that Columbus 'discovered' America. It is now generally acknowledged that the presence of existing indigenous peoples suggests that someone else knew about America before he did, and there is also now good, well-known evidence to suggest that the Vikings also reached North America by boat some time before Columbus. And this is in the context of 'facts', not a subject where knowledge is not a single, straightforward entity. Even in our equivalent, we might look to the authorship of the plays of Shakespeare, many of which, modern scholars of literature are arguing with increasing certainty, were co-authored with others in part or in whole (e.g. Petersen, 2010). Not that whether William Shakespeare the man from Stratford wrote in whole or in part the plays attributed him is generally considered to be important knowledge in relation to the study of his works in school. Disciplinary 'powerful knowledge' is generated through social and historical processes and therefore does not exist outside social hierarchies: knowledge is 'arguably always in a dialectical relationship with power and identity' (Green, 2018, p. 24).

Another theme that recurs through the book is the constraints and affordances of curriculum, and how teachers can and do work within them. Despite the burdens placed on schools and teachers to 'close the gap' of structural inequality, it is not within their capacity realistically to solve all social ills. We must acknowledge as a profession that we have the power to reinforce social structures of inequality, but we also have the power to resist and undermine those structures if we think critically about them.

Terminology

It would be remiss not to talk about terminology in a book about knowledge in English Literature, but it belongs in all chapters and none, so I have chosen to include it here. Terminology is among the required knowledge now assigned for 16-year-olds to be assessed on in England:

> such as, but not restricted to, phrase, metaphor, meter, irony and persona, synecdoche, pathetic fallacy.
>
> *(DfE, 2013, p. 5)*

I adore terminology, particularly the huge range of Greek and Latin terms which can be widely encompassing, or indeed so narrowly specific as to leave one wondering when it would be appropriate to use them. I commend the *Silva Rhetoricae* (The Forest of Rhetoric) to you as an online list of the most amazing Greek and

Latin terms.[1] My personal favourite is *bdelygmia*, a party trick for any speller (the 'b' is silent), which is defined in the *Silva Rhetoricae* as a statement 'Expressing hatred and abhorrence of a person, word, or deed'. Sadly, this is the first useful purpose I have found for this knowledge, other than helping my sister, a teenager when I learned the term, to annoy her English teacher. Terminology does not exist in a vacuum: it is only useful when applicable, and it is not useful to shoehorn into discussion as a result of feature spotting, prompted by having learned something and being determined to use it. Rather, you should first identify your point of interest, then find the terminology that is required to describe it.

The structure of this book

Each of the following chapters takes a particular approach to the concept of knowledge in English Literature. Chapter 2 takes an overview of how knowledge works within the discipline, and in particular the characteristic pedagogies that we employ in our teaching, and what those can tell us about knowledge. It debates the old chestnut 'There's no such thing as a wrong answer in English' and considers the case of genre as a particular type of knowledge in English Literature. Finally, it touches on the role of retrieval practice in classrooms and how that interacts with the kinds of knowledge we teach in English Literature.

Chapter 3 focuses on shared reading experiences, both in terms of things that we have read which other people have also read, and on the sharing of reading experiences within the classroom. This chapter also considers the origins of English Literature as a colonising tool within the British Empire, and draws some links to the discourses around the texts that are taught in schools today. The core section focuses on the way we read texts together in classrooms and how that affects the kinds of knowledge we develop about texts.

In Chapter 4, I consider Shakespeare and his works, utilising his 'case' to discuss interpretation and context more widely in the discipline. I draw on *Macbeth* as an example to think about what kinds of knowledge are valuable in relation to studying Shakespeare, and also some of the broader considerations of the relation between his name, wider culture, individual plays and the development of disciplinary knowledge. The chapter also considers a characteristic pedagogy in relation to Shakespeare – that of 'Active Methods' and what kinds of knowledge those methods can engender.

Chapter 5 deals with questions of representation and inequality as they relate to the 'canon' and to the English curriculum, in terms of race and gender. It begins by considering the mechanisms of canon formation. The majority of the remainder of the chapter focuses on race, and the framing of 'other' within the curriculum. The chapter considers what texts are available on exam specifications in the UK and also comments on two widely taught texts: *Of Mice and Men* and *To Kill a Mockingbird*. It also asks readers to consider the experience of Black students within the classroom and to think about the social responsibilities of the English teacher within the context of structural inequalities.

Chapter 6 'pins down' poetry and poems – and the difference between knowledge of poetry and knowledge of a poem. It considers different forms of knowledge – cognitive, aesthetic and affective as they relate to poetry and how it is conceptualised. It goes on to explore the question of the authoritative 'answer' to a poem, and who 'owns' the meaning of a poem in the classroom, critiquing some of the effects of the concentration on poetry in the context of high-stakes assessment.

Finally, in Chapter 7 I untangle the concepts of cultural capital, cultural literacy and cultural hegemony, and complicate the question of using English Literature as a means of developing either of the first two by suggesting that, in doing so, we are not enabling individual students but rather cementing social inequalities that already exist.

Throughout, my main aim is to bridge the debates between 'progressive' and 'traditional' approaches to knowledge, to suggest that the two sides are closer than has been promoted by debates on Twitter, and, above all, to think carefully about knowledge in English Literature in the secondary classroom.

Note

1 http://rhetoric.byu.edu

2

THE CONSTRUCTION OF KNOWLEDGE IN ENGLISH LITERATURE

Characteristic pedagogies are pedagogical approaches that typify different subjects: the practical in science, for example, or the workshop model in creative writing. This chapter explores the particular contribution made by the characteristic pedagogies of English to the ways in which knowledge is created in the English classroom and discipline. It contextualises English as a discursive, interpretive subject and considers the balance between contextual knowledge, understanding and the ultimate purposes of learning in English. I will consider the favourite phrase 'There's no such thing as a wrong answer' and the specific case of genre in English Literature as a case for thinking about the way knowledge develops in a discipline. Finally, this chapter considers the testing effect and how it relates to knowledge and teaching in the secondary English Literature classroom.

Characteristic pedagogies

Every year, I ask my beginning teachers of English to define literary non-fiction: it is an exercise in discomfort for them, as we try to examine the features that make something literary. Definitions of literature range widely and might encompass the Arnoldian 'best that has been thought and said' (2006, p. 46). The 'Accidental Professor', John Carey, wrote:

> My definition of literature is writing that I want to remember – not for its content alone, as one might want to remember a computer manual, but for itself: those particular words in that particular order.
>
> *(Carey, 2005, pp. 173–4)*

He also suggests that:

> a vital element in all literature is indistinctness, and this empowers the reader. The reader, that is, not only can but must come to some kind of accommodation with the indistinctness in order to take meaning from the text.
>
> *(Carey, 2005, p. 214)*

This indistinctness is important for the way in which we construct knowledge in the English Literature classroom. I would suggest there are two characteristic pedagogies that are important to English Literature across the varieties of classroom across the globe. The first is the communal reading of a text, with interspersed glossing, which may be either commentary directly by the teacher or via the use of questioning of students. The second is the guided discussion of a text, a conversation that uses textual evidence to explore questions of interpretation, of character, of context and of values. As such, knowledge in English is always contingent:

> In English Studies, the semantic and formal incompleteness of the text, its nigh inexhaustible potential for multiple interpretations, is mirrored in the open system of the seminar. Each seminar or class (like each reading of a text) is an exercise in the production of values. Ideally this represents a communal and democratic process of sifting, of deciding (in gestalt terms) which semantic item is figure, and which ground.
>
> *(Knights, 2017, p. 5)*

While some may 'see books and teachers as neutral, truthful and reliable sources of knowledge' (Teifouri, 2018, p.169), 'English very often deals with the ineffable and the unknowable' (Day, 2018, p. 127). English Literature as a discipline is a conversation within and between students, texts and teachers:

> However naive it may be to say so, however it ignores the hidden and not-so-hidden power dynamics of the seminar room, English is a discipline in which all readers are presumed to be equal before the text, and therefore have as much right to contribute to discussion as everyone else.
>
> *(Denith, 2017, p. 177)*

I question if this assumption applies equally to the discipline of English Literature in the secondary classroom, in which we might see there being a reader who is 'more equal than others' in the person of the teacher. The rules of classroom interaction (Ingram & Elliott, 2016) also mean that the 'right to contribute to discussion' is always the teacher's in most formal classrooms: the teacher then delegates to particular students when they want to. However, the principle that all students have as much right as any other student to contribute, and that their reactions to the text should be given due consideration, is a good one, flippant and time-wasting comments aside. This, then, is another tension in the construction of knowledge in the English classroom: that we have the right to speak but within the constraints of power relationships that reside in classrooms, whether on a personal or a societal level. Dentith (2017) half mocks and half makes the case for 'what do you think of this, then?' and finding 'a good bit' as important levelling pedagogies within English. The personal response, which has waxed and waned in terms of assessment priorities in school English Literature, remains an important part of the subject.

These two characteristic pedagogies – the communal reading of a text and the later discussion of that text – tell us things about how we construct knowledge in English. The first is that the text is intrinsically important: we draw on detail, on a close reading, to construct our knowledge. An encounter with the text itself is a key component of knowledge in English Literature; while we might argue about whether that textual encounter needs to be committed to memory or merely held in the pages of the text, we all agree that textual detail, plot points, structure, language, imagery and quotations are what provide the raw material for the construction of knowledge. The textual encounter in itself is not enough, however, for true knowledge in the discipline. Having read a text is necessary but not sufficient. The types of commentary are also significant in terms of understanding the nature of knowledge. 'Labelling isn't what we want students to do in English' (Bleiman, 2020, p. 66), but some of the commentary does achieve labelling, in that it identifies mechanisms by which effects are achieved. Largely, starting from the effect and moving to the mechanism is a more effective way to understand a text than moving the other way around. It is true, however, that it is often easier to teach a mechanism (metaphor or simile, for example) in isolation, and then effectively prompt students to engage in technique spotting.

The second characteristic pedagogy, of discussion, moves us further on: we construct knowledge through discursive means, as a community. Even scholars of English Literature in the ivory tower of the academy work through interaction with others, whether that is in person or through reading and responding to their critical works. Knowledge within the academic discipline of English Literature is not produced in isolation; it is produced through argument with others, whether real or imagined, as we work through possible interpretations and make the case for our own particular take on a text. To me, the exploratory talk of Neil Mercer represents the ideal form of discussion about literary texts in the classroom:

> [P]eople ask questions; people share relevant information; ideas may be challenged; reasons are given for challenges; contributions build on what has gone before; everyone is encouraged to contribute; ideas and opinions treated with respect.
>
> *(Mercer, 2008, n.p.)*

In the literature classroom, we do not need to seek 'agreement for joint decisions' (Mercer, 2008, n.p.) because the decision on any given interpretation lies with the individual and their response, but in many classrooms a joint decision on a particular question relating to a particular text *is* reached by negotiation between discussants. Knights (2018) argues that literary studies is 'carried out through a specialised form of dialogue: this form of conversation starts with what looks like confusion and moves towards a provisional order' (p. 40).

The vision I have laid out here of the generation of knowledge within the classroom might be challenged as being unrealistic; the counter view would be that of the knowledge residing with an expert teacher who transmits that knowledge to the students. The knowledge of the text – the interpretation, the argument that supports it – is already generated (from a discussion outside the classroom, either from scholarly sources or between teachers writing departmental resources, or schemes of work created centrally). One difficulty with this model is that it denies the multiplicity of interpretation which is one of the characteristics of literary study: to offer one authoritative reading is impoverishing the student. I would also argue that this is not true study of English Literature – it is merely memorisation of one dimension, akin to learning a text by heart. To return to the question of validation, it might be validated in terms of being adequate for assessment, but it is not enough for progression within the discipline. In truth, it might well not be adequate for assessment either, in that it is essential to be able to adapt arguments to work with the particular focus given in an examination question, and simple learning of one potential argument, even with supporting evidence, will not enable the student to do this. However, even if this is the approach that has been decided on for school students, the fundamental nature of the construction of knowledge has not changed – it has merely shifted outside the classroom. In doing so, it moves the students in the classroom to a lower level of engagement with that disciplinary knowledge.

We might also consider the different ways in which teachers and students read texts together to be characteristic pedagogies of the English Literature classroom: round-robin, teacher reading or 'popcorn' reading, where the teacher picks on individuals out of predictable order, or the use of assigned parts for dramatic readings (including, often, the stage directions). These will be considered further in the next chapter. Here, I think it is enough to say that these collective experiences of the text are further evidence of the communal nature of knowledge within English: that it is developed within a social context, not an isolated one.

There's no such thing as a wrong answer in English[1]

'There's no such thing as a wrong answer in English' is a reassuring maxim, designed to encourage students to attempt to answer questions when they are not sure, and to prevent the development of the attitude that there is but one right answer that students must regurgitate to please the teacher. It is completely untrue. There are plenty of wrong answers in English Literature: Jane Eyre did not write *Sense and Sensibility*, for example. There are, however, also plenty of right answers. The maxim is perhaps better expressed: there are no right answers in English. Or at least: there is usually not a single right answer in English. 'Subjective responses to writing are a feature, not a bug' (Warner, 2018, p. 67).

The very nature of knowledge and 'correctness' in English Literature is that it is generated not in a simple authoritative statement, but in the evidence and argument that is supplied to support that statement. There are indeed better and worse arguments, which may mean that we accept or reject an answer. I can make the case, for example, both that Magwitch acts entirely selfishly in the matter of Pip and that he is a selfless benefactor. A more reasonable answer might lie between the two. Seamus Heaney's 'Storm on the Island' makes another interesting case: for some, this is a poem entirely about a storm and the ravages of nature; for others, it is a poem that is entirely allegorical, about the Northern Irish political situation and the Assembly at Stormont (a cryptic clue in the first eight letters of the title). The poem works well on both levels, as so many great works of literature do. The 'correctness' of the interpretation lies in its justification, in the evidence selected to support it, and the consideration of both halves of the argument. I shall return to this debate in the context of poetry in Chapter 6, where I draw on interviews with beginning teachers about the teaching of poetry. All supported the concept that as long as a student could support their response with evidence, then any justifiable interpretation should be accepted, and one acutely noted that 'there are far fewer ways to be wrong about a poem than there are to be right'. That is, given your students are not busily *trying* to be wrong by claiming *Macbeth* is really about custard manufacturing.

Any justifiable interpretation seems to me to be a good rule of thumb for the validity of knowledge in English Literature. One chain of schools in England produced some examples of its 'Mastery' curriculum via PowerPoints which were widely shared and critiqued for their interpretation of *The Tempest*, in particular for the fact that they shared just one interpretation of Caliban, which was heavy-handed and tone-deaf to the post-colonial context which teaching *The Tempest* requires in the 21st century. Practical Criticism is a well-acknowledged approach in English Literature, perhaps more so in practice than in name than it was twenty years ago: looking at the text stripped of contextual information and working on the basis only of the words within. Interestingly, I. A. Richards, the Cambridge-based English lecturer who coined the phrase in a book of that name was in fact reporting the results of an experiment in getting his undergraduates to interpret texts without contextual cues, the results of which were a variety of mis-readings of greater and lesser degree (Richards 1929).

In 2014, I argued that the curriculum reforms in England and Scotland, in the focus on 'British' texts in England and the introduction of the compulsory Scottish texts in Scotland, were intended by their progenitors to inculcate a sense of nationhood and national belonging (Elliott, 2014). Michael Gove, speaking at the first Conservative Party conference after the formation of the UK Coalition Government in 2010, told the Conservatives that:

> [T]he great tradition of our literature – Dryden, Pope, Swift, Byron, Keats, Shelley, Austen, Dickens and Hardy – should be at the heart of school life. Our literature is the best in the world – it is every child's birthright and we should be proud to teach it in every school.

> *(Gove, 2010)*

Similarly, the then Cabinet Secretary for Education and Lifelong Learning in the Scottish government, Michael Russell, boasted that:

> Scotland's contribution to literature is marked down the generations. Burns, Walter Scott and Robert Louis Stevenson have provided work that has lasted the test of time, along with contemporary writers like Irvine Welsh and Liz Lochhead. We want our children and young people to have the chance to learn about our literary tradition and to inspire the future generations of Scottish writers
>
> *(Russell, quoted in Denholm, 2012)*[2]

But in order to construct a national story (what has sometimes been promoted in the British context as 'Empire 2.0' before being shouted down) from national texts, particularly from canonical texts, the issue of 'any justifiable interpretation' becomes problematic. A decolonised (or, one might say, appropriate) reading of Victorian literature should deal with issues of Empire as they relate to Austen, Dickens and Hardy. The national myth built on the greatness of Britain founders when you begin to think, for example, about the plantations that fuel the wealth of William Elliot in *Persuasion*, and it becomes less easy to cheer for Mrs Smith when one realises her final happy ending is based on the restoration of slaves and slave labour to her as their 'rightful' owner. Dickens himself constantly undermines the myth of Victorian greatness by showing the underbelly of society in terms of poverty, workhouses, crime and the contrast with the genteel and the rich. To adhere to the traditions of our discipline in English Literature – that is, the critical reading of texts in context and to understand the multiple interpretations – is to be in direct conflict with a model that promotes a singular knowledge of the greats as the route to social success (see Chapter 7).

What do we teach when we teach literature?

Although I return to this question throughout the book, there are some things that we can say in preparation. We teach many things when we teach literature, and what those things are is steeped in context: in history, in emotion, in curriculum, in geography, in society, in danger, in identity, in theory, in power, in constraints, in possibility.[3]

The relationship between the curriculum and assessment can reveal some of the most interesting and important questions about the teaching of literature. As a subject, we rely largely on the use of the essay as a form for assessing knowledge, which has well-known difficulties – studies of the problem of reliably marking essays were being carried out as early as 1926 (Thompson & Bailes, 1926). Gibson has light-heartedly described 'the deep but tortured relationship between English Studies and the essay':

> Although constituting a genre whose raison d'etre is to be assessable, [essays] are notoriously hard to pin down: the difficulty of analysis and 'marking' or 'grading' has a mystical quality that withers when exposed to the light.
>
> *(Gibson, 2017, p. 99)*

I would argue that the essay is, if not a characteristic *pedagogy*, certainly a characteristic *form* for the study of English Literature, and what has been termed the 'core scholarly unit' of the discipline (Hartley, 2019, p. 20). It can also tell us a great deal about the ways in which we think about knowledge in the subject. Taking as the simplest structure one that is quite familiar in the classroom, that of PEEL – Point, Evidence, Explanation and Link – we can see that knowledge in our subject is expected to be supported by evidence. That evidence is not simple or self-sufficient, because we need an explanation. We do not speak of 'proof' but of 'evidence'. We expect knowledge to be made up of more than one discrete unit; it is rather composed of a series of linked elements which go together to make up an argument. Even if we reject the scaffold 'PEEL' and look for more complex approaches to essay and paragraph writing, we still look to a lengthy piece of writing in which an argument is built, drawing on quotation or exemplification from the literary text under consideration, which requires a close textual familiarity – what we might call knowledge also – and which, ideally, deals in both points and counter-points, to create a written discussion that eventually reaches a conclusion in relation to a question about the text. That conclusion is knowledge only because of the argument behind it. Without that evidence, without the weft of the essay, it is assertion. So at least part of what we are teaching when we teach English Literature is the knowledge of how an argument is constructed, and how to propose a point, listen to the ideas of others, and propose counter-arguments; we are teaching some aspect of written communication; and we are teaching the idea of knowledge as a complex construction of language.

But the essence of the subject does not only lie in what can be assessed. Gerzina asks, for example: 'How do we assess whether a student has gained a larger vision of humanity by reading *King Lear*?' (Gerzina, 2017, p. 27). I discuss the particular relationship between Shakespeare and 'a larger vision of humanity' in Chapter 4, but for many teachers, this is one thing that we teach when we teach literature. To express this in a less grandiose way, other phrases such as 'walking a mile in another's shoes' mean much the same thing: when we teach literature, we are teaching students about a multitude of experiences that they will never have. There is also a sense in which the 'larger vision' suggests that we are introducing them to the possibility of a better world via the part of teaching literature that deals with the examination of character and motivation, helping them to deconstruct and consider their own actions. This is related to what Maxine Greene (1995) termed the 'social imagination': essentially that in order to change the world we have to be able to imagine it differently than it is. Similarly:

> So much depends on how successfully we may oppose as teachers the crippling, disempowering determinism so prevalent in the current climate. We need instead to foster a sense of purpose, and an underlying sense that human beings may work together to bring about change for the better.
>
> *(Stevens, 2018, p. 157)*

This 'larger vision' also ties into both the Personal Growth model and the Cultural Analysis model (the ability to critically analyse the world around you) of the Cox models of English teaching (Goodwyn, 2016). We are never *merely* teaching literature. In order to contextualise the texts we teach, we often also teach a vast range of other subjects: history, sociology, psychology, geography, politics – the list goes on. Teaching literature encourages us to look outwards, beyond our own time and place, and to disrupt our routine assumptions. The question of how we use contextual knowledge recurs through the later chapters in this book, explored in the context of specific areas of study. It is an essential part of literary study, however, and of the construction of knowledge in the discipline, whether you adopt a new historicist approach or a presentist approach to any given text. In schools, we tend to consider most acutely the context of production of a text, of an author. The temptation to use biographical renderings to explore the poems of Sylvia Plath, for example, or the use of information about country dances to inform readings of *Pride and Prejudice*, one of which might be seen as more appropriate than the other. But we also use texts to think about our current contexts and current concerns. In a secondary classroom, insisting on ecocritical readings of Chaucer (as one beginning teacher complained her Year 8s were doing) may seem less valid than it would in a university classroom. But it is a potential approach to literature, albeit one that we would not pursue in the junior classroom because of the need to learn to walk before you can run.

To return to that central question of what it is we teach when we teach literature, I would direct almost anyone to a chapter by Robert Eaglestone in *Teaching Literature*. 'English is a more communal subject than many others' (2017, p. 75), he tells us. When we teach English rather than 'facts', we are teaching 'ways of thinking' (p. 70), an argument that resonates with me, to the background of Gradgrind's bristling forehead. Some of these ways of thinking – the use of discussion of stimulus text as a characteristic pedagogy, the use of justified argument – are more universal than others – the use of one or other critical theory as an approach to the analysis of text, for example. Eaglestone also challenges us:

> This sense that English is a subject more linked to its community than to the object or series of objects that it studies is the principal reason why the discipline has always been so riven by debates about its own nature. Because it has no one object, no one methodology, its tribal rules are even more dependent than most disciplines on what the tribe happens to say they are at any given moment. Part of the tradition of the tribe is precisely debate and argument about what is and is not part of the tradition. The tradition in English consists in conflict over what English is.
>
> *(Eaglestone, 2017, p. 74)*

The tension for English teachers is that we know both that we are asking for multitudes, that we understand the multiplicity of interpretations that are possible, and indeed the ambiguity of any given text, and yet we also at the end of the day (scheme of work, term, qualification) ask students to come down on one side of the argument and generate a single acceptable answer to a question. Hartley writes of university-level teaching in the US:

> I constantly wrestle with the implicit paradox of my own course structure where, on the one hand, I try to open up the plays we are studying to multiple interpretations, but end the semester requiring what most of us demand: a thesis-driven paper. Students are asked to produce what we as scholars are used to thinking of as the core scholarly unit of our field: a textual analysis which makes a compelling case for a particular reading of the play, one which badgers and banishes all contrary elements and the critics who have voiced them, in pursuit of that most hallowed of scholarly objects, an essay which is closely attentive to the text, while being single-minded in its focus, clear in its exposition, and so logical in its conclusions that, at least for a time, the reader is convinced that no contrary position is intellectually viable. The result is a kind of critical unicorn, beautiful, elegant, and pointed.
>
> (Hartley, 2019, p. 20)

In a discipline where the tradition is conflict over what English is, and where we have such tensions between the different outcomes that we are teaching for, the question of what knowledge *is* is in constant flux and debate, even for any given individual to come to a conclusion, let alone for an entire profession to come to a complete consensus. There are some things we can all agree on, perhaps, and others we need to negotiate.

Genre – a threshold concept for English?

Genre is a particularly interesting concept in relation to knowledge in English Literature. It illustrates, for example, the difference between the simple acquisition of facts and the application of those facts into something that becomes knowledge (or indeed a skill). Knowing a list of generic features does not mean you can write that kind of text successfully, nor does it give a framework by which you can analyse a text completely or come to know everything about it. Further, I think that there is a strong case to be made for genre as a threshold concept in English Literature.

'Threshold concepts' were introduced by Meyer and Land (2003), as being important thresholds of learning in all subjects. They linked it to the idea of 'troublesome knowledge' (Perkins, 1999); this is 'knowledge that is conceptually difficult, counter-intuitive or "alien"' (Meyer & Land, 2003, p. 1). For teachers, the importance of threshold concepts is that they are often points when learners struggle, and they represent leaps forward in conceptual understanding. This is an approach that you may be able to recall from your own school days, particularly with science, where if you continue to the next stage, KS3 from primary, GCSE from KS3, A level from GCSE, you come to understand that what you had been taught previously about any given concept was a useful fiction which told some but not all of the truth.

The key aspects of a threshold concept, according to Meyer and Land, are that it can be: *transformative* – that is, it occasions a significant shift in the perception of a subject; *irreversible*, in that it was unlikely to be forgotten, or might only be unlearned through considerable effort; and *integrative* which they defined as 'exposing the previously hidden interrelatedness of something' (Meyer & Land, 2005, p. 373). For me, genre fits the concept of threshold concepts in the study of English Literature, thinking about both curriculum and assessment in secondary English but also looking forward into the undergraduate syllabus and potentially further. Genre starts via a taxonomic approach – that is, one that is about sorting into categories – and moves into a more complex understanding in late school or in undergraduate study (or, indeed, postgraduate study).

Concepts of genre in early secondary school are largely learned from writing. The 'genre approach' to teaching writing has been dominant for some years, under the influence of the long-defunct National Strategies. Genre-based approaches originated in Australia and aimed to promote socio-economic parity by explicitly teaching the kinds of generic knowledge that some children assimilated from their home environment (Wyatt-Smith & Murphy, 2001). This is the model in which 'these are the features of this kind of text' is taught and students are expected to assess work with reference to the presence or absence of generic features for an answer of how good or bad an example of that kind of text it is. This is a taxonomic approach, which is completely in line with a traditional Aristotelian vision of genre in which texts belong in specific generic buckets (even if it is a little unfair to blame Aristotle when his categories in *On Poetry* were rather broader than modern generic categories!). In this model, 'genre comes to be seen as a rigid trans-historical class exercising control over the texts which it generates' (Frow, 2015, p. 24).

The reading that early secondary students do is fairly firmly placed within this vision of genre as a taxonomy. 'Genre fiction', as it is termed in modern publishing parlance, is also strongly influential in children's and young adult literature. For the most part, texts studied up to age 16 are placed in generic categories and taught as such, based on their main storyline or subject. We tell students 'this is a detective novel' when teaching *The Sign of Four* or we teach a Dystopia-based scheme of work. We ask students to identify the kinds of things they like to read as 'science fiction' or 'real life'. This is also the approach to GCSE poetry which is clustered into theme-based groups such as 'war and conflict' or 'love and relationships'. When I interviewed some beginning teachers about poetry teaching in schools (described more fully in Chapter 6), one of them commented that this clustering approach gave a scaffold for her students to approach the poems and tackle the initial unseen analysis, in effect by giving them a sense of generic features they could look for. In Shakespeare teaching, the one constant author in English studies to 16, at least in England, we teach plays with strong generic identification, to the extent that the 'problem plays' are very rarely taught below and not often at A level, because of the difficulty of understanding what sort of a thing this is.

The more sophisticated vision of genre presents a challenge. Anne Freadman has identified two false assumptions within a taxonomic view of genre:

1 That a text is 'in' a genre – ie that it is primarily or solely describable in terms of the rules of one genre, and
2 That genre is 'in' a text ie that the features of the text will correspond to the rules of a genre.

(Freadman, 1988, p. 73)

Before the age of 16, we tend to ignore the ways in which a novel does not correspond to the rules of 'its genre' in order to emphasise the way it does – for understandable reasons in terms of getting students not to be distracted by subtleties when they are still dealing with the basics. However, beyond the 'threshold' we move into a version of genre that draws on Derrida, who suggests that rather than belonging, genre is a case of *participation*, with a text participating in one or more genres. In his book *Genre*, John Frow (2015) makes the case for genre as a 'more reflexive model in which texts are thought to use or perform the genres by which they are shaped' (p. 27). He goes on to say that 'genre is not a property of a text but a framework we impute to it; but this imputation is neither arbitrary nor idiosyncratic, since the conventions of a genre are shared by members of a discourse community' (p. 133). So we might understand, for example, that *Frankenstein in Baghdad* (Saadawi, 2018) draws on the genres of science fiction, but also magic realism and fantasy (the monster in the novel has no scientific origins), satire and war fiction. To assign it to just one of these genres would be to do the novel an injustice. In marketing terms, it might be 'literary fiction' or 'literature in translation', neither of which is very informative from an analytical point of view. It draws on and participates in multiple genres.

We might suggest that the transition to this understanding of genre is one that needs to be completed in order to have a successful career as an undergraduate English student, but it is certainly true that enough of this framework of genre has influenced A level that genre can be a very troublesome kind of knowledge indeed in the final stage of literary study at secondary level in England. A-level specifications approach genre in a variety of ways. For some, it reflects the GCSE poetry approach so that you get modules such as 'the Gothic'. However, the significant change is that a major part of generic study is considering how texts both do and do not reflect the 'rules' of the genre, or how those rules might change over time. Context, a key Assessment Objective, covers how a text speaks to the tradition within which it appears, or indeed the tensions it is held in, within it.

Currently, there is a genre-based specification in the form of the 'B' specification published by the Awarding Body AQA. It has a traditional, even Aristotelian, approach in the first year, studying comedy or tragedy, but in the second year the focus moves to a choice of 'Elements of crime writing' or 'Elements of social and political protest writing'. Among the set texts for the former is *Hamlet* and for the latter *Henry IV, Part 1*. The specification for this A-level syllabus describes 'Elements of crime writing' in the following way:

> [M]any of the texts pre-date the crime fiction genre that emerged as a recognisable literary genre in the mid-19th century and with academic recognition in the 20th century. However, in all the texts a significant crime drives the narrative, and the execution and consequence of the crime are fundamentally important to the way the text is structured.
>
> All set texts are narratives which focus on transgressions against established order and the specific breaking of either national, social, religious or moral laws. The focus in this component must be on 'Elements' and students need to consider the elements that exist in each of their texts.[4]

This is a severely weakened version of generic identification. The generic identification has been built around the characteristic of 'having a crime as part of their narrative'. While specific narrative content does play a part in the dialogue of generic characteristics – the revenge tragedy, for example, has to have a crime in it as well – specific tonal, structural or formal characteristics also have a part to play. Frow (2015) has posited that generic characteristics are a complex set of relations, a 'set of conventional and highly organised constraints on the production and interpretation of meaning' (p. 10). The view of crime writing as having just one driving force, which is hardly a constraint at all on the 'production and interpretation of meaning' provides a major challenge for 17-year-olds' understanding of genre by casting it wide open. It is almost as meaningful to suggest as a group all texts that contain food and drink as a key element of their plot (would anyone care to pair *Alice in Wonderland* with *Titus Andronicus*?). This approach goes beyond a Derridan model of genre, to place strain on the concept of genre existing at all. However, we can see how for more advanced study it is useful to consider *Hamlet* not just as simple tragedy; and indeed it would be interesting and productive once a student had moved beyond an initial understanding of the play to analyse it with regard to some of the facets of the crime genre as it is traditionally understood: the maverick detective perhaps, or the femme fatale, as Hamlet and Gertrude respectively. This kind of approach centres a text in the context of reception rather than production, and examines how we read it in the light of our 21st-century attitudes and understandings. (For more on *Hamlet* as detective fiction, I have written on this particular instance of generic identification in Elliott, 2019.)

Study at A level, then, whether in a traditional generic approach or a more unusual and creative one such as this, requires students to undergo at least somewhat of a transformation in their understanding of genre – they have to come to see texts as selecting or participating in specific generic characteristics, rather than matching a full checklist of features. This is not quite enough to bring them over the threshold of genre, however, because the change in understanding is not necessarily irreversible, to refer back to Meyer and Land's (2003) definition. Culturally, we are all very deeply influenced by the strong use of generic identification in the marketing of fiction. We buy our books from tables in which they are clustered with other books of the same 'type'. A book must be 'crime' or 'sci-fi' or 'chick lit' or 'LGBQT+', and it must be instantly recognisable as such. It is not that long since publishers were reissuing *Wuthering Heights* with a cover carefully designed to mimic the covers of the *Twilight* novels in order to emphasise its generic identification as Gothic romance – a far more profitable one than the 'classic fiction' pigeonhole it had been languishing in for some years. The transition to seeing genre in a Derridan rather than an Aristotelian mode involves overcoming a lifetime of conditioning in terms of teaching at earlier levels and in terms of exposure to the publishing industry in bookshops and popular imagination. It is a troublesome concept, but the transition to seeing genre as a participation rather than a 'bucket' taxonomy is one that revolutionises your understanding of texts.

Significantly, a threshold concept is difficult to learn – it is not necessarily a natural development or progression in student thinking. It often needs explicit teaching, but it can be a hard thing to teach as well as learn. Even the most committed Derridan will often find the language of generic taxonomy emerging in their everyday talk about books. Genre, therefore, represents a particular line of both continuity and discontinuity in English Literature from 11 to 21 and beyond. It is a fruitful area of discussion and for analysis of texts, and for understanding how 'knowledge' in English develops differently through various educational stages.

The testing effect and interleaving learning

The recent cognitive turn in education, both in the UK and across the world, has led to the sudden (re)discovery of some well-evidenced phenomena, such as retrieval practice. Also known as the testing effect, this is the mechanism by which returning to test knowledge (rather than simple revision of it) – that is, practising its retrieval – helps to increase long-term memory of information (Rowland, 2014). Regular low-stakes testing has become a familiar feature of classrooms around the world; lessons often begin with a recall session of some kind. Despite the contemporary labelling of this as a 'memory platform' or a 'knowledge recall' or 'retrieval practice', it is not fundamentally different from the long-standing classroom practices of asking questions about the learning from the last lesson to prime students to restart their reading of *Much Ado About Nothing* or *To Kill a Mockingbird*, or the use of questions on a passage just read to check comprehension and instil an understanding of the key points of that text. The advantage of testing is that every child tries to retrieve the information, as opposed to being able to opt out of the process of trying to remember as they sometimes can in some structures of classroom discourse (such as who nominates the speaker who answers, and when that nomination happens (Ingram & Elliott, 2016)). Contrary to the silos constructed between 'traditionalists' and 'progressives' on EduTwitter, I am a firm believer in retrieval practice.

There has been some suggestion that because we know 'what works' in terms of learning, pedagogies should be limited to those practices. However, it is important to think carefully about what can be learned easily using some of these pedagogies and what is valuable and useful knowledge going forward. It is possible to consolidate and embed valuable knowledge that has previously been constructed together in the English Literature classroom using low-stakes quizzing. It is not as easy to do so as it is to use low-stakes quizzing to embed low-level factual knowledge which can be delivered via a handout and simply learned. Some of that knowledge is necessary, but it does not lead to a better student of English Literature. A simple example from my last year in school, when my incoming Year 7s could happily define all manner of parts of speech for me, but on being asked to highlight the adverbs (for example) in a piece of text, they struggled. Low-stakes quizzing can help us to learn definitions but not necessarily to apply them, unless we think about it carefully. One answer is to use low-stakes quizzing to embed the application of the knowledge – that is, requiring the highlighting of the adverbs in that case. Even then, that is not as valuable as being able to think about and decide for yourself why one adverb is more effective than another – a question to which there is not a right answer, and which therefore does not lend itself to the low-stakes quizzing and rapid marking approach.

Interleaving asks us to remind students of learning not just from the last lesson, but also from last week, last month, last term, last year. This is something which might be particularly useful in the construction of an overall understanding of English Literature as a discipline, rather than each individual text as a start and end point in itself. Barbara Bleiman uses the example of understanding Dickens' caricature approach to characterisation, which might then be usefully applied in a more nuanced way to an understanding of Mrs Bennet in *Pride and Prejudice*, or Mrs Reed in *Jane Eyre* (Bleiman, 2020). Interleaving can help to make links between texts and concepts, to create a larger schema of how literature works. But it can also simply make sure that we remember who wrote *Jane Eyre* and some simple facts about Scrooge's character in *A Christmas Carol*. Which you use it for, which you value, is up to you. But like all tools, retrieval practice and interleaving are not good in and of themselves: it is the content that makes the difference as to whether they are useful practices in developing knowledge in English Literature. So my concern about retrieval practice in the current climate is that it is often mandated on a school level because it 'works' with little consideration of *how* it works in individual subjects. It is easy to implement retrieval practice for low-value knowledge; it is much harder to implement for high-value knowledge, and as a result the approach has the potential to steer classroom practice in the wrong direction.

Conclusion

Knowledge is constructed in English Literature, I have argued, through discursive means, and supported by evidence. The justifiable argument is the key to any interpretation and the validation of any individual claim to knowledge. The question of authority and the right to 'own' an answer will be considered in later chapters, particularly in Chapter 6, in relation to poetry. One of the key problems for knowledge in English Literature, however, is not just how that knowledge is constructed in the first place, but that there are different levels of knowledge, some of which are more valuable than others. It is axiomatic that the more valuable the knowledge, the more difficult it is to teach it, and to learn it. Through the example of genre, I have suggested that the nature of the discipline changes at key progression points. Therefore, it is more pertinent to learn how to construct knowledge yourself than to imbibe a pre-ordained version of it, in terms of preparing students for progression. The recurrent tension between teaching all students for foundational reasons and teaching the smaller group who could go on to further study is therefore once again relevant and will continue to be explored in later chapters.

Notes

1 I am particularly indebted to my colleague Nicole Dingwall for vigorous debates on this topic over the years.
2 We could note here that the Scottish tradition reaches down into the present day, whereas the 'great tradition' of Gove's list had all been dead for quite a while at the time of his speech.
3 In writing this section I have drawn on two excellent books: *Teaching Literature: Text and Dialogue in the English Classroom* edited by Ben Knights (2017) and another book in the Routledge NATE series: *International Perspectives on the Teaching of Literature in Schools: Global Principles and Practices*, edited by Andy Goodwyn, Cal Durrant, Louann Reid and Lisa Scherff (2018). I highly recommend both of them to the teacher of English Literature.
4 www.aqa.org.uk/subjects/english/as-and-a-level/english-literature-b-7716-7717/subject-content-a-level/texts-and-genres

3

SHARED EXPERIENCES OF READING

For Robert Eaglestone, the nature of literature rests in 'collaboration and dialogue' (2019, p. 28), not only between people but between books. He draws on Bakhtin to support this argument and notes that Bakhtin suggests 'that those who seek to dominate this conversation and arrest it completely – shouting, accusing, excluding – are tyrannous' (2019, p. 29). Thus for Eaglestone, 'in literary studies the aim is to help develop a continuing *dis*sensus about the texts we study in order to root, explore and develop our own selves and distinctiveness' (2019, pp. 28–9). The nature of knowledge in English, then, is fractured, contested; there is no single agreed account of the meaning of any given text. In this chapter, I explore the nature of English Literature as a conversation – as a communal subject, drawing on its history as a colonising, nationalising and homogenising force. The chapter will explore questions of reading lists and common experiences, invoking questions of what teenagers 'should' be reading; the use of subject English (Literature) as a political football, and the thorny question of why or indeed if it matters if 90 per cent of all teenagers study *Of Mice and Men*. This chapter will explore the way in which what we read at school continues to be an important part of our adult life, and whether it is deployed as a positive or a negative experience (the communal bond of all having 'suffered' the same texts?).

English as a subject is itself already fractured. Green and Cormack (2008) remind us of 'the various and complex associations with which the term [English] is invested, referring at once and at different times to the *language*, the *nationality* and the *(school-)subject*' (p. 257). In this chapter more than any other in the book, the other 'parts' of English intrude upon the discussion of literature, because shared reading is not just part of teaching literature. It is also a more fundamental aspect of literacy, as we learn to decode and comprehend, skills that underpin knowledge in literature (and in almost all academic subjects) without rising to the level of disciplinary knowledge.

The history of English Literature as a subject

English Literature was not, originally, a subject worth the name. If students in universities around the world studied literature in the 18th and 19th centuries, it was the literature of the Greeks and Romans. The study of 'Belles Lettres' or 'beautiful writing' was not a serious one.

The subject of English Literature as a university discipline in the UK emerged at a time of distinctly Romantic sensibilities; Green and Cormack (2008) argue that this imbued the subject with a particular nationalism and set of sensibilities that have remained in how we think of a literary education today. That emergence of the subject also coincided more or less with the expansion of the British Empire and the development of schools and curriculum across the Empire to consolidate and underpin British rule (Kenway et al., 2017). Raffles (1819), writing his *Minute on the Establishment of a Malay College at Singapore* in 1819, wrote of the importance of providing the 'light of knowledge' as part of the 'benefits of civilisation' wherever a British flag flew around the world (p. 14). Sir John Robert Seeley (1870), a political essayist who ended his career as Professor of History at Cambridge, wrote of his concern for the 'cultivated men' of the Empire (i.e. the Englishmen abroad) who would be living 'in the midst of a vast half-barbarous population' and therefore that there was a need for education to 'enlarge' the views of that population (p. 240). Morgan (1990), discussing the establishment of English studies in Canada, notes that 'significantly, English as a school subject began in the colonies, in Africa, India, Scotland and Ontario long before it was initiated within secondary schooling at "home"' (p. 205).

One of the ways that English Literature was utilised in the curricula of schools across the Empire (whether in countries remaining under direct control or later in countries in transition such as Australia) was in the development of a particularly English culture in students, an 'Englishness' (Morgan, 1990). Green and Cormack discuss this with particular reference to the development of English as a subject in the early years of the 20th century in Australia:

> In this view, literature could be put to work in building and inspiring the child as a particularly 'English' (or 'British') citizen. English Literature was brought into the centre of the curriculum as a site where the progress of the nation and race could be affirmed and its future assured through the training of the young. In Australia, that theme was complicated by its role as a colony and, after 1901, a dominion of the British Empire. In this conception of English, the child in a State school in South Australia was, first and foremost, a member of the British race and the Empire and, at the same time, a prospective citizen of a newly formed Australian nation.
>
> *(Green & Cormack, 2008, p. 262)*

The modern use of the English Literature curriculum in terms of nation-building will be discussed later in this chapter. Green and Cormack (2008) also note the continuity between the previous centuries' studies of Classical literature and the relatively new subject of English Literature was an emphasis on the 'moral-ethical education' such literature could provide (p. 263); this continuity can be seen stretching forward to Michael Gove's assertion that:

> Whether it is Austen's understanding of personal morality, Dickens' righteous indignation, Hardy's stern pagan virtue, all of these authors have something right to teach us which no other experience, other than intimate connection with their novels, can possibly match.
>
> *(Gove, 2011, n.p.)*

Other resonances abound: Lord Macaulay in 1835 highlighted the quality of literature written in English in recommending it be taught throughout the Empire (London, 2003) – the resonances with Gove's assertion that 'our literature is the best in the world' (Gove, 2010, n.p.). Stepping outside the argument to consider the logic of that statement for a moment is to see its absolute arrogance. No one can judge British literature to be the 'best in the world' who is not intimately acquainted with the national literatures of all countries in the world, which would involve, one suspects, a lifetime of study even working in translation. As Morgan (1990) pointed out, 'school editions of "Standard Authors" served as [the] literary armature' of British imperialism; 'at one level the expansiveness of the claim that English Literature embodied the essential truths of "the human condition" is no more than the cultural counterpart to the military domination of a global empire' (p. 205). The deliberate Anglicisation of literature curricula in British colonies around the world continued for decades. Textbooks (called 'The Royal Readers') for the study of English in Trinidad and Tobago during the 1930s and 1940s centred around 'great English writers' like Charles Kingsley, Dickens, Goldsmith and Swift (London, 2002). In this context, calls to 'decolonise' the discipline of English Literature take on a new light; we need to consider how much of our subject's shape today is due to its long partnership with Empire and colonialism (for more on 'canon', see Chapter 5).

Perhaps the best-known example of the use of English Literature in education as a means of promoting the interests of the British Empire is Shakespeare, who came 'to represent the ultimate sign of English literary-cultural authority, the best distillation of Englishness, and thus all that was sacred to colonial elites' (Morgan, 1990, p. 212). It is in this way that Shakespeare was utilised in colonial Indian education to perpetuate 'the myth of English cultural refinement and superiority – a myth that was crucial to the rulers' political interests in India' (Singh, 1989, p. 446). This formed part of a systematic use of English Literature education to maintain the interests of colonial rulers in India, utilising the 'civilising mission of English Literature in relation to various subordinate classes and groups' (Viswanathan, 1998, p. 11), in the light of a consensus that rule in India could only be achieved by means of a co-opted elite group drawn from the Indian native population to act as a 'conduit of Western thought and ideas' (p. 34). Through education, intellectual manipulation reduced the need for coercive military control of colonies of the British Empire. Bhatia (1998) notes that there was debate over whether it should be English Literature or Classical Literature that formed the basis of this educational 'civilisation'; that the debate ended up on the side of English Literature is one of the main drivers behind the international dominance of Shakespeare as an author for study. Interestingly, Shakespeare also becomes from the beginning a means by which resistance, adoption and adaption by Indian authors operate in creating a counter-culture (Singh, 1989).

Reading lists and extra-curricular reading (including 'The Classics') – keeping us all reading the same thing

While the issue of the canon in terms of canonical reproduction and (lack of) representation are considered in Chapter 5, it is worth considering here 'The Classics' and the idea that there are some 'need to have read' books for the educated person, and the sometimes concomitant imposition of these books as the only acceptable extra-curricular reading in schools. A Sky Arts poll in 2019 revealed a number of books that Brits tend to lie about having read: *The Odyssey, To Kill a Mockingbird, War and Peace* and *1984* among them (O'Connor, 2019). Thirty-one per cent of the survey respondents said they lied about having read them in order to appear more intelligent, while 37 per cent said it was in order to join in a conversation about the book, which in itself offers an insight to how we approach reading and texts as acquisitions, not opportunities for learning. Jess Mason, reporting the initial findings of her research on Identity and Reading on Twitter, mentioned both that readers were more likely to lie by omission and allow people to assume that they had read texts rather than outright lying (2020a) and also that a lot of English teachers felt guilty about not having read more of 'The Classics' (2020b).

'The Classics' is a term that is ill-defined: we all know what it means, but the exact texts that it encompasses are difficult to pin down. In England, we would almost certainly include the Brontës, Dickens, Austen, Eliot, Hardy, Stevenson and (Mary) Shelley as 'Classic authors', but beyond that we might find it hard to agree. Is it anything that has been published as part of the Penguin Classic brand? Perhaps, until Morrisey's autobiography was set among their ranks. We might rather suggest a text that is sufficiently old so as to be out of copyright and therefore published by several imprints is a 'Classic'. Age is not sufficient, however, or we might be reading *Varney the Vampyre* at the same rate as *Dracula*. Italo Calvino, in his book *Why Read the Classics?* offers us the following possibilities:

- A classic is a book which with each re-reading offers as much of a sense of discovery as the first reading.
- A classic is a book which even when we read it for the first time gives the sense of re-reading something we have read before.
- A classic is a book which has never exhausted all it has to say to its readers.

(Calvino, 1999, p. 5)

In these terms, we might expand the list of Classics to be much wider than it is traditionally conceptualised, but we might also make an argument for excluding some of the novels that are included simply because of their 19th-century credentials.

A short while ago, thinking about the arguments that are made for the need for every teenager to read large chunks of the canon, I asked a group of my friends – all university educated, a number holding doctorates, university lectureships or high-status professions like patent attorney or teacher – what they read as teens, and specifically whether they had read 'The Classics'. The one thing that united a group of highly educated people was a dislike of Hardy, having been made to read his novels in school; the exception was the person who read *Far from the Madding Crowd* before her class studied it. The majority of us had read mostly among the favoured teen genres of sci-fi and fantasy, but also more widely. The novels of Jean Plaidy came up more than once. One person mentioned having enjoyed *Silas Marner*, which is at least a recommendation for it as a GCSE text. We all had something in common, but none of us had everything in common: we most certainly had not read the entirety of Penguin Classics. Given that this is a group with high 'cultural capital' for the most part, the argument that the force-feeding of Austen, Brontë, Dickens and Hardy into impressionable young minds will promote their social mobility becomes tenuous.

There was also a distinct sense of 'the right book at the right time'. 'Remember that the book which bores you when you are twenty or thirty will open doors for you when you are forty or fifty – and vice versa. Don't read a book out of its right time for you' (Lessing, 1964/2014, p. 18).[1] Many of us felt that we had been exposed to certain Classics too young, or at least at the wrong stage for us. I was among only a few who had enjoyed *Lord of the Flies*; similarly to the Hardy lover, I had read it before encountering it in class and it was re-reading and gaining a sense of how it worked as literature and particularly as a text dripping with symbolism which endeared it to me.

One dissenting voice was raised in favour of having a common set of texts: an American friend who recalled that the case studies he had read in business school were standard cases that were studied by all his contemporaries in business schools across the country. These formed an instant way of bonding with new workmates or colleagues at conferences, with a common set of references. Similarly, Kemmis and Fitzclarence (1986) emphasise the key role of education in 'maintaining inter-generational continuity' (p. 88); we might say one advantage of reading the Classics is that they give us common ground with our parents. Not for English the problem of parents not understanding the 'New Math': they can also remember reading *Middlemarch* at school. There might also be a sense that having suffered through a particular set of texts is a rite of passage which unites both generations and individuals within a generation. A set of common reference points is the basis of cultural literacy (see Chapter 7) but it also once again raises the question of which are the common reference points that we should adopt if we insist on all the references being in common. If, instead, we embrace a wider reading experience that enables us all to have something but not everything in common, the problems of elitism and assimilation become instantly less.

One of the advantages of a shared reading experience in terms of extra-curricular reading is to enable conversations about books and reading with a set of common reference points on which to draw. Those conversations promote the profile and the love of reading, it is to be hoped – there is a joy for a fluent reader in having hated a book and being able to excoriate it. (I maintain the best thing about *Wuthering Heights* is the Ukulele Orchestra of Great Britain's rendering of the Kate Bush song of the same name.[2]) For a less fluent reader, the hatred of the single book may not be distinguishable from the reading experience, and the same potential pleasure or desire to discuss may not be gained – another argument for the right book at the right time.

In late 2019, I had the pleasure of observing one of our PGCE interns[3] guiding his Year 10s in a discussion about their silent reading books (the school required them each to carry a book and read for five minutes at the beginning of English lessons). His enthusiasm was palpable and infectious as the students discussed their reading choices. By the time I saw the same class again four months later, a number of the class had tackled *The Weight of A Thousand Feathers* by Brian Conaghan, which for many of them was a significant step up in literary quality and weight of content from their previous reads. It was not mandated: they had simply enjoyed the class conversations about the book. A 'shared' reading experience in this case started out simply being the act of talking about reading; for some of those students, it translated into a shared experience of a text, but in all cases the students' view of reading as something interesting grew.[4]

If there is one book that has been read by more students in England than any other, it is surely *Of Mice and Men*. During the curriculum reforms of the Coalition Government, it was held up as an example of what was wrong with the examination system because 90 per cent of all teens in England answered their GCSE Literature question on this text. It was certainly a text I read at school in the 1990s, as I remember being so overcome with grief at the end of the book that I could not complete my homework assignment on it. When teaching it, I always managed to dodge reading that final chapter aloud because I could not rely on being able to read it without collapsing in sobs. *Of Mice and Men* is a text we joke with beginning English teachers about in the first few sessions of the PGCE course: a shared text which we can laughingly 'spoiler' for them. (George shoots Lenny, in case you are not familiar with the ending.)

English teachers turned out to have such affection for *Of Mice and Men* that when it was removed from the Key Stage 4 syllabus in England, it was swiftly moved to Key Stage 3. (One of our PGCE interns reported being told by a Year 8 at her placement school that they loved *Of Mice and Men* because it was the only text they studied in three years that had any reference to race in it at all – in a highly multicultural school. The problems attendant upon that statement are discussed in Chapter 5.) The clarity of the symbolism, characterisation and plot contributed to its being considered a good text for teaching, as did its shortness as a text for GCSE. In mentioning this, I am not being pejorative, as many of those who mocked the backlash were; shortness can be a real asset in a class text in that it enables teaching time to be dedicated to the meaty analysis of text and understanding across the whole novel. Simply reading a novel is only the beginning of literary study, and the simple economic truth is that many schools in England cannot afford to allow students to take books home because they cannot afford to replace them, and they must therefore read the text in class. If having a common set of reference points to draw on is an ideal of the English curriculum and the development of cultural capital, does it then matter if 90 per cent of students study the same text? *Of Mice and Men* might perhaps particularly serve that purpose of the commonly suffered text, but that might be my personal relationship with the novel colouring my interpretation.

It is true that there does not seem to be the same concentration on a single text in quite the same way in the reformed GCSE specifications from 2015 on, to judge from the examiners' reports. In Pearson GCSE English Literature in 2017, for example, an examination with over 40,000 candidates, the single most chosen text was *An Inspector Calls* at 26,500 candidates.[5] Even *Macbeth* only attracted 23,000 candidates. One might cynically suggest that the problem with *Of Mice and Men*'s dominance was mainly its American origins, given the emphasis on British texts in the new specifications (and see the next section). But in principle it does not seem problematic for us all to study one text. Many schools rely on a shared reading experience as a transition project from Years 6 to 7, where feeder primary schools read the same novel before it is picked up by the secondary school in September of Year 7. It is perhaps down to the specific desires behind the shared read which make a text appropriate or not. One argument against this is the question of teaching expertise, and its narrowing to a few specific texts, or the concentration of resources on a narrow range, which prevent teachers branching out or finding more suitable texts for their classes. On the other hand, even if students all learn the same text, when it is only one of (I hope) at least four novels they will encounter through English Literature teaching, the range provided by the other three prevents that fear of the narrowed range of teacher expertise.

The class reader

The class reader is a very particular case of a shared reading experience, of thirty or so pupils in the room at once, synchronously reading the same text, or having it read to them by an expert reader.

If one of the reasons we teach the class reader – or encourage any reading of any sort in school – is to promote the love of reading that we know is so important in developing future prosperity in both wealth and happiness terms (e.g. OECD, 2002), then it is a good question as to whether the way we approach class readers is actually doing that, in terms of the traditional 'round-robin' reading, which can draw on teacher or student reading. Westbrook et al. (2019) conducted a study with 20 teachers who read two whole challenging novels in 12 weeks at a faster pace than usual with their classes of average and poor readers aged 12 to 13. 'Simply reading challenging, complex novels aloud and at a fast pace in each lesson repositioned "poorer readers" as "good" readers, giving them a more engaged uninterrupted reading experience over a sustained period' (Westbrook et al., 2019, p. 60). The poorer readers made unprecedented levels of reading gains on stan-dardised tests.

When we think about knowledge and reading, we rarely think about this aspect: the knowledge of what it means to read rapidly and with understanding, to gain the satisfaction of a meaty and interesting text without being so bogged down by its being broken into pieces, or by struggling over individual in-fluencies that we lose track of the overall narrative. If you think about your own reading habits, think about the qualitative difference of a novel read in snippets over a long time and the novel devoured next to a holiday swimming pool, or in the bath on a weekend morning if you are lucky. It is evident from the record of my own reading that if I read a book rapidly, I am more likely to rate it highly, and although there is some two-way causality here – in that if I am enjoying a book, I will read faster – it cer-tainly *is* two-way. To return to *Wuthering Heights*, I finally read the whole of it in two days in order to be able to tutor a student on it during a revision course. I still find the characters to be detestable, but in forcing myself to read it over a short period I came to appreciate the artistry of the writing and the structure. I now acknowledge that it is a great novel: I just do not like it very much.

Oral reading of a shared text is an intrinsic part of English Literature study – one that I have suggested is a 'characteristic pedagogy' in the previous chapter. Westbrook et al. (2019) documented one of the advantages of the teacher reading aloud, particularly at a rapid pace. Reading around the class, or 'round-robin reading', is also widely used in schools around the world (e.g. New Zealand, Brooks & Frankel, 2018; the USA, Ariail & Albright, 2005; and the UK, Warner et al., 2016). Warner et al. (2016) surveyed 360 teachers across a range of subjects in England and found that student and teacher reading aloud was valued highly by teachers across a range of subjects; those who valued teacher reading also valued student reading. Teachers valued reading aloud to the class for various reasons – for their enjoyment (more so English teachers than other subjects); to quieten the class (a far less common reason, although again more selected by English teachers); to reinforce instructions; and to aid in understanding the text. This last reflects the success of Westbrook et al.'s (2019) approach. Interestingly, Frager (2010) links oral reading back to the traditions of the church – with the Bible or tracts being read aloud to congregations in church or to monks in the refectory. In another context, we might also think of the traditional evening reading aloud of the newspaper by patriarchs in working-class mining communities.

Warner et al.'s (2016) data also show high levels of teacher agreement across the curriculum that not knowing when they would be asked to read kept students concentrating. We might also note that for some students reading aloud is a stressful experience (e.g. Gibson, 2008) and it is likely that not knowing when you will be called on to read increases that stress. Warner et al.'s (2016) English teachers were more likely than any other subject other than modern foreign languages to give students time to rehearse reading before being asked to read to the class (with similar levels shown by teachers in support and intervention).

One important aspect of the class reader is the production of the schemata – the mental maps – representing the text in the head of each pupil. When we as teachers read a novel with students in the classroom, we are almost always re-reading that novel, whether it is after a single read to prepare to teach it for the first time, or after multiple re-readings of the novel as part of teaching (Giovanelli & Mason, 2015). Often we are reading it in the context of experience of previous exam questions, sometimes of critical material, of discussions with previous classes, or departmental debates about teaching. The phrase 'contexts of reception' is not usually considered in this light, but sample assessment material is perhaps the most important contextual material that a teacher uses to understand a text and to develop pedagogical content knowledge relating to it. That responsibility, either at A level or at university level, shifts to the student, who uses past exam papers to prepare and structure their knowledge of a text and *what* knowledge of a text it would make sense to develop. More broadly, the contextual knowledge we possess also pre-figures the text and how we make sense of it: preparing to read a Shakespeare play as a tragedy or a comedy, for example, or reading *The Murder of Roger Ackroyd* with a knowledge of the conventions of detective fiction, but also the socio-historical knowledge we have that might be used to understand non-contemporary texts.

That a teacher is always re-reading and bringing a particular context to that reading changes the way we experience the novel and the things we seek to highlight as we read it with each new group. Think, for example, of foreshadowing. While some foreshadowing is heavily emphasised by authors to ensure readers pick up on it (think of *Romeo and Juliet*'s prologue, for example, with its 'star-cross'd lovers', their 'misadventured piteous overthrows' and 'death-mark'd love'), some is only visible in hindsight. Think, for example, of the pathetic fallacy at the beginning of *Great Expectations*. A re-reading teacher will pick up on this and make a heavier point of it than the initial reader, even if they are looking for pathetic fallacy. Thus our reading of the book is framed in a different way than it would be otherwise. Giovanelli & Mason (2015) argue that this prevents 'authentic' reading experiences, through a careful dissection of a lesson on *Holes*. They argue that teacher-led discussion of a text changes what is 'figured' (Stockwell, 2009) – that is, what is brought into the focus of the attention, and what is ground, from how a student would naturally encounter the text. This directly undermines Knights' argument about the 'communal and democratic process ... of deciding ... which semantic item is figure and which ground' (2017, p. 5), discussed in the previous chapter. In the classroom, we might learn mostly from 'discourse *about* the text' (Mason, 2016, p. 67) rather than reading the text itself as we would in a natural reading environment. Students re-read before they have even read. (Interestingly, books for very young children are often written and illustrated with the very expectation of re-reading in mind. The illustrations in the *Winnie and Wilbur* books often contain elements that will only make sense – or even be noticeable – on re-reading. Each reading offers more than the previous reading, which leads me to ask whether they meet Calvino's definition of a classic?) Mason and Giovanelli (2017) go on to examine how the school editions of texts structure the development of schemata further, through the use of pre-reading questions which direct students what to notice where. They argue that this 'pre-figuring' privileges some interpretations over others. One difficulty of this is that where a student embraces a dissenting interpretation from the set of pre-approved interpretations, it is likely to be disregarded or assessed as 'wrong knowledge' despite the principles of the discipline discussed in the previous chapter. The damaging effects of this where the interpretation is a feminist or critical race one are considered in Chapter 5.

Frager (2010) argues that one of the issues with reading aloud in the classroom at all is that it prevents one of the key mechanisms that enable us as readers to make sense of the text: going back to revisit, re-read or check, all of which are enabled by silent reading. He also notes that oral reading by the teacher in particular has the effect of limiting meaning-making in a similar process to that described by Giovanelli and Mason:

> [I]t is unlikely that students listening to an oral reading of a story will employ the same meaning activities – predicting, visualizing, asking clarifying questions, and summarizing – that they would in silent reading. Because the author's feelings are re-constructed and transmitted by the oral reader, the listener's engagement with the text is more passive than in silent reading. Creating a mental image or asking a clarifying question is possible while listening, but it isn't necessary because the oral reader will use cues – emphasis, pauses, and volume changes – to signal to listeners when to engage their emotions or to give special attention to an idea.
>
> *(Frager, 2010, p. 33)*

In contrast, Collins (2005) discusses the value of this 'storytelling' aspect of reading aloud in capturing primary readers, choosing the words of one Year 3 girl that the teacher was 'dragging me into the story' as her title quotation. It is also important to note that Frager's point assumes a level of ability at effective silent reading which is not true of all readers in all classrooms. We might argue that the oral interpretation of a novel by a teacher is a way of modelling the understanding and reading of text, as well as modelling what it means to read aloud. Both of these are valuable forms of knowledge although they relate more closely to decoding and comprehension than to the discipline of literature in a more specific way.

There is a counter-argument that the kind of pre-figured reading noted by Giovanelli and Mason is what the study of literature is – distancing ourselves from mere 'reading' of the text. It might deal with Frager's objection to oral reading removing the possibility of re-reading and checking textual meaning, because it gives a structure. However, it also ties in, as Mason and Giovanelli (2017) highlight, to the knowledge turn and the privileging of cultural literacy and knowledge about texts over reader response and authentic reading. I would suggest that in pre-framing the reading of a novel in this way, we reduce the elements that students have to draw on in developing their schema. We might view this as being a hindrance to the development of a key part of knowledge in English Literature – how to read and develop an interpretation of a novel independently – or we might also view it as a key means of modelling that development of interpretation, if it is worked through questioning as opposed to instruction. It is also possible that the best of both worlds might be obtained through the rapid reading of the text without guidance to the 'important parts' followed by an in-depth study of the text as a whole. The fact that we often ask A-level students (and, in some schools, GCSE students) to read texts independently before the class study suggests that unconsciously English teachers are scaffolding the development of these skills.

John Yandell (2013), however, argues for a very different conception of the act of novel reading. He argues that our conception of the act of silent, private reading, and the classroom experience as a poor substitute for, or at best a preliminary to, that private reading stage, is to oversimplify and misunderstand the role of novel and society. He is arguing primarily for the social construction of meaning within the classroom – that is, the kind of argumentation discussed in Chapter 2 which is part of the characteristic pedagogies of English Literature – but I think it also speaks to the wider issue of how we develop our understanding of any given text that has some form of shared reading associated with it. There is a natural urge on the part of readers to tell about a text, to find someone else who has read it and to discuss it, which is perhaps particularly developed in fluent readers for pleasure, but is also present in those who have been made to read books they disliked. In conveying our opinion, or rather our judgement of a text, we enter into a dialogue that enables us to confirm or change those judgements and to incorporate new information. Our justified arguments may require extra rationalisation, or we may discover that we cannot justify them after all, and in doing so have to consider alternative interpretations and valuations of a text.

National shared reading

I touched briefly on the possibility of the English Literature curriculum as a nationalising force in the previous chapter. As well as the 'British' (but principally English) texts of the curriculum reforms of the Coalition Government in the UK, and the use of Scottish texts in Scotland, Australia also has mandated teaching of Australian texts in schools, although the take-up is debatable (Cheung, 2019). An insistence on British texts in England could speak to
'two anxieties':

> one of reverse colonisation by the overgrown infant that is the USA, particularly evident in that concern over the prevalence of *Of Mice and Men* at GCSE; and one that the centre cannot hold in the wake of devolution and the increasing assertion of independent nationalist identities of Scottishness and Welshness.
>
> *(Elliott, 2014, p. 193)*

Bell (1994) discusses the tensions in the construction of a 'national' English Literature curriculum in the context of New Zealand, where in the 1990s there were differing discourses of nationhood, one looking towards the European origins of its settlers and the other locating itself firmly in the Pacific diaspora:

> Discursively, the former defends the continuance of a predominantly white, male national culture, best signified by the name 'New Zealand'; the latter promotes voices traditionally marginal to that culture – those of Maori, women and Pacific Island immigrants and best signified by the indigenous 'Aotearoa'.
>
> *(Bell, 1994, p. 173)*

There has been some movement towards the importance of incorporation of national literature in English-speaking countries around the world, to reformulate English Literature as literature *in English* rather than literature *from England*. Justice (2018), in the context of Canada, argues for the importance of indigenous literatures in part as a way to enable people to learn to be human within the contexts of their own community. In many of the former British colonies around the world, I would argue that the study of texts by indigenous authors is essential for everyone, to understand the context of the country in which they live. In England, with its lack of indigenous population,[6] the shouts of white nationalism can drown out the importance of having texts that speak to the range of peoples living in the country now. I make the case for this importance in Chapter 5.

Linda Colley, in her book *Britons: Forging the Nation 1707–1837*, considered the idea of Britishness to have been principally constructed against the 'other' of French Catholicism during the long 18th century. In her preface to the second edition, now almost two decades old, she wrote:

> Given the unprecedented level of change we are all now living through (and this is emphatically not just a challenge felt by the British), it is understandable that many people hunger for some kind of renewed anchorage, and often for a narrower, more traditional and seemingly more secure sense of who they are.
>
> *(Colley, 2002, p. xvii)*

It is a view that has increased resonance in the late 2010s and early 2020s, as we see more nationalist rhetoric being used by politicians and in the media, and the closing of borders as we seem to be heading towards more insular nations. There must be a temptation for many politicians, where the curriculum is part of their remit, to utilise it as a tool to support that nationalism. In doing so they conceptualise the nation as one particular thing and co-opt their readings of texts to support that thing. The colonialist, Empire-based view of the world which was explored in the first section of this chapter was also shown to have strong links to the rhetoric around the study of English Literature in the curriculum in England today. This promotes a set of texts which are white in their authors, characters and concerns, and which, because they draw on a romanticised past, strongly linked with Empire, ignore the multicultural and diverse nature of literature in English in the 21st century. Nationalist approaches to literature rely on assimilationist models, not multicultural ones.

> Assimilationist ideas are racist ideas. Assimilationists can position any racial group as the superior standard that another racial group should be measuring themselves against, the benchmark they should be trying to reach.
>
> *(Kendi, 2019, p. 29)*

As I contend in Chapters 5 and 7, this assimilation is not only racial but also class-based in some of the ideas being promoted in English education today. However, the implementation of text selection as a tool is left to classroom teachers, and unless they choose to emphasise the nationalist aspect and to drive home a message of national pride based in the literary heritage of that country, it seems unlikely to be a productive tool. Knowledge of a text is not fixed: there is no set list of useful political talking points that all students can be set to learn from any given text. This gives us a clue to the nature of knowledge in English Literature, but also how it is regarded in some political circles and why the English curriculum has become such a fiercely used tool. For some elites, knowledge about texts is fixed: there is one interpretation – theirs – and that is the 'right' interpretation.

The selection of national texts may, therefore, be a useful *rhetorical* tool in a politician's armory, which returns us to the state of play in the 19th century when the subject of English was utilised to drive pro-British rhetoric throughout the Empire, and to contribute to the development of the truly colonised indigenous group which then operates in the interests of the coloniser. Gary Snapper (2018) has argued that as English teachers we need to utilise these discourses explicitly in the teaching of literature: 'the cultural and political challenge to the status quo offered by devolution – the post-colonial spirit of it – [offers] us the opportunity to put cultural and literary politics more centrally and more explicitly into our teaching' (p. 213). In highlighting this opportunity, Snapper returns us to the question of what it is we are teaching, and recalls to me the words of John Carey:

> [L]iterature gives you ideas to think with. It stocks your mind. It does not indoctrinate, because diversity, counter-argument, reappraisal and qualification are its essence. But it supplies the materials for thought. Also, because it is the only art capable of criticism, it encourages questioning, and self-questioning.
>
> *(Carey, 2005, p. 208)*

This is perhaps a rather naively hopeful note, but it expresses the full possibilities of the subject and challenges the simple promotion of nationalist rhetoric through literature syllabi. The 'ideology sold' is not necessarily the 'ideology bought by the pupils it was intended for' (Morgan, 1990, p. 229). This is a salutary reminder for all of us, because it is also a caution about the efficacy of the strategies suggested elsewhere in this book about improving representation: it is not only what we teach but how we teach it that makes a difference to what pupils learn from (and about) the text.

Conclusion

Shared reading is an intrinsic part of English Literature in terms of pedagogies and of content. It has been used historically as propaganda, and there are contemporary attempts to use it in the same way. As a pedagogy, we do not often stop to think about our underlying assumptions about collective oral reading in the classroom, and in terms of content, we need to think carefully about what shared reading we are promoting and why. Questions here about the nature of 'The Classics' will be picked up in the discussion of the canon in Chapter 5 and of cultural literacy and cultural capital in Chapter 7. I have followed Giovanelli and Mason in considering reading in the classroom to be largely 're-reading', which echoes the discussion in Chapter 2 of ways in which knowledge is constructed in English Literature in the light of conversation with others, whether those others are inside the classroom or outside it, in the space in which the teacher works. The nature of discussion around texts makes it a powerful tool for learning but also for the creation of community within classrooms, across generations, and across society (of which more will be discussed in the final chapter).

Notes

1 I encountered this quotation thanks to Robert Eaglestone's masterful *Literature: Why It Matters* but it led me to reading *The Golden Notebook* for myself.
2 www.youtube.com/watch?v=FF0VaBxb27w
3 Students on our PGCE programme are known as interns.
4 I should thank this intern – Joseph la Porte – for a number of stimulating discussions about encouraging reading for pleasure with reluctant students, and for being able to draw on our discussion of his PGCE assignment about these Year 10s.
5 https://qualifications.pearson.com/content/dam/pdf/GCSE/English%20Literature/2015/Exam-materials/1ET0_01_pef_201708231.pdf
6 My original academic background was in the medieval history, languages and literatures of the British Isles, Ireland and Scandinavia. If there is one thing that the study of such a period shows us, it is that the white population of the UK is a thoroughly mongrel mix and there is no such thing as an indigenous English person. We also know that there have been Black people living in Britain since at least the Roman era.

4

THE CASE OF SHAKESPEARE

Ewan Fernie, addressing the question 'What good is Shakespeare?' answers with the argument that Shakespeare is freedom:

> I propose that Shakespeare can help us to see freedom less as a substantial thing or concept and more as a specific and welcoming disposition towards life. For the plays suggest that the forms of freedom are as various as life is; they suggest freedom can be found wherever life is affirmed. As often as not in Shakespeare, freedom is a thrilling surprise, a kind of secular blessing or grace.
>
> (Fernie, 2017, p. 5)

In this chapter, I consider the specific and unique place of Shakespeare in the English curriculum and explore debates over Shakespeare and what it means to have studied Shakespeare. I begin with an exploration of the knowledge required for teaching a single text, *Macbeth*, which is the most popularly taught play in the UK, before considering what the case of Shakespeare can tell us about interpretation and context in the discipline more widely. I explore how pedagogies and especially 'active methods' can affect the kinds of knowledge of Shakespeare we develop, and consider his apparent universality.

Macbeth: the national play of the UK?

What knowledge would I need to teach *Macbeth* (as a teacher)?[1]

The first thing that springs to mind when I start answering this question is that initially I might not need very much knowledge about *Macbeth*. I would need a broad understanding of how to read Shakespeare, and then I could come up with some of the most fundamental 'knowledge' aspects:

- The outline of the plot;
- The characters, their relation and some of their characteristics;
- The major themes in the play;
- The structure of the play.

Even if I had knowledge of the play from my own school days (which I do), I would want to re-read the play to remind myself of nuances and to identify key moments or images which I would want to draw to a class's attention.

Then I might need – or at least appreciate – some contextual knowledge of the time of the play's production:

- The context of James VI and I's inheritance from Elizabeth I of the English throne and the potential that had to affect Shakespeare's livelihood;
- James VI and I's obsession with witches (and his writing of a book about them called *Daemonologie*);
- An understanding both of the Divine Right of Kings and of Shakespearean attitudes to religion, morality, heaven and hell;
- Staging conventions as they relate to ghosts, invisible daggers, castles and moving forests.

Then there is a vast range of contextual knowledge that might or might not be useful for understanding the play or simply appreciating it:

- What 'from his mother's womb untimely ripp'd' means in a modern context (and the tradition of speaking the truth while lying in relation to all sorts of creatures associated with magic);
- The tradition of the comic break in a tragedy (the Porter);
- The cultural significance which *Macbeth* has come to have in terms of modern politics;
- The fact that the Queen Mother was born at Glamis Castle (although that probably would not enter into my discussion with under-18s these days!);
- The tradition of the *femme fatale*, or even the blaming of Eve for the Fall of Man, in relation to Lady Macbeth.

I would also want to know some alternative interpretations. My own English teacher, Mrs Gadd, who was a formative influence on me in more ways than one, argued strongly that Lady Macbeth was not the instigator of the regicide, but was in fact acting the loyal wife and doing what her husband had heavily hinted that he wanted her to in his letter, persuading him to an action which he wanted to be persuaded to. This was backed up – as it must always be! – with textual citation and argument based around the ways in which the Macbeths react to the actual killing, and the final fate of Lady Macbeth who fades away once her use to her husband is over. This is the interpretation that I have always loved to promote to classes, who usually argue fiercely with me, drawing on textual evidence to support. That, to me, is knowledge in action. *Macbeth* is a Scottish play for a Scottish king, but there is perhaps also a ghost of Elizabeth I in Lady Macbeth, and an implicit sigh of relief for having a male back on the throne.

If I were, on the other hand, making a list of essential knowledge about *Macbeth* to put in a knowledge organiser and issue to Year 8, I would almost certainly not have the list above. A knowledge organiser would almost certainly say something along the lines of 'Lady Macbeth bullies her husband into killing the king'. If I were to write instead that 'Lady Macbeth feels she has no choice but to persuade her husband into killing the king, after he makes clear he wants her to do so', many might rightly object. The value in either proposition is *not in the proposition itself* but in the argument and discussion around it. Knowledge in English, to return to the argument of Chapter 2, is contested and constructed. That Lady Macbeth is Macbeth's wife is an acceptable and useful fact, but it hardly gets us further into unpacking the play or any deeper understanding of literary knowledge.

I last taught the play more than ten years ago, and although I have seen dozens of productions over the years, the last was roughly contemporaneous with that teaching (and I can remember nothing about it save that Macbeth was played by a TV actor who was rather short and, by accident or design, his characterisation was Napoleonesque-short-man-complex). I can recall a handful of quotations that may or may not be those that I would want to emphasise to students, but a knowledge organiser approach would probably include some key quotations. The 'knowledge' I would prefer to teach is how to select the quotations you want to use.

In her experiment of this nature, Bleiman (2020) distinguishes between 'door opening' knowledge, which can be built upon, about the key questions in literature, which quickly blurs into the domain of 'skills', and the 'Trivial Pursuits' type of facts (p. 59). This is a point that will be returned to in Chapter 7. Some of those Trivial Pursuits facts are interesting and useful in moving us forward in an understanding of the text, but it is their application that is important, and too many of them are simply frivolous and unimportant, but easily tested for recall.

There are other kinds of knowledge that I would want English teachers to know about *Macbeth*, which would not necessarily be the kind of knowledge they would pass on to their students, but would inform their teaching. *Macbeth* is one-fifth of all Shakespeare play-teaching in the UK (Elliott & Olive, 2019): I would ask teachers to think about why this is, and if it is really the most suitable play for their students. (Perhaps it is, I have regular debates about this with myself. I think there are good reasons why *Macbeth* is particularly suitable as a play for teenagers, not least that it has a relatively simple plot, easily distinguished characters and some useful violence, all features identified in our survey as good for Shakespeare teaching (Elliott & Olive, 2019).) I might then ask them to consider the fact that the play that occupies the '*Macbeth*' slot in the USA is *Julius Caesar* and to think about the relationship between each play and the system of government, and indeed attitude to rulers, in each country. This is knowledge about *Macbeth* too which brings us further into our understanding of the play, but also of society and our relationship to it. In autumn 2019, the *Guardian* ran an opinion column entitled 'Like Macbeth, Johnson is too steeped in blood to turn back' (Rawnsley, 2019). This is the part of knowledge that runs into cultural literacy (not capital) as we start to be able to engage in political debate and the life of society through our recognition of the allusion, to both play and specific quotation:

> I am in blood
> Stepped in so far that, should I wade no more,
> Returning were as tedious as go o'er.
> (3.4.142–144)

Perhaps we as a subject are 'stepped in so far' that returning is too tedious – we do run the risk of 'knowledge of Shakespeare' being largely limited to 'knowledge of Macbeth' and one other play, most likely to be *A Midsummer Night's Dream* (Elliott & Olive, 2019). That limitation applies to two groups – both the students who study a limited range of plays, but also to their teachers. This is a more real danger than the narrowing of the pool of expertise in novels to *Of Mice and Men*, discussed in the previous chapter, because the number of Shakespeare's plays taught to each student is usually fewer than the number of novels. We know that beginning teachers draw on their knowledge of plays that they were taught at school (Elliott, 2014), so may feel most confident in teaching a text that they were taught via the kind of pedagogies they need to use. We also know that time and resources are short and that this can prevent the change to new texts (Elliott & Olive, 2019). If we posit the existence of a communal pool of professional knowledge, in the form of shared resources and helpful colleagues, whether that it is on a departmental level or on the level of the subject community, then there needs to be a critical mass of people teaching different plays to keep the pedagogical content knowledge of those plays alive, or we run the risk of having completely honed our ability to teach *Macbeth* but to be at a loss should we have to switch to *Henry V*. (I have argued elsewhere that awarding bodies tend to maintain continuity on specifications in order to make them attractive to time-poor teachers who do not want to have to change their entire teaching repertoire with every new reform of a qualification (Elliott, 2017).)

I think we also run the risk of teaching by rote and becoming blind to new interpretations or becoming bored by our texts as teachers, which does not make for an ideal teaching or learning experience. One of the joys of teaching texts (reflexively, at least; possibly not from a set list of required knowledge points) is discovering new gems buried in the text:

> My favourite metaphor for this [discovering new things while teaching plays again] is that of a large country house, a stately home that one has visited repeatedly, finding a new room or passage or even a whole wing that one didn't discover on the last visit.
> (Jackson, 2019, p. 76)

Even more so is the joy of finding your way through a new Shakespeare play with a group of students, providing you have the confidence and the support to do so.

Interpreting Shakespeare's plays

One of the delights of Shakespeare's plays is what Emma Smith calls 'the sheer and pervasive gappiness' of Shakespeare's drama (Smith, 2020, p. 2). One of the consequences, therefore, of studying Shakespeare has to be the induction of the student into this key component of knowledge in English Literature: that interpretations are many and varied, as explored in Chapter 2 and throughout this book. Shakespeare provides a useful way into this concept because of the obviousness of the variety of interpretations – *Hamlet* has become a by-word for the debate around its main character, for example. The lack of stage directions coupled with the ways in which interpretation is couched in performance provides if not a blank canvas then certainly a Rorschach test of a picture. I have spoken of genre as a threshold concept in English Literature and I wonder if the concept of interpretation as separate from text is another.

Sitting with ambiguity is an essential part of working with Shakespeare in other ways, in that there are some parts of his language in terms of words or phrases which are simply lost to us – or potentially which were never sufficiently embedded in the oral language around them to be passed on in other ways.

> The more of Shakespeare's words one looks up, the more one discovers that, time after time, according to the OED, he turns out to have used language in wholly individual ways or (more often) to have originated usages that subsequently became established in the language.
>
> *(Brewer, 2013, p. 345)*

Based on the 'first usage' data in the Oxford English Dictionary, Brewer (2013) estimates that one in ten of Shakespeare's lexemes (i.e. not counting different forms of the same word) was a new usage. It is hardly surprising that our students are not entirely confident with all of them, particularly since a number of them only appear in Shakespeare's works. Yet even teachers are nervous of not being able to explain every word and its meaning in a play (Elliott, 2014). We have the ability to model different sets of knowledge here: first, we can show how to draw on the resource of the edited play text, or the internet, to search for meaning; but we can also model the ability to sit with ambiguity, and to work with a text where not every individual word is comprehensible, but the general gist is. Above all, I think we have a responsibility to model a lack of fear of not understanding, to model a kind of confidence with the text and a belief that it is not beyond our reach or the reach of our students. It is for this reason that I find *No Fear Shakespeare* or other 'translations' of the text to be counter-productive. It is important to know what is going on, but to treat Shakespeare as a foreign language is to ramp up students' anxieties about the texts and the consequent potential for them to reject it as too difficult.

Ambiguity extends further, however, into the interpretations of the plays themselves, and here there is a further tension:

> We all know that Shakespeare's plays sustain multiple interpretations, which is part of what makes them Shakespeare, and that those interpretations are subject to individual interpretation and evolution over time, yet we persist in demanding that our students pretend, at least for the duration of a paper, that one interpretative approach trumps all the others.
>
> *(Hartley, 2019, p. 21)*

We may even engage in that fiction ourselves, at least in regard to some elements of the plays, while restricting the vantage point of multiple interpretations to specific instances when it is most relevant: Are the witches real? Are Macbeth's visions (the dagger and Banquo) real? These instances are most readily expressed in questions for debate when it comes to study below sixth form, and perhaps always. Is Bianca really the 'good' child in *The Taming of the Shrew*?

But this raises another question: To what extent can or should we restrict the range of interpretations our students engage in when it comes to Shakespeare's plays. In thinking about this, I would like to consider three questions: How should we read *The Tempest*? Is Othello Black? Is Isabella to blame in *Measure for Measure*?

To take the last case first: in my last year of teaching, I had a sixth form class who were studying *Measure for Measure* with their other English teacher. I had not studied the text myself at that point, nor yet seen it in the theatre. But I was very sure that the interpretation of Isabella's character that my students were putting forward was not justifiable. They entirely blamed her for her troubles with Angelo, labelling her a tease and knowing in her interactions with the male characters. This in itself would not be an infeasible interpretation if it were not for the fact that it was simply based on a dislike of the character, and their interpretation and their dislike were reinforcing each other. Without any sympathy for her character, they were unable to see that any other interpretation was possible, and as a result neither justified their argument nor took the play as a whole, in a text where ambiguity and counter-balancing are key themes. This is the risk of personal response: it can become *too* personal. It is part of developing knowledge in English Literature to understand the difference between this kind of personal reaction to an individual character and an appropriate analysis of presentation of character, backed up by textual detail.

Othello, meanwhile, has been the subject of a number of discussions about his racial origins. Some disputants maintain strongly that he is not what we would call Black today but is merely darker-skinned than the allegedly typical pale Englishman of his time. To insist on this interpretation in the classroom is to engage in an act of erasure of the only *potential* leading Black character in Shakespeare. Othello may be a tragic hero, and he may murder his wife, but he is also presented as charismatic, brave and successful before his downfall. As Butler (2015) has pointed out, the question of whether or not he is actually Black is by no means the most interesting question in the play; but to insist that he is not, or possibly even to allow the debate in the classroom, is an act of potential symbolic violence (see Chapter 5) and certainly an act of erasure.

Finally, let us consider *The Tempest*. It is possible, perhaps even likely (especially in the first years of secondary school), that this play is taught with an emphasis on the magical elements coupled with the romance, in a way which entirely avoids questions of post-colonialism, the racist portrayal of Caliban, and the question of slavery in terms of both Caliban and Ariel. Even if this teaching choice was not enforced by deliberate avoidance, and would be complemented by responsive teaching should students raise these questions, it would be highly likely to miss out some of the most significant elements of interpretation of the play. It is a possible interpretation that this is a light-hearted play about magic with no real difficulties to be considered, but is it at all justifiable given our contemporary understandings? Is it really a true 'knowledge' of the play if these complications are not at least acknowledged?

I worry that in raising the latter two questions I am privileging my own interpretations and worldview, and risk being too 'right on'. (I am confident that basing your interpretation of the text on like or dislike of a character is not acceptable!) We necessarily tend to simplify difficult issues at the lower end of the secondary age range, which might be when we focus on the magical elements of *The Tempest* at the exclusion of the others; simultaneously dealing with difficult questions in sixth form, which is when *Othello* tends to be taught, is to be expected. The overall point is valid, however: that to promote one interpretation in the context of multiple interpretation is a responsibility which must be carefully considered. There is also the responsibility to the student, when it comes to the context of examination texts, to provide a sufficient range of interpretation and interpretative knowledge that will enable the student to make a response which meets the approbation of the examiner. I am most concerned, however, that when teaching Shakespeare to 11- to 12-year-olds, teachers are most likely to elide challenging interpretations and to present the equivalent of Bowdlerised texts, via not the text itself but the analysis of that text. The most popular text for teaching to 11-year-olds in the UK is *A Midsummer Night's Dream* (Elliott & Olive, 2019): this is a play featuring threatened honour killings, forced marriage, date rape drugs, spousal abuse via coercive control, bestiality and mockery of the working class, to name but a few of the issues in it. For the most part, it is taught as a hilarious play about fairies and poor acting. If we elide the most challenging aspects of Shakespeare at the start of secondary school, we also arguably elide the most important feature of the way we utilise his work as adults and in society, as discussed in the final section of this chapter.

Using Shakespeare to explore contextual knowledge

Shakespeare's plays are a particularly useful case for exploring contextual knowledge in English Literature. As students will study at least two plays over the course of their school career in England (the regulations mandate two in Key Stage 3 and one in Key Stage 4, but there is no need for the one in Key Stage 4 to be a different one from the two, a somewhat important oversight), and elsewhere are likely to study more than one play, generic sociohistorical context of Shakespeare and his times is also often taught. Indeed, the introduction to Shakespeare may well be this kind of contextual knowledge of Shakespearean times and of the Globe Theatre. This means that most students will have some generic knowledge of gender relations in Tudor times, but in a broad-brush way which can lead to some deeply inaccurate contextual statements in the opening lines of GCSE essays. Women may have been subordinate legally, but that is complicated in a country ruled by a woman, and they were not the entirely passive objects that they are sometimes made out to be. Sociohistorical contextual knowledge can obscure students' knowledge of the realities of human nature; the rebellion of Juliet in *Romeo and Juliet* reflects some of that underlying aspect, no matter what the historical context.

Thus, Shakespeare helps us to consider the difference between useful, specific contextual knowledge and the more generic knowledge which is less useful for interpretation. For example, considering the fact of candlelit stages in original productions helps to illuminate (pun intended) the imagery of *Romeo and Juliet*, for example, in a very concrete way, whereas generic knowledge about the role of women does not, unless linked to very specific elements of the play. What you need is knowledge that takes you further into the text.[2]

In a similar way, Candido (2019) talks of the increase in understanding that can be given by considering where on stage in the Elizabethan theatre some speeches take place. Playing between the canopy (heaven) and the trapdoor (the entry to hell) brings a very real sense of danger and 'a much richer level of irony' (p. 54). He lists several examples such as the prayer scene in *Hamlet* or the attempted rape of Isabella in *Measure for Measure* in which this aspect is important. This is a very different approach to treating the play as play and not as text than many of the 'active methods' (discussed below) which emphasise play as enacted. In raising this kind of contextual awareness

> the sole aim of the exercise is to get students to think creatively about the myriad symbolic and thematic possibilities that the mere physical aspects of an Elizabethan theatre provide for them
>
> *(Candido, 2019, p. 59)*

I would suggest, however, that there is currently an exception in terms of where sociohistorical knowledge of a more general kind could be usefully taught in schools, and that is in relation to 19th-century texts, given that in England the unseen texts in the GCSE examinations will at least partly be drawn from this era. So while workhouses, pickpockets and a generic knowledge of Victorian attitudes to poverty are necessary for understanding *Oliver Twist*, they may also provide valuable background for later examination. In this, we see again the tension between teaching for everyone, who will be expected to achieve a qualification in English, and developing the necessary understanding of how contextual knowledge works to support interpretation, through the introduction of specific items of context, for those who will go further in the discipline of English Literature.

Assessment and Shakespeare

In the introductory chapter, I suggested that one way we could validate the kinds of knowledge that we teach was by looking to examination and assessment. Shakespeare provides an excellent case study for this validation. A few years ago, I became the custodian of what might be formally called an archive, but informally is two plastic crates containing manila folder after folder stuffed with every English exam paper a local teacher, Michael Matejtschuk, had collected over the course of his long career, a gift for which I was immensely grateful as it fed my twin interests of English and assessment. Sifting through, I was immediately struck by the early Shakespeare examination papers for A level. In 1966, the first question on the paper tells candidates to:

> Choose **two** of the following passages, of which **one,** but not more, must be taken from passages (*a*) to (*d*) and then:
>   (i)   Rewrite each of your chosen passages in full in MODERN ENGLISH. Your chief object is to make the meaning as clear as possible.
>   (ii) Indicate the *exact* context of each in not more than two or three sentences.
>   (iii) Comment on those aspects of each passage which contribute most towards its particular poetic and dramatic effects.
>
> *(UCLES, 1966)*

There follow seven passages of approximately 14 lines verse or the equivalent, two each from *Othello* and *Antony and Cleopatra* in (a) to (d) and then one each from *Love's Labours Lost, The Tempest* and *Henry V.* A second section asks for two essays, with the same choice of plays. The entire paper has a time allowance of two and a half hours. There is no indication of the weighting of different aspects of the paper. By 1968, the format has changed: although the first question is still extract-based, each passage has one specific question about italicised lines in the passage and a second one relating it to the play as a whole. Nevertheless, these extracts demonstrate that at one point assessment suggested that one of the most important forms of knowledge about Shakespeare's plays was the ability to 'translate', although that is not the word used, the Renaissance English into Modern English – that is, to produce what we might now see as part of 'No Fear Shakespeare'; second, that the students were expected to know with extreme detail the events of plays and where any given speech was to be found within the text (no scene references are given in the exam paper).

To a modern eye, this is extremely unusual as an advanced examination question: it is both too simple, not requiring any of the argument construction or advanced thinking about texts we would expect, and too difficult – how many of us would expect our students to be absolutely fluent in Shakespearean language, or indeed would feel comfortable ourselves? I have known teaching students whose first act with any Shakespeare was to go online to find a plain English parallel text. Being able to read Shakespeare's language with ease is a decided advantage for studying English Literature, but it is not a skill that we require of all students. Indeed, the language aspect is one of the most problematic for students, and for teachers in their motivation of those students. When I researched trainee teachers' feelings of readiness to teach Shakespeare in relation to their own school days, one recalled that 'No one in the class could pronounce the words correctly and I was frustrated and bored' (Elliott, 2016, pp. 204–5). All 12 of the student teachers who provided narrative data for that study had some sort of anxiety about teaching Shakespeare in relation to the language and lower-attaining students, although several noted that these anxieties had not in fact been realised in the classroom. However, in terms of validation of knowledge for progression, we might suggest that a comfort, or, as I have termed it in the previous section, a confidence, with 'translating' Shakespeare might well be a necessary skill even if not one that is formally acknowledged or assessed.

The essay questions are also of interest to the modern English teacher, in that they are more quixotic, less predictable and potentially more difficult than the questions in contemporary exam papers which have to follow a set pattern for reasons of validity and reliability in marking.

> **Either** (a) 'The "free and open nature" leads innocence to destruction.' Is this an adequate comment on the character of **either** Othello or Desdemona?
>
> **Or** (b) Consider *Othello* as a dramatic poem.
>
> **Either** (a) Discuss the part played by the 'war between the sexes' in *Antony and Cleopatra*.
>
> **Or** (b) Estimate the contribution which the poetry makes to the total effect of *Antony and Cleopatra*.
>
> **Either** (a) 'Armado: "The words of Mercury are harsh after the songs of Apollo. You that way: we this way."' Discuss the importance of these final words of *Love's Labour's Lost* in an interpretation of the play.
>
> **Or** (b) Write an essay on the use Shakespeare makes of pastoral conventions in *Love's Labour's Lost*.
>
> **Either** (a) 'For Shakespeare forgiveness is the supreme virtue, but a virtue that must be achieved through suffering.' To what extent does this statement give you useful insight into *The Tempest*?
>
> **Or** (b) Show how Shakespeare differentiates his characters by the nature of the verse which he employs in *The Tempest*.
>
> **Either** (a) 'A historical play calls for a succession of episodes.' Show how Shakespeare has welded the episodes of *Henry V* into a dramatic whole.
>
> **Or** (b) How far do you consider that Shakespeare demonstrates in *Henry V* that patriotism is an inadequate motive for human conduct?
>
> *(UCLES, 1966, p. 6)*

These questions are all closed book, I assume, given that the first section requires students to locate the passage precisely within the play. They demonstrate considerably less framing than contemporary A-level questions. Some do represent a familiar approach in providing 'critical' interpretations of plays in the form of an unattributed quotation to which a response is required. There is also an emphasis on Shakespeare as poetry, which would be unusual, I think, in a modern classroom. The questions on forgiveness and the final question on patriotism as a motive for human conduct also speak to an engagement with Shakespeare's plays psychologically with a wider relevance than just the text.

To know or not to know? That is the question

Shakespeare is a unique author in England, having been the only author named for compulsory study on the National Curriculum since its inception (Olive, 2015). He is also widely studied across the world, whether in translation or in the original. There are few students in English-speaking countries who have entirely avoided Shakespeare in their educational careers. In our survey of UK Shakespeare teaching, 91 per cent of respondents thought teaching Shakespeare was important, and 74 per cent agreed that study of Shakespeare should be compulsory, although we particularly enjoyed the response of one Scottish teacher of English who said that making Shakespeare compulsory in Scotland was the equivalent of 'cultural imperialism' (Elliott & Olive, 2019, p. 6). His work has certainly been the instrument of cultural imperialism throughout the British Empire at one time or another (see Chapter 3).

Even accepting that we should be studying Shakespeare, there is the question of what it means to 'know' Shakespeare. Does knowing one play well suffice? Or should we rather have a broad knowledge of which plays he wrote, with perhaps some basic knowledge of their plots, and no close study required? Shakespeare is a particular case of the cultural capital question, in that it is no doubt important to be able to have some reference to his work, and there is a shibboleth attached to enjoying Shakespeare in performance or being able to quote some key lines. I would say that I know Shakespeare pretty well, and I certainly enjoy his plays in performance, but I do not know all of the plays well, and some of them I know not at all. What I do have is a certain level of confidence with Shakespeare – which returns us to the question of cultural capital and whether it is based in knowledge and specific learning experiences or more centred in enculturated attitudes (see Chapter 7). If I had studied one play (or even one sonnet), would I say I knew Shakespeare? I would not claim to know Dickens on the basis of having read *Our Mutual Friend*, or indeed that in addition to having studied *Great Expectations* and *A Christmas Carol*, which largely made up my experience of his work before the age of 18. Shakespeare seems to be uniquely embodied in his plays and particularly in a handful of them, not so much as an author but as a textual shorthand.

The sonnets provide an interesting example in relation to Shakespeare. Although most will encounter, at a minimum, one or two sonnets in their educational career, when we talk of studying Shakespeare, we almost always refer to his plays. For one thing, the challenge of a play-length text in Shakespearean language is considerably more intimidating as a prospect and will also provide a much larger chunk of a year-long curriculum than a handful of sonnets. However, we do tend to study the sonnet form, and the form we study is largely the Shakespearean, not the Petrarchan, sonnet. In this, Shakespeare has come to silently dominate the English education system's understanding of the sonnet, in terms of the three quatrains and the couplet, whether that expresses a verso or a summation of the content that went before. In a similar way, Shakespeare has come to dominate the study of plays, almost entirely eliding his contemporaries such as Marlowe or Webster at school level, to the frustration of enthusiasts of that time, and scholars of the Early Modern period who do not specialise in Shakespeare. One of the results of this is that we assume the blank verse that dominates his plays is the standard for the Early Modern period, when reading a handful of his contemporaries demonstrates it is not.

Embodied knowledge: the pedagogy of the rehearsal room

One of the driving forces in Shakespeare pedagogy in secondary schools for the last two decades has been the 'active methods' approach, which has come to prominence particularly through the education teams of the Royal Shakespeare Company (RSC) and Shakespeare's Globe. Active methods find their roots in the embodied dramatisation of Shakespeare, through movement, action and speech.

> Active methods of teaching Shakespeare are particularly powerful in aiding student development because they accord a greater degree of responsibility to them than traditional ways of teaching. They are rooted in co-operation with others to make some form of presentation. Active approaches to Shakespeare satisfy the creative impulse (How can we stage the shipwreck that opens *The Tempest?*) and offer free play to the imagination (How should our Ariel appear, move, speak, vanish?). Such methods are vocally and personally demanding because they involve students in making presentations of many kinds. They are a source of deepening self-awareness as students find ways to express their understandings and feelings in physical action (How can I overcome my inhibitions about acting in front of others?).
>
> *(Gibson, 2016, p. 4)*

Comprehensive sets of activities drawing on these principles can be found in Rex Gibson's *Teaching Shakespeare* (2nd edition, 2016), James Stredder's *The North Face of Shakespeare* (2009) and the RSC's *Shakespeare Toolkit for Teachers* (2011), as well as in many different resources for individual plays. Active methods are popular in the UK – a third of English teachers use them regularly and a further quarter use them 'a bit' – but there is also a large proportion of teachers (40%) who do not know what active methods are (Elliott & Olive, 2018).

The main reason for discussing active approaches to Shakespeare here is because they represent a different kind of knowledge to that developed through traditional classroom approaches to the play. Their proponents (of whom I am one) argue that active methods promote understanding of the meaning of the language and imagery in the play, and can be key to engaging reluctant students. However, they also have an important function in understanding the text as a play, a performed object, whose meaning is created through movement and interaction with an audience, as well as through text on a page. There are few teachers who would not want their students watching a play either via film or in a theatre to grasp the meaning more thoroughly; active methods bring some of the decision making and the vital experience of that to students. But they also draw on what is called 'embodied' knowledge, the 'identification of an abstract idea with a physical entity' (MacLachlan, 2004, p. 2). By using the stimulus of enacted approaches, knowledge is generated which links physical movement with intellectual understanding, and the two reinforce each other. Think, for example, of the opening to *Romeo and Juliet* and how the two sets of servants encounter each other in the street. By experimenting with the constraints of space, students can connect this encounter with, for example, rubbing up against others in school corridors and the impossibility of avoiding conflict when pressed into close contact with your rivals.

Winston (2015) explicitly connects these approaches to the rehearsal room, in his examination of the pedagogies promoted by the RSC. Members of a theatre company preparing to produce a Shakespeare play need to understand exactly what every utterance means and is doing: that is the heart of the clarity of performance. Rehearsal room explorations, which are similar to the types of activities undertaken in active methods, are aimed at that understanding. Choral reading, rehearsed speaking, walking of punctuation (perhaps particularly paying attention to punctuation given the issue that students have with blank verse, and expecting sense breaks to come at the end of the line rather than at punctuation points) all enable the understanding of language in a way which round-robin reading of Shakespeare does not, even further than in terms of class readers as discussed in Chapter 3.

Actors also need to understand the options for action and character interpretation at every stage – a similar understanding to that required of students in terms of multiple possible interpretations. Actors will then decide on a final interpretation, which does move away from ambiguity, but having gone through the process, students will have considered the range of possibilities and chosen their final position for a reason, which returns us to the concept of justified argument.

Some Shakespeare scholars view active methods with deep suspicion, criticising the concentration on performance over language (although the discussion above suggests why that may not be a reasonable critique); it is true, however, that those who have progressed to a career in academia based on Shakespeare are more likely to have a personal preference in favour of desk-based literary criticism. Active methods have also been used successfully at undergraduate level, most notably in the 'Shakespeare Without Chairs' module at Warwick University, originated by Professor Carol Chillington Rutter. But the critique leads us back to the question of what we are teaching. Many of those who do not use active approaches in the classroom at secondary school say that one of the reasons is the lack of time in the curriculum. It is true that active approaches require a greater investment of time per scene than reading around the class, although I would argue that the time *is* an investment – in the understanding of students. For a majority of our students, reading through a scene is not enough to understand what is going on, so must be supported by direct instruction of what is essentially information rather than knowledge, enough to pass but not excel at examination. This provides a veneer of cultural literacy (see Chapter 7) but is not sufficient to fulfil what Neelands and O'Hanlon refer to as the 'double entitlement' that Shakespeare provides:

> This double entitlement to Shakespeare is grounded in the desire to establish purpose and rewards in learning that may lead, by choice, to other life-long and life-wide outcomes, in particular giving a broader range of children and young people the choice of Shakespeare, now and in later life, as a source of pleasure and as a reference point for understanding the complexities of their own and other lives.
>
> *(Neelands & O'Hanlon, 2011, p. 240)*

This points back to the supposed uniqueness of Shakespeare – to his position as 'the Bard' – and the usefulness of his works to inspire and comfort. What Neelands and O'Hanlon are pointing out is that without the kinds of pedagogies that enable students to truly grasp and enjoy Shakespeare, we are still confining the major benefits of studying his works to the highest attainers and to those whose parents can afford to regularly take them to the theatre, and value doing so.

If we really believe in the value of learning Shakespeare, it is not the value of being able to write analytically about a single play or two; it is about seeing his work as a cultural resource which former students can draw on all their lives. The power of learning Shakespeare in terms of a lever for personal development and reframing can be seen from the numerous Shakespeare-based rehabilitation programmes in the USA; Nicklin (2020) demonstrated the ways in which incarcerated individuals were able to utilise their new knowledge of Shakespeare and his words to vocalise and advocate for themselves, feeling a new sense of pride in that knowledge. They relied on playing with and adapting his language, not just regurgitating rote learning.

Winston (2015), in theorising the use of embodied learning through the rehearsal room pedagogies, specifically in relation to the RSC, refers back to the educational philosopher John Dewey and the value of learning through experience. Many of the arguments he makes in favour of active methods are those which are linked with so-called 'progressive' teaching, rather than knowledge-based direct instruction. However, one of his points is that active approaches reject the mind-body dichotomy of Descartes and instead understand our minds as situated in bodies. When we think of the ways in which hairs rise on the back of our necks, or our breath quickens as we watch a play, read a poem or rush to finish a cliff-hanger, we can be in no doubt as English Literature specialists that our minds are embodied, and that our bodily reactions are a significant part of the way that we experience texts. Second, Winston argues, much of the meaning-making in performance, particularly in Shakespeare, is non-verbal. This is part of considering plays as plays but it is also an additional resource to enable our students to understand the text.

All things to all men

Shakespeare's unique place in our education system also reflects somewhat the unique place he holds within culture more generally. One of the claims made for his works is their universality – their application at all times and in all places. His work becomes a combination of the *Sortes Virgilianae* (a form of divination in which you open the works of the poet Virgil at random and select a line to apply to your situation), a secular Bible to offer comfort in times of need, and a universal self-help book (see the extensive use of Shakespeare in leadership courses and also prison rehabilitation). We are told that we can make any play relevant to our students because they deal with universal themes and the human condition. I have to say that while I agree it is usually possible to do this, I am not sure that 'relevance' is always the Holy Grail to be pursued in studying any text with students. Universality is also the basis of the claim that one outcome of studying Shakespeare's plays is to pursue a 'larger vision of humanity' (Gerzina, 2017, p. 27). I would argue that this outcome is at least partially present in any teaching of literature, given that we consider questions of character and motivation, of good and evil, of love and hate, delving into some of the deepest concerns of human life. Proponents of Shakespeare see this as a particular strength of studying his plays.

The claim to the universality of Shakespeare, however, also poses a problem. Bhatia, in writing of the place of Shakespeare in colonial India argues that

> the 'singularity' imparted to Shakespeare through claims about 'universality' and 'timeless transcendentalism' was disrupted by multiple reconstructions and local appropriations of 'Shakespeare' which made the iconic status of the bard's authority a contested one and imparted new meanings and experiences to Shakespeare. Thus, over time, numerous versions of Shakespeare came to be deployed for multiple purposes: for the subversion of colonial and hegemonic ideologies, for the revival of ancient Hindu culture during a time of rising anti-colonial nationalism, and for popular entertainment. The singularity of Shakespeare, as presented in claims about 'universality', hence acquired a plurality that was shaped by the heterogeneity of alternative reproductions in historically specific and local contexts.
>
> *(Bhatia, 1998, p. 97)*

Ironically, it is almost this writing back to Shakespeare that emphasises his universality: he and his works can be adapted and co-opted to different causes and for different purposes. In playing with his language, characters and plots, we can utilise his work for ourselves. His work provides sufficient recognisable reference points for a vast range of afterlives. There are the ways in which his plays are written into golden-age detective novels: Lisa Hopkins' *DCI Shakespeare* (2016a) and my personal favourite, her work on Shakespearean allusion in the detective fiction of Georgette Heyer (2016b); the almost entirely surface-level engagement with the plays (and Stratford) in the BBC daytime odd-couple drama *Shakespeare and Hathaway*; the many, many young adult novels based on *Hamlet* which variously gender swap (Lizbeth Zindel's *A Girl, A Ghost and the Hollywood Hills*), set it in the glitzy world of celebrity and social media (Michelle Ray's *Falling for Hamlet*) or simply switch to Ophelia's viewpoint and change the ending (Lisa Klein's *Ophelia*); and the numerous films which use his plays as a jumping-off point, to a greater or lesser extent (such as *Ten Things I Hate About You* or *She's the Man*), to name but a few. He is also the source of many intertextual Easter Eggs, so that I was delighted to find, reading *The Southern Book Club's Guide to Slaying Vampires* by Grady Hendrix, a sudden raising of the point that the pie at the end of *Titus Andronicus* would have had to be exceptionally large to fit in Tamara's full-grown children.

'Universality' does raise other questions, however. In maintaining his place as our national poet, we often work ourselves into knots in justifying how *The Merchant of Venice* can be read as a challenge to anti-Semitism, rather than racist in its portrayal of Shylock (and the play's supposedly happy ending); or how *The Taming of the Shrew* can be read as a proto-feminist play. Emma Smith in *This Is Shakespeare* identifies *Shrew* as one of Shakespeare's 'most controversial' plays:

> Everything, from the name of its heroine to the ideology of its gender relations, is contested, to the extent that it's impossible even to begin with a neutral synopsis of the play.
>
> (Smith, 2020, p. 7)

She goes on to demonstrate that this contestation is not just down to the 400-odd years which separate the play from us:

> Sometimes we assume that what seem to us ambiguities in Shakespeare's plays – whether Henry V is a good king, or *Othello* a racist play, for example – are the result of different ethical frameworks then and now. So, this argument goes, scenarios which were quite unproblematic to early modern audiences have gained moral complexity because our attitudes to race, or military expediency, or, in the case of *The Taming of the Shrew*, the relationship between the sexes, have changed since Shakespeare's time. But actually it seems that *The Taming of the Shrew* was always ambiguous, right from the start.
>
> (Smith, 2020, pp. 13–14)

As evidence, she brings two contemporaneous plays which also deal with 'shrews', one of which was written in direct answer to Shakespeare's play, and one of which is a much more explicit taming. Smith argues that the questions raised by *The Taming of the Shrew* are not questions of history, but are questions intrinsic to the language and structure of the play, right down to the omission of any explicit choreography at the end of the play. In this, she says, lies Shakespeare's claims to universality, because his plays are written so that we can bring our own concerns to them, and think of them in our own way. Or we can if we are reading them: I have seen plenty of *Shrews* whose directorial vision has been almost painful in their commitment to the domestic abuse angle and which deny any other reading.

Others have not always agreed, and see specific plays as promoting specific values – not always good. In post-war Berlin, the Office of Military Government of the USA in the American sector circulated lists of works that were proscribed and of those which were

> deemed to be of benefit to a defeated, traumatised populace in need of radical political re-education. The black list featured two major pieces by Shakespeare: *Julius Caesar* and *Coriolanus*. Performances of these were roundly banned, in the light of their supposed 'glorifications of dictatorship'. The white list contained *Macbeth* and *Hamlet*, the former held brusquely to affirm that 'Crime Does Not Pay', the latter's inclusion more curiously justified on the basis of its alleged treatment of 'corruption and justice'.
>
> *(Hawkes, 2002, p. 66)*

The significance of the interpretation made of a work becomes immediately clear in these categorisations. I think both the post-war Office of Military Government and Smith would agree with Fernie's declaration that:

> Unlike Wagner, Shakespeare makes no attempt to give us an overarching myth. He offers only a series of plays. One comes to an end; another begins. There is no final, definitive synthesis.
>
> *(Fernie, 2017, p. 7)*

It is this, perhaps, which makes it hard to distinguish between 'knowledge of Shakespeare' and knowledge of one (or more) of his plays. There is not an overarching knowledge to be gained. In terms of the discipline of English Literature, there are important elements of knowledge to be explored: contextual, linguistic, multiplicity of interpretation. In terms of culture, there are references to be known (see Chapter 7) but also a certain level of confidence to be gained, the teaching of which may be more difficult than the simple knowledge of a single play's plot, character and themes.

Conclusion

Shakespeare has become a unique case in the discipline of English Literature, who is peculiarly celebrated among authors and who has come to dominate certain aspects of the subject at school level and in the popular imagination. As such, his work provides a useful mechanism through which we can think about aspects of knowledge in English Literature, while always being mindful of the fact that because he is unique, knowledge in relation to Shakespeare may not be the same as knowledge in relation to other texts and forms. In particular, Shakespeare has been the focus of a number of arguments around pedagogy, and the site of a number of anxieties for both teachers and students. Shakespeare as a person and as a play-wright is also the source of significant economic value to the UK and is also considered to be of particular cultural value of the kinds that will be discussed in Chapter 7.

Notes

1 It is worth noting at this point that Barbara Bleiman's *What Matters in English Teaching?* conducts a similar thought experiment to this with Dickens' *Great Expectations,* and I think comes to largely similar conclusions (Bleiman, 2020).
2 I am indebted to Peter Ellison for this example, which perfectly captures the relationship between contextual knowledge and textual interpretation.

5

RACE AND GENDER IN THE ENGLISH CURRICULUM

This chapter deals with two of the structural inequalities in society and how they play out in the curriculum and the classroom of English Literature: race and gender. A third structural inequality, class, is touched on, and will be further examined in Chapter 7. In thinking about all three of these issues, I acknowledge that they interact with each other strongly, and that the concerns relating to one are often mirrored in relation to another. I have not included, but could have done under the same umbrella, representation and treatment of LGBTQ+ authors, issues and texts within the curriculum. The construction of the canon, which often excludes texts and authors on the basis of their position in relation to race, gender and class, forms the first section of the chapter, as a foundation on which to consider all the other issues. I draw on research on the representation and the framing of women and Black, Asian and Minority Ethnic[1] authors and texts within the literature curriculum to look at how representation works in English Literature in schools, and how that impacts students.

While we cannot teach everything, decisions about what we do and do not teach, particularly when mandated at the political level, speak volumes about what we consider to be valuable and important, and, most importantly, can have a concrete impact on educational attainment.

In 2014, Claudia Rankine, the African American poet wrote a book-length poem called *Citizen*, of which one extract in particular has resonated widely:

> because white men can't
> police their imagination
> black men are dying

(Rankine, 2014, p. 135)

This is the urgent flipside of representation in the curriculum. It is essential that we reach a place where the imaginations of all students are populated with a wide range of visions for Black, Brown and White lives. This is the root of unconscious bias – the population of our imaginations. There is a frequently told story of the Black researcher working on the Implicit Association Test programme at Harvard – a test which measured reaction times of people linking positive and negative words to Black and White faces at random. The researcher did the test every morning, and usually had a negative association for Black faces, despite his own ethnicity. Then one day he went to work and found the opposite – a strong positive association for Black faces instead. It was during the Olympics and the morning news had been full of stories of Black American success and excellence, instead of the usual emphasis on crime.[2] Whether we are aware or not, we populate our imaginations with the things we consume every day, from the people in our communities, to news, social media, television and, of crucial relevance to an English teacher, books.

We have a race problem in education in England.[3] One aspect, but not the only one, can be seen in relation to assessment. The 'gap' in attainment between different groups in the school population is intensely intersectional: ethnicity, class background and gender all intersect in terms of attainment. While the all-encompassing 'Black' and 'White' groups do not differ hugely in their attainment at present (seen in the 2019 'Attainment 8' measure for GCSE[4]), Black Caribbean heritage students do much less well than their Black African heritage counterparts. The least well-attaining group is White British boys from low socio-economic status backgrounds, something that has led the Department for Education to investigate 'ethnic minority resistance to the effects of deprivation on attainment' (Stokes et al., 2015), and which has served to divert attention from some of the structural racism in education. Black Caribbean, Black African and Mixed-Race students are all less likely than White students to take three STEM subjects at GCSE (used as a proxy for 'highly academic' subjects) (Henderson et al., 2018). Both girls and certain ethnic minority groups do better at school-level educational attainment. Yet by the time they complete university (if they do), the attainment gap has reversed in favour of being male and White; this gap simply goes on to increase in terms of the likelihood of employment, promotion and pay. (Research has consistently shown since the 1960s that people with ethnic minority names have to make far more job applications (on average 60% more than 'White' names, and in some cases 100% more) to get to interview in Britain than White people do (Di Stasio & Heath, 2019).) Burgess and Greaves (2013) have shown that there is systematic under-assessment of Black children by teachers compared to their standardised test scores; this has implications for (for example) university entrance, which is largely worked on predicted grades, and for setting decisions in schools, which has consequent knock-on effects. In terms of permanent exclusion, Roma children and Irish traveller children are three or more times more likely to be permanently excluded than White children.[5] Other examples of the structural aspects of discrimination (in terms of race and gender) will be considered throughout this chapter.

The so-called universal

One of the defences mounted in favour of the canon and of classical literature is that they are for all time, and universal in their concerns. The canon, after all, is the canon because it has remained in use: this collection of texts, largely by White middle-class men, is defended on the grounds that it has been generated purely on the grounds of quality, and that that quality is what has kept texts prevalent.

Exactly what that canon consists of has been a matter of long-standing debate for critics and literature scholars. F. R. Leavis, whose imprint is seen everywhere in the discipline of English Literature – described as the 'single most influential figure in twentieth-century English literary criticism' (Norris, 1988, p. vii) – defined the 'Great Tradition' as being just four authors, two of whom were women: Jane Austen, George Eliot, Thomas Hardy and Henry James (Leavis, 1948), a balance rarely seen in a list of canonical texts. Miernik (2015) notes the inherent tension in the creation of canon lists, in that the selection of a canon is 'arbitrary and often ideologically charged on the one hand; on the other, it is placed in a privileged position and often is approached with reverence' (p. 86). A canonical text is revered because it is canonical. Because it is canonical, it is continually taught. Over time, this becomes a virtuous – or a vicious – circle.

John Guillory (1993) argues that canon formation is in fact principally about the social forms by which it becomes institutionalised, not about the inherent value of the texts themselves, or at least not solely: 'evaluative judgments are the necessary but not sufficient conditions for the process of canon formation' (p. vii). Canonical literature is not defined by the accumulated aesthetic judgements of informed minds, but by the 'institutional forms of syllabus and curriculum' (Guillory, 1993, p. vii), reproduced and created by educational norms which may be stimulated by many other things than simply 'the best which has been thought and said' (Arnold, 2006. p. 46) (as discussed in Chapter 3).

This reproduction of canon means that 'it is only by understanding the social function and institutional protocols of the school that we will understand how works are preserved, reproduced and disseminated over successive generations and centuries' (Guillory, 1993, p. vii). While the 'school' to which he refers is the American college, the same holds true of the secondary educational canon, although it is not only the institutional protocols of the school that matter, but those of the government and, in the case of the UK, those of the Awarding Bodies who set the text lists that become the effective canon for secondary education. Writing about historical narratives and what comes to be regarded as 'fact', Michel-Rolph Trouillot (1995/2015), a Haitian scholar, noted that 'the production of historical narratives involves the uneven contributions of competing groups and individuals who have unequal access to the means for such production' (p. xxiii). In relation to canon, the phrase 'history is written by the victors' points us to look at the symbolic violence of education (defined in the next section) in relating to the power disparities involved in its construction and to the 'hidden curriculum'. This is not to say that canon is a deliberate conspiracy, but neither is it a value-free absolute that stands apart from society – it is constructed by social means and reinforced and reproduced by those same means of power.

This is not the only issue that the canon has, however; in addition, historical factors combine to mean that there are simply fewer examples of non-White non-male literature to be found before a certain period. As Lola Olufemi (2020) points out: 'Art requires will. But it also requires, as writer Virginia Woolf recognises, a room of one's own. A set of social and financial circumstances that enable creativity to take place' (p. 88):

> The divide between politics and art is not real. It is politics that dictates who creates art, how it is consumed and sold, the conditions in which it is created, the subjectivities that dominated it. Poor women do not get to make art.
>
> *(Olufemi, 2020, pp. 87–8)*

Therefore, where we insist on the canonical, we are merely reproducing the inequalities produced through social conditions of one or two hundred years ago.

It is possible to introduce new texts into institutional canons, and over time they too become canonical; in the late 1970s, there was a 'canon opening' movement (see, for example, Fiedler, 1981), and we have seen a similar movement in the last few years in the campaigns at universities such as 'Why is my curriculum white?' and the 'Decolonise the Curriculum' movements which have spread across the US and the UK in particular. Once texts are taught, they are available for institutional reproduction of the sort described by Guillory. In the meantime, however, the traditional texts and classics continue to be considered as the texts of value for curriculum.

> If it's not crunchy and canonical, we're not going to teach it
>
> *(Head of English in an elite private school)*

This leaves us in a position where the texts that are valued – the canon – are left to represent all that matters in English Literature. They are, in the words of Ben Jonson on Shakespeare, 'not of an age, but for all time'. The word often used of Shakespeare, and to justify the continued relevance of historical texts, is that they are 'universal'. In doing so, 'Whiteness positions itself as the norm. It refuses to recognise itself for what it is. Its so-called "objectivity" and "reason" is its most potent and insidious tool for maintaining power' (Eddo-Lodge, 2017, p. 169). The same thing applies to class in education. The middle class positions itself as the norm, as the 'Standard English', and positions those outside the White middle class (and often male) as in deficit, lacking in 'powerful knowledge' and 'cultural capital' (as discussed in Chapter 7). As Eddo-Lodge also argues, in the UK:

> Neutral is white. The default is white. Because we are born into an already written script that tells us what to expect from strangers due to their skin colour, accents and social status, the whole of humanity is coded as white. Blackness, however, is considered the 'other' and therefore to be suspected.
>
> *(Eddo-Lodge, 2017, p. 85)*

The content we teach in schools and the way it is presented contribute to that presentation of Whiteness as neutrality. An insistence on White as the majority and the norm prevents all of us seeing the wider ways in which we are similar and can integrate. As others have argued:

> It is useless to pretend that Dickens 'spoke the language of humanity' or that white male authors can articulate other experiences unaffected by their positionality. The effect of the white curriculum is such that we have imbued white male writers with the power and authority to speak for everyone; marginalised students often find themselves grasping at texts that were not written for them in an attempt to find a shared humanity that is based on their exclusion.
>
> *(Olufemi, 2019, pp. 57–8)*

One of the challenges in overcoming this false default, and, indeed, the happiness of a large part of White Britain to accept it, lies in the way that immigration and specifically Black immigration from the Commonwealth has been framed historically. This same framing led to the Windrush scandal and deportation of many British citizens to countries where they had either not been since they were children or, in some cases, never been to. The mass of Black immigration into the UK in the 20th century was at the behest of the British government, who needed them to fill jobs and demographic gaps left after the Second World War. But beyond that:

> The government and the education system failed to explain to white Britain that, as the academic Adam Elliot-Cooper puts it, we had not come to Britain, but 'rather that Britain had come to us'. They did not explain that the wealth of Britain, which made the welfare state and other class ameliorations possible, was derived in no small part from the coffee and tobacco, cotton and diamonds, gold and sweat and blood and death of the colonies. No one explained that our grandparents were not immigrants, that they were literally British citizens.
>
> *(Akala, 2018, pp. 6–7)*

I would suggest that one of the ways in which we can ameliorate this omission is by the inclusion of texts that represent the range of Black experience in both historical and contemporary terms. Barbara Bleiman (2020), in suggesting pairing of contemporary or diverse texts with the 'crunchy canonical ones', argues that 'Creating literature, reading and studying literature are all about responding to other texts and making them speak to different readers, in different times' (p. 49). In this, she pinpoints one of the difficulties for English; perhaps more so than for other school subjects, English is prioritised for what it can do for everyone, and preparing students for further study or lifetimes in that subject is less recognised as a function of school English (literature in particular). Yet for all children, to study only the ancient, the canonical, is to obscure the possibilities for literature in their own future. To see the contemporary response of Patience Agbabi (2015) to Chaucer's *Canterbury Tales*, for example, or Soniah Kamal's (2019) retelling of *Pride and Prejudice* set in contemporary Pakistan, *Unmarriageable*, is to understand the role of playful adaptation and response, and to exemplify what it is in those classic texts that does stand the test of time, as well as showing a less limited world.

But to decolonise the curriculum (or to degender it) is not only about inserting representation into the curriculum; it is also about consistently thinking about the ways in which we read texts in the classroom. When we think about *Jane Eyre*, do we also think about the myriad ways in which Empire intrudes into the text, through furniture (Freedgood, 2010), through the missionary destination of St John Rivers, through the origins of the first Mrs Rochester, and the racist origins of her depiction as violently delusional, on account of her Creole background (and also the exoticisation of her appearance)? To reject the so-called universal 'common sense' approach to texts and to examine them in terms of historical context, gender, class and race is to truly represent our island story.

In 2010, Arizona's state legislature passed a law that prohibited the teaching of courses in schools that advocated ethnic solidarity or were designed primarily for students of a particular ethnicity, with a penalty that the state could withhold 10 per cent of funding from a district where such teaching was found to take place. This led to the abolition of a highly successful and popular Mexican American Studies programme at the direct instruction of the state superintendent of education, which in turn led to student protests in which the teens chained themselves to the chairs of the school board members. The protests made national news in the USA and debate about the situation raged (all related in Cabrera et al., 2014). Cabrera et al. went on to examine the more fundamental question, which debaters on all sides claimed to be their priority: What was the effect of the course on student attainment?

To put this in context, Hispanic students in the US are the most likely of all groups except for Native Americans to drop out of high school, with a rate of 8.2 per cent in 2017 (compared with Native Americans/Native Alaskans 10.1%; Black 6.5% and White 4.3%).[6]Cabrera et al. (2014) took administrative data from the Arizona school system to look at the relationship between student participation in the Mexican American Studies programme and their rate of passing the state stan-dardised tests, and of graduating high school. There was a significant positive rela-tionship, and the positive effects on testing and graduating increased with every extra Mexican American Studies course the student took. These findings provide empirical evidence that there is a positive effect on educational attainment of having representation of your own home culture or race within the official school curriculum. The effect, however, was also found for non-Mexican American stu-dents who took courses in the Mexican American Studies programme. Repre-sentation matters (although the nuances of this will be discussed below), but, importantly, diversifying the curriculum is not just for the benefit of those who are now represented, but ultimately everyone. Britain is different from the majority of other English-speaking countries in that we do not have an indigenous population to consider, which has sometimes enabled issues of race and representation to be swept under the carpet. In English-speaking nations that were historically colonies of the British Empire, there is a compelling case – indeed, a moral imperative – for teaching texts that represent the indigenous people as well as the contemporary population. In this chapter, I make the case for the English Literature curriculum in the UK to represent the full range of the students who are subjected to it.

Being Black in the UK education system

> My history is the screams shouting out through the silent slots in syllabi.
>
> *(Suhaiymah Manzoor-Khan, 'Where is my history?')*

It is an unavoidable truth that most teachers of English are White. We cannot know what it is like to be Black in the UK education system. Luckily, we are in a profession where we understand the use of reading to see through another's eyes. In 2019, I read in rapid succession a number of autobiographical memoirs and guides to education which created a powerful sense of what it is to be Black in a White education system. The quotations that follow give a sense of the meaning of 'symbolic violence'[7] visited upon our Black students by schooling.

Many authors reflect on the lack of representation in school and university curriculums. In 2015, a Black student on our PGCE course, who had been an Oxford English undergraduate, told us that it was not until she got to university that she even knew that Black people could be writers: in her multicultural inner-city London state school, she had studied only White writers all the way to A level, with the exception of the foreign poets in the 'Poetry from Other Cultures'. Yet not even universities necessarily provide this respite:

> When I, as an English student, cannot formally study a single person who looks like me for the first two years of my degree, what I am being subjected to is a violent form of erasure.
>
> *(Olufemi, 2019, p. 56)*

Olufemi is not describing a school curriculum here, but a university curriculum in which there is supposed to be choice and direction to follow one's own interests. To be unable to do so is equivalent to being told that there is no value in knowledge of works in which someone who 'looks like' you is figured. This is the implicit message too of our school curriculums, to both Black and White students. This erasure is familiar from the work of poet and critic Adrienne Rich, who came to this realisation from her feminist position as a White woman, but whose words also reflect the violence of this erasure:

> When those who have power to name and to socially construct reality choose not to see you or hear you, whether you are dark-skinned, old, disabled, female, or speak with a different accent or dialect than theirs, when someone with the authority of a teacher, say, described the world and you are not in it, there is a moment of psychic disequilibrium, as if you looked in the mirror and saw nothing.
>
> *(Rich, 1994, p. 99)*

Rich highlights an important point: that the teacher is a figure of authority. Akala credits the fact that his parents defended him against 'the system' rather than telling him that his 'negative experiences' in school were the result of his own behaviour as the reason that he did not drop out of school (Akala, 2019, p. 84). We are very often, as teachers, concerned with maintaining authority in the face of defiance and the all-consuming behaviour management challenge, and do not always recognise that that authority carries with it other implications about the ways in which we frame the world are received by students. It is not merely the curriculum but also the way that the student is then framed within the classroom.

> It was rarely open aggression or contempt shown by peers or tutors at uni-
> versity but more a dislocating feeling that you, your history, your thoughts,
> your experiences don't matter and a resultant fatigue.
>
> *(Mohamed, 2020)*

This sense of fatigue has been noted by other researchers as a result of having to work within White norms in the classroom. Thein (2018) draws on a range of research in the field of Critical Emotion Studies to show that particular 'emotional dispositions (empathy, self-control, delayed gratification, optimism, etc.)' which are promoted within schools as 'neutral life skills' are 'normatively white, Protestant, middle-class identities' (p. 59) that have the power to marginalise or even sanction particular responses to texts, such as anger from Black students towards racism. Conventional and approved emotional responses in the classroom put the burden of emotional work on to ethnic minorities to avoid triggering reactions of shame or denial by White teachers and classmates. Thein makes a compelling case that the emotional work should be done instead by the (White) teacher, to suppress their need to deny their racism (see above) or complicity in White privilege. This then allows the Black student the space to make an authentic response to texts without having to be conscious of censoring themselves: an outcome that must be seen as important for the teaching of English Literature given the aspects of personal response and the need for individuals to engage in the construction of authentic knowledge.

When there is representation in the curriculum, that representation also has impli-cations. Writing on the history curriculum, Ogunbiyi writes that for a Black person:

> The only times you might see someone who looks like you represented in
> your curriculum will be at the mention of slavery, colonising, lynching and
> maybe political corruption in African states – a dehumanising experience.
>
> *(Ogunbiyi, 2019, p. 70)*

In English, the main texts that deal with race which are widely studied are *To Kill a Mockingbird* and *Of Mice and Men* (in which it is hardly a main theme). There are implications of seeing race (and specifically racism) as primarily an American 'pro-blem'. This theme is picked up below in a section on how the Black experience is framed in the English curriculum.

I would strongly recommend that any teacher spends some time engaging with a number of the (at least partially) educational memoirs that have been published in the last few years: Akala's *Natives*, Reni Eddo-Lodge's *Why I Am No Longer Talking to White People About Race*, Afua Hirsch's *Brit-ish*, Chelsea Kwakye and Ore Ogunbiyi's *Taking Up Space: The Black Girl's Manifesto for Change*, or *A Fly Girl's Guide to University* (Lola Olufemi, Odelia Younge, Waithera Sebatindira and Suhaiymah Manzoor-Khan). It is notable that there has been a distinct move in the publishing industry over the last few years that has made these texts possible, so that the opportunities for White teachers to understand the experiences of Black and Asian students are far more numerous than they were, or than books that represent the Roma or Traveller experience of school.

It is worth noting that our schools and curriculums do not work in a vacuum. Kendi, writing of his adolescence in the US, talks about his internalised fear of Black bodies – like his own – as a teenager, stimulated by media depictions and public discourse, dominated not by the mundane everyday but by the occasional violence: 'if it bleeds, it leads' (Kendi, 2019, p. 78). Akala (2019) also noted the contrast between the money pumped into the system to alleviate the under-achievement of Black boys and the daily portrayals of young thugs in the media. We cannot control the media, but we can and should offer an alternative, a different envisioning – or many different ones – of Black lives. We can offer the materials for White people to 'police their imagination' (Rankine, 2014, p. 135).

In 2017, Bansi Kara, then an assistant headteacher in London, speaking at the inaugural BAMEEd conference, argued that decolonising the curriculum is not about removing 'white knowledge' but was rather:

> for the inclusion of more knowledge, not less, for the sole purpose that our students deserve to be able to do more than fit into the culture of one country. They might, if we find space to colour in the black and white, learn the interconnectedness of the world they live in.
>
> This is not about diversity for the sake of audits or political correctness. It helps students to be part of the narrative of now – not just the narrative of the colonial past.
>
> When I was a teenager, I had a moment of realisation. I didn't fit into the narrative of England, the country I was born in. I couldn't find myself in any of the stories; as a student of literature, I was desperate to feel like I had a place. I sought it out many years later, but I recognise my privilege in being able to. Perhaps that is what we owe our students: including knowledge in the curriculum that exists outside of the narrow lens of colonial history.
>
> *(Kara, 2017, n.p.)*

Any teacher must recognise the duty of care to their students to make sure that they do find a way to fit into the narrative of their country. As English teachers, we understand the value of stories and being able to lose ourselves in them – or find ourselves. Although it is simply impossible to represent everyone equally, it is about showing more than 'a single story' (Adichie, 2009), and demonstrating the rich breadth of literature in English. The next two sections consider that breadth of representation more deeply in relation to gender and race.

Gender representation in English Literature

The question of gender representation has been a topic of debate in academic literature for far longer than that of race, and even in a subject like English Literature which is often considered to be deeply feminised (Daly, 2000; Thomas, 2006), there is a substantial bias in favour of male writers in the curriculum. Of the set texts for examination at age 16 in the four countries of the United Kingdom before the most recent update by Pearson, there were 69 text options by male authors (66%) and 36 text options by female authors (34%) (Elliott, 2017, as with the other numbers given in this paragraph).[8] In the Northern Irish GCSE specification at the time of the analysis, there was not a single drama text written by a woman available for study. Overall, there were 66 male protagonists (seven of which are in texts written by women) and 31 female protagonists (five written by men). Four of the text options by a man but with a female protagonist were *Never Let Me Go*, showing that this combination is even rarer than an initial glance would suggest. The female experience is rarely centred in the set texts for English Literature. This analysis did not even include Shakespeare, partly because he is a special case and partly because he would skew the numbers even further towards males.

> There is a well-quoted statement by Geena Davis that in crowd scenes in Hollywood, if a third of those present are women, they are perceived by men to be in the majority (although despite its being quoted often, the research evidence to back the statement up is elusive). It is tempting to suggest that when it comes to lists of set texts, if a third of the authors present are women, it looks like equality.
>
> *(Elliott, 2017, p. 57)*

Writing in 1975, Lobban argued that we 'need new reading schemes which show equal numbers of real females and males participating in the variety of activities and occupations that they do actually participate in' (p. 209). It seems that more than 40 years later we have not achieved that balance in our set texts in English.

Feminist critics adapted the term 'covert' or 'hidden' curriculum for this kind of systematic bias which considers the ways in which gendered behaviour and expectations are embedded within the curriculum (Deem, 1978; Riddell, 1992). The original 'hidden curriculum' is a Marxist critical view:

> The inculcation of values, political socialization, training in obedience and docility, the perpetuation of traditional class structure – functions that may be characterized generally as social control.
>
> *(Vallance, 1974, p. 5)*

I would consider the hidden curriculum to be equally applicable to race, and the false 'universal' of White voices, as well as to heteronormativity.

The example of gender representation demonstrates how long we have to wait for 'passive revolution' (Gramsci, 1971) to bring about change. Those with potential agency to make change happen faster are those who designate set texts – Awarding Bodies in the UK, and those in government who can mandate certain requirements for study. If we can say that students must study Shakespeare, we can also say that they must study at least one female-authored text at GCSE and at least one text written by a Black author. Teachers also have agency in what they choose, although it is often constrained by what is in the stock cupboard, or resources to support the study of new and different texts. In the trade-off for teachers' time and energy, introducing a new text to the school can lose out on grounds of urgency.

There are two places where it is easier to bring in change in both gender and race representation in the curriculum, and those are the beginnings and ends of school. A-level texts have a somewhat broader focus, and, importantly, there is scope within non-examined assessment (NEA), formerly known as coursework, to choose texts that have not even entered the consciousness of Awarding Bodies. Similarly, at Key Stage 3 the English curriculum has the freedom in it to encompass a broad and varied curriculum. In England since the reform of the GCSE, there seems to have been, from the curricular documents shared on the internet, an increased emphasis on 19th-century texts in order to prepare students for what they will encounter at 14, and indeed an increased emphasis on so-called cultural capital (see Chapter 7) which has had some unfortunate side effects on the range of texts chosen for study. I have seen several slightly worrying Key Stage 3 maps which included a single 'Women Writers' scheme of work over the three years (or the equivalent), with the clear implication that the norm was to be male and also that the other units over the three years did not incorporate women. It seems crass to see this for women: it is equally crass but far more widespread to see it applied to the inclusion of Black Asian and Minority Ethnic writers in Key Stage 3. In either case, the equal implication that this single characteristic can be used to group writers of huge diversity of style, form, interest and topic is somewhat confusing. If we had a 'White male writers' scheme of work, it would rightly be decried as being a facile grouping. The equivalent is also true.

Framing race in the English curriculum and in UK culture

For a long time, 'Poetry from Other Cultures' was the main representative of non-White literature (though not wholly so) in the English curriculum in England. Asha Rogers (2015) argued that such a framing has the potential to make a powerful impact on the way we read and understand texts. She noted that the anthology in which these poems were contained de-historicised the poems, stripping them from their contexts (which we noted in Chapter 2 has some problems for interpretation and to which we will return in the context of anthologies in Chapter 6). Instead of being framed by their contexts of production, the main framing of these poems was as 'other'. My own experience of teaching them left me with the strong impression of one cluster about 'life in other countries is different' and one about 'the difficulties of assimilation and dual cultures'. 'Two Scavengers in a Truck, Two Beautiful People in a Mercedes' by Lawrence Ferlinghetti (a White poet), for example, framed by the 'Other Cultures' label, encouraged an anthropological view of the people within the poem, and that anthropological view extended towards the other poems in the cluster.

The framing of how we encounter a text makes a difference to the way we interpret it and the way we enter it into our mental schemata. Meeting *Hamlet* in the context of a Crime Writing module or a Gothic one, as I have discussed, changes the way that we engage with it. The framing can be strong, as in the case of 'Poetry from Other Cultures' or it can be weaker, and it is this weaker framing with which we are concerned here, in relation to texts by Black, Asian and Minority Ethnic authors, or other texts that deal with issues of race.

The traditional books that deal with racism in the UK curriculum are actually by White authors, which in itself is interesting. Secondary students almost universally encounter at least one of *Of Mice and Men* and *To Kill a Mockingbird*. To encounter the theme of race only in American novels stokes the impression in the UK that racism is a peculiarly American problem and continues the narrative of denial that racism exists in the UK. Not only that, but *Mockingbird* in particular centres the *White* experience: it is about Atticus Finch and his experience of defending a Black man, not Tom Robinson's experience of living as a Black man in the highly racist South. Indeed, Ibram X. Kendi has pointed out that:

> The novel's most famous homily, hailed for its antiracism, in fact signified the novel's underlying racism. 'Mockingbirds don't do one thing but make music for us to enjoy,' a neighbour tells the lawyer's strong-willed daughter, Scout. 'That's why it's a sin to kill a mockingbird.' The mockingbird is a metaphor for African Americans. Though the novel was set in the 1930s, the teeming Black activism of that era was absent from *To Kill a Mockingbird*. African Americans come across as spectators, waiting and hoping and singing for a White savior, and thankful for the moral heroism of lawyer Atticus Finch.
>
> *(Kendi, 2017, pp. 369–70)*

Of Mice and Men presents another challenge: the presence of the N-word in the text. Ijeoma Olua (2019) points out that this is 'a very powerful word with a very painful history' (p. 132) and argues that 'the history of a word matters as long as the effects of that history are still felt (p. 131). The impact of hearing the N-word spoken in the classroom on a Black student is symbolic violence; but more than that, even if the teacher says 'N-word', the entire class of students is staring at the word written out in full, and is conscious of the Black student in their midst. I do not have an answer to this if we are to continue to teach *Of Mice and Men* but I do know that saying the word in full even in an all-White classroom without discussing the history of this word is not an acceptable route.[9] This also demonstrates an important point: simply having Black characters in existence in texts is not enough to redress imbalances, because without thoughtful treatment they can simply reinforce those imbalances. For another example of this, see Carter (2007) in which she explores the classroom experiences of two young Black women in the US who were negatively positioned through the analysis of Sonnet 130 ('My mistress' eyes are nothing like the sun') and its emphasis on skin colour as a feature of beauty.

The main exception to the dominance of American novels in tackling race is and was the inclusion on some GCSE specifications of Meera Syal's comic novel of growing up in the West Midlands, *Anita and Me*.[10] (This novel is framed in the Welsh GCSE English Literature specification as 'Different Cultures Prose' which always makes me laugh in disbelief, having worked in initial teacher education in the West Midlands – I'm not sure whether it is insulting, racist, appropriate, or merely a commentary on the difference a few miles over the Welsh border makes.) Reni Eddo-Lodge quotes David Oyelowo speaking to the *Radio Times* about his frustration at producers refusing to make historical drama with Black characters in them: 'you are stopping people having a context for the country they live in and you are marginalising me' (*Radio Times*, 2015, quoted in Eddo-Lodge, 2017, p. 55). The same issue pertains to the literature we read in school: powerful knowledge must surely encompass giving people the context for the country they live in.

One concept which comes from Canadian multiculturalism is that of 'recognition' (Taylor, 1994):

> The thesis is that our identity is partly shaped by recognitions or its absence, often by the *mis*recognition of others, and so a person or group of people can suffer real damage, real distortion if the people or society around them mirror back to them a confining or demeaning or contemptible picture of themselves. Nonrecognition or misrecognition can inflict harm, can be a form of oppression, imprisoning someone in a false, distorted, and reduced mode of being.
>
> *(Taylor, 1994, p. 25)*

This concept shows why the framing of texts in the curriculum matters, not representation alone. Looking to A level first, the greater number of texts recommended for study, and the fact that many specifications suggest wider reading for key texts, and possibilities for the free choice of texts for NEA means that there are many more texts by Black, Asian and Minority Ethnic authors mentioned in the specifications.[11]

Although AQA 'A' does not include any texts by Black authors on the list of suggestions (primarily because the suggestions focus on pre-1900 texts), the first example question is:

> John. R. Reed (1973) has suggested that the 'unacknowledged crime' of Wilkie Collins' *The Moonstone* is the colonial guilt of the British Empire for its

annexation of the entire Indian sub-continent rather than the theft of a single exquisite diamond.

Compare and contrast the presentation of British attitudes to race and ethnicity in *The Moonstone* and in Zadie Smith's *White Teeth* in the light of this view.[12]

This is a relatively refreshing moment in the A-level specifications, directing students directly towards the potential use of a post-colonial lens to enable race to form a key focus of study even when they have to include a pre-1900 text.

OCR's list, which is the most extensive because it recommends comparative reading for core set texts, is themed along the following lines:

- **American Literature 1880–1940:** Richard Wright, *Native Son*
- **The Gothic:** Toni Morrison, *Beloved*
- **Women in Literature:** Zora Neale Hurston, *Their Eyes Were Watching God*; Toni Morrison, *The Bluest Eye*
- **The Immigrant Experience:** Timothy Mo, *Sour Sweet*; Jhumpa Lahiri, *The Namesake*; Monica Ali, *Brick Lane*; Andrea Levy, *Small Island*

Of these eight texts, only three are by British authors, two of whom are of Asian descent, and the other five are by Black American novelists (of whom Toni Morrison appears twice). *Native Son* deals explicitly with themes of race and particularly among poor urban Black families in the USA. It is interesting but not surprising that one of the ways in which half of these novels are included in the specification is through 'The Immigrant Experience', echoing the 'Poems From Other Cultures' theme of problems with assimilation.

OCR's suggestions for NEA texts are similarly themed:

- **War Through Time:** Chimamanda Ngozi Adichie, *Half of A Yellow Sun*
- **Caribbean Experience**: Derek Walcott, *Omeros*; Richard Hughes, *A High Wind in Jamaica*
- **Young Women:** Chimamanda Ngoszi Adichie, *Purple Hibiscus*
- **The City:** Jeet Thayil, *Narcopolis*

For AQA 'A', the two potential set texts are themed under 'Modern Times: Literature from 1945 to the present day' and are Indian author Arundhati Roy's *The God of Small Things* and American Alice Walker's *The Color Purple*. The two texts of AQA 'B' are divided between two modules – 'Aspects of comedy' for Andrea Levy's *Small Island* and 'Elements of social and political protest literature' for Khaled Hosseini's *The Kite Runner*.

The Northern Irish Awarding Body, CCEA, also set *The Color Purple* under 'Women in Society' and Toni Morrison's *A Bluest Eye* [sic] under 'Childhood'.

Edexcel's five set texts provide the widest range:

- **Childhood**: Alice Walker, *The Color Purple*
- **Colonisation and its Aftermath**: Sam Selvon, *The Lonely Londoners*
- **Science and Society:** Kazuo Ishiguro, *Never Let Me Go*
- **The Supernatural:** Toni Morrison, *Beloved*
- **Women and Society**: Khaled Hosseini, *A Thousand Splendid Suns*

The three poems they include in their 20 poems post-2000 (which are used as preparation for unseen poetry in the examination) are: Patience Agbabi's 'Eat Me'; Tishoni Doshi's 'The Deliverer'; and Daljit Nagra's 'Look We Have Coming to Dover'. This collection is the least strong framing of all the texts, being simply contemporary poetry.

Some patterns can be seen across these specifications; you will have noted several repeated texts: *Beloved* (2); *The Bluest Eye* (2); *The Color Purple* (3) (each in a different thematic context) and *Small Island* (2). The texts are also almost always modern prose, which is partly due to availability but also implicitly rejects the presence of Black people in Britain before the second half of the 20th century, which we know not to be true (see, for example, Miranda Kaufmann's *Black Tudors*). Texts are often by African American authors, reinforcing the concept of race and racism as 'not a British problem'. Most interestingly, perhaps, there seems to be a strong association between texts written by Black or Arabic authors with themed study of women or children, which potentially reflects an unconscious bias developed from historical racism.

At GCSE, although reform of qualifications has removed 'Poetry from Other Cultures', students still study modern poetry in addition to compulsory Romantic poets and war poetry. Four out of 45 poems across three clusters on the OCR specification are by Black authors, and an additional two by Asian poets. AQA has three poems across 30 by BAME authors, two of whom are Asian. Edexcel initially had five poems spread across two of its three clusters by BAME poets, one of whom was Asian. However, they diversified their GCSE set texts in 2019, which will be further discussed below, and added a cluster called 'Belonging'. Leaving aside the six poems representing the compulsory pre-1914 (and therefore default White) section, the rest of the poems are by three Black poets, two White, one each of mixed-race Asian heritage and mixed-race Black heritage, one Asian poet and one Kurdish, presenting perhaps the most diverse set of texts anywhere in British education.

Eduqas/WJEC has two GCSE specifications, one each for the English and Welsh markets, which operate under different regulations. Eduqas, the English specification, has one poem by an Asian poet and one by a Black poet out of the 18 in its anthology, but it also names 29 poets recommended for study in order to prepare for the unseen poem element of its examination, eight of whom are Black and one of whom is Asian. The same list is given for WJEC, the Welsh specification, which does not list specific poems for study. In Northern Ireland, which also operates under different regulations (not that these address in any way the representation of race in the curriculum), CCEA does not name a single non-White author in any area of its set texts.

TABLE 5.1 Set texts at A level

Awarding Body	Number of BAME set texts	Number of BAME suggested comparative reading	Number of BAME suggested NEA texts
OCR	1	8	5
AQA 'A'	2	n/a	0 (see below)
AQA 'B'	2	n/a	0
Eduqas/WJEC	0	n/a (but 'read widely')	0
CCEA	2	n/a	0
Edexcel/Pearson	5 plus 3 poems out of 20	n/a	0

WJEC in its Welsh specification has a category specifically called 'Different Cultures' which is composed of the following novels: *Of Mice and Men* (Steinbeck); *Anita and Me* (Syal); *To Kill a Mockingbird* (Lee); *I Know Why the Caged Bird Sings* (Angelou); and *Chanda's Secrets* (Stratton). Three of the five authors of these texts are White, and *Chanda's Secrets* in particular is a little problematic as the author is a White Canadian writing about a young Black girl in sub-Saharan Africa dealing with the consequences of an AIDS epidemic. The other four texts deal explicitly with racism, and three of them are American: *Anita and Me*, as I have said, does deal with racism (in a nuanced way) in the context of the West Midlands.

Edexcel is clearly leading the way on diverse texts, but it is interesting to note that the two novels introduced in its diversification exercise are specifically young adult, or even children's novels, with the implication that race adds an element of difficulty (although no one would challenge the complexity of *Boys Don't Cry*!). One of the two plays is an adaptation of a children's novel. The other is one I was not familiar with; *The Empress* was written for the Royal Shakespeare Company and deals with the relationship between Queen Victoria and Abdul Karim (also recently dramatised in the film *Victoria and Abdul* (2017)), blending that story with that of the Indian ayahs who came to Britain in the 19th century. What is laudable is that Edexcel has supplied a set of resources to accompany these texts, in the form of schemes or part schemes of work, and a set of 'knowledge organisers' for the poetry cluster mentioned above. I have noted elsewhere that one of the difficulties in expanding or changing the range of texts in schools is that teachers are hard-pressed for time, and teaching new texts is a risk in accountability terms, so a lack of resources can be a limiting factor in change (Elliott, 2017); the provision of resources is therefore a praiseworthy element of Edexcel's diversification.

Most notable about the choice of 'ethnically diverse' texts in GCSE specifications, however, is that schools have, in the most part, the option of *Never Let Me Go* or *Anita and Me*, suggesting a severe failure of imagination on the part of Awarding Bodies. Edexcel, the only board that does not permit *Never Let Me Go* for GCSE, has it as an A-level text. *Never Let Me Go* has already been noted in this chapter as one of the few options for a female protagonist in GCSE set texts: it is doing hard work for diversity. However, although Ishiguro is of Japanese heritage and has written novels set in Japan, he also works within the realm of quintessential Englishness (*Remains of the Day*). *Never Let Me Go* is an interesting text to read through the lens of race: its clones are second-class citizens, who are subordinated to the medical needs of the non-cloned, evoking the life of Henrietta Lacks, perhaps. Josie Gill has argued that 'despite appearing postracial, the world of the novel is saturated in racialized forms of discrimination', and identified

> correspondences between the exploitation of the clones and the marginalization of Britain's nonwhite immigrants and migrant workers, as well as similarities between the clones' functional education and the education of the colonized.
>
> *(Gill, 2014, p. 846)*

Similarly, the concern of the clones to prove their 'realness' through art or through true love echoes themes of non-humanity that were used to justify slavery in the 16th to 19th centuries. However, sample assessment items from the Awarding Body suggest that GCSE study is more likely to consider questions of empathy and morality more generally, without touching on race as a component. One would hope that might arise with A-level study, but the framing of 'Science and Society' means that it would not necessarily do so.

Interestingly, the Scottish texts selection, which represent the only 'set' texts in the Scottish syllabus for English, and which are much more balanced on gender grounds than the texts in the other three countries of the UK, have only one Black author: Jackie Kay, a set of whose poems is one of the text options for study at age 16.

Within the curriculum, then, the representation of Black texts is limited, although less so at A level than at GCSE. The strong framing of 'other cultures' is now relatively set aside, in favour of weaker framing in which the most striking element is an association with women and children, and there is also the less surprising framing of 'immigrant' or 'colonisation'. It is refreshing to see some direct consideration of race in some of the specifications. There is a strong bias towards American literature in terms of Black representation, and this has the potential to leave students associating racism with America; *Anita and Me* does deal with anti-Black racism, but it is subtle and not foregrounded as the anti-Asian racism is, which again has the potential to suggest something about race relations in the UK. But the truth of the matter is that students could easily go the whole of their examined lives in English Literature without studying a single book or play by a non-White author, and perhaps only one or two poems. Students who only study English Literature to 16 – that is, the vast majority – are far less likely to encounter texts by Black authors, unless they study Edexcel's syllabus.

We are left with a problem in terms of the material we have to populate our imaginations with, whatever our own racial background, both in relation to the

TABLE 5.2 Set texts at GCSE

Awarding Body	Number of set texts by BAME authors	Texts
OCR	2	Kazuo Ishiguro, *Never Let Me Go* Meera Syal, *Anita and Me*
AQA	2	Kazuo Ishiguro, *Never Let Me Go* Meera Syal, *Anita and Me* Additionally, a prose anthology of short stories includes two (out of seven) stories by BAME authors.
Eduqas	2	Kazuo Ishiguro, *Never Let Me Go* Meera Syal, *Anita and Me*
Edexcel 2015–2019	1	Meera Syal, *Anita and Me*
Edexcel/Pearson from 2019	5	Meera Syal, *Anita and Me* Tanika Gupta, *The Empress* Benjamin Zephaniah, adapted for the stage by Lemn Sissay, *Refugee Boy* Jamila Gavin, *Coram Boy* Malorie Blackman, *Boys Don't Cry*

authorial role models and to the texts they produce. Malorie Blackman's *Boys Don't Cry* is perhaps the most interesting novel in relation to this, in that it upends the stereotype of the neglectful Black father by telling the story of a successful teen, about to go to university, who instead is left literally holding the baby he did not know he had, and how he rises to that responsibility. There are some classics of great literature spread about the specifications, but it is the simple truth that if you only study one novel by a Black author, you read it through that frame, and it represents the single story that you have access to. I am thinking of *Beloved*, a text I taught under 'The Gothic' for A level as a beginning English teacher. It is a wonderful novel, rich and layered, but it is also embedded in the immediate aftermath of slavery in the USA, and that is an intrinsic part of its plot, themes and tone. To hark back to Ogunbiyi's point quoted earlier in this chapter, slavery is not the only story we can or should be telling about Black people in our classrooms.

In order to support the possibilities of other narratives about Black protagonists, I would like to finish this section by pointing to a set of three articles that appeared in NATE's *Teaching English* magazine in May 2020, on 'Changing the Narrative' in relation to race and texts in the classroom, which provide useful ideas for further reading. I argued for the use of Black-authored texts for NEA and made some suggestions for good pairs with more traditional texts, Lesley Nelson-Addy showed ways of diversifying the 'single story' at Key Stage 3 by incorporating a diverse range of Black experiences, and Gary Snapper suggests use of critical questions like 'Why is My Curriculum White?' to stimulate debate and students' wider cultural awareness (Elliott, 2020; Nelson-Addy, 2020; Snapper, 2020).[13]

Postscript: 'It's too political for our school'

In the summer of 2020, after the murder of George Floyd by police in the USA, the world erupted into Black Lives Matter protests, and it felt as if there might be a moment for change. I hope that by the time you are reading this, that moment has been sustained into the beginnings of real transformation. But there needs to be willingness for that transformation.

In June 2020, in the midst of a mass sharing of resources and suggestions from educators in England, some schools responded to suggestions that they needed to tackle this moment head-on with their students, and do some work on anti-racism, with the statement was that this was 'too political for our school.' I felt this chapter could not be left without addressing this.

The most radical and uncompromising attitude I take in this book (not to me, but potentially to others) is my espousing of Ibram X Kendi's definition of racist and anti-ractist:

> A racist policy is any measure that produces or sustains racial inequity between racial groups. An antiracist policy is any measure that produces or sustains racial equity between racial groups. By policy, I mean written and unwritten laws, rules, procedures, processes, regulations and guidelines that govern people. There is no such thing as a nonracist or race-neutral policy.
>
> *(Kendi, 2019, p. 18)*

I accept that things are either racist or anti-racist: there is no neutral here. The neutral position by default upholds White supremacy, because of the history of colonialism and the structures in our society. In education, we have a racial attainment gap that is not based on merit, but on the inbuilt problems in society, the education system and the curriculum. To say that tackling racism is 'too political for our school' is to say 'we are a racist school'. Not by action, perhaps, but by inaction. It is a position of ultimate White privilege to be able to say that something is too political for you: for those whose skin colour is politicised simply by virtue of being, it is not possible to step back from this fight. The same has been true and still is, to a lesser extent, for women.

A school is political by its nature: we are engaged in turning out citizens for the future. We can equip them to be critical, engaged citizens or we can equip them to be unquestioning upholders of the government, or anything in between. The point is that any action is a political action. It is just that some actions are less visibly political because they align with the status quo.

Schools and teachers are all too often charged with righting the wrongs of societal inequalities in ways which they cannot. But it is true that we have the opportunity to do some things that can make a difference if we resolve to, to start working for a better future for all our children, via all our children, not just the ones whose skin colour marks them out as unavoidably 'political'.

Conclusion

The instinct when confronted with issues of structural racism is to knee-jerk into an 'I'm not racist' response. However, it is absolutely crucial that our response should not be to deny personal guilt, but to always think: How can I mitigate the effect of structural racism on my students? What can I do to prevent racism recurring? In this chapter, I have explored the framing of race in the literature curriculum, as well as issues of representation, arguing that the non-canonical provides a source of valuable knowledge in and of itself, because canon is constructed via historical inequity. However, it is also essential that we acknowledge the powerful role that literature can play in enabling wider interracial understanding in society, and the consequent effects that can have on students' lives.

Notes

1 A note about terminology: B(A)ME – Black and Minority Ethnic or Black, Asian and Minority Ethnic – is the most common term used to describe non-White people in the UK. It is decidedly problematic, given that it can obscure more specific inequalities relating to different groups within that category. BIPOC (Black and Indigenous People of Colour) is used in the US and elsewhere, while others have made the case for Black and Global Ethnic Majority as a better representation of the relative populations globally. Race also encompasses a number of White ethnic minorities, such as Roma and Traveller communities. I have used Black where I mean Black and BAME as an imperfect category elsewhere, acknowledging that this is partly in order to sit the analysis in this chapter in the tradition of educational research in the UK. Similarly, the question of whether to capitalise 'white' in the same way that 'Black' is capitalised is a fraught one with many arguments on each side of the debate. In this chapter, I have chosen to capitalise 'White' to defamiliarise it, because one of the points made in a later section is that Whiteness is framed as the universal in our curriculums.
2 For further details on this, see Malcolm Gladwell's *Blink* (2005, p. 97).
3 www.runnymedetrust.org/uploads/publications/pdfs/Runnymede%20Secondary%20Schools %20report%20FINAL.pdf
4 www.ethnicity-facts-figures.service.gov.uk/education-skills-and-training/11-to-16-years-old/gcse-results-attainment-8-for-children-aged-14-to-16-key-stage-4/latest#by-ethnicity-gender-and-eligibility-for-free-school-meals
5 www.ethnicity-facts-figures.service.gov.uk/education-skills-and-training/absence-and-exclusions/pupil-exclusions/latest
6 Statistics from the US National Center for Educational Statistics, https://nces.ed.gov/fastfacts/display.asp?id=16
7 Symbolic violence is a term coined by the French sociologist Pierre Bourdieu (whose work on cultural capital will be explored in Chapter 7). It is a term for the non-physical violence created by the power differentials between different groups; it is not typically a deliberate violence, but simply created by the reinforcement of the status quo under which members of some groups are disadvantaged and disempowered. It can refer to class, race, gender, nationality, sexuality and gender orientation.
8 There are substantial overlaps between the different set texts of the Awarding Bodies which issue specifications for GCSE in England. Each text option – that is, repeats of the same book – was counted individually.
9 For a useful support in these discussions, the chapter in Oluo's book *So You Want To Talk About Race* (2019) called 'Why can't I say the "N" word?' lays out the arguments and contexts extremely well, albeit in a US context.

10 I should also say that this novel features the N-word as the name of the (White) Anita's family dog, although part of the point of that naming is to directly address the unthinking racism of doing so.

11 The Awarding Bodies in the UK that pertain to England are: AQA (the Assessment and Qualifications Alliance), which has two specifications for A-level English Literature; OCR (Oxford, Cambridge, RSA – a historic grouping that is now run by the Cambridge Assessment organisation); Edexcel, owned by and sometimes known as 'Pearson'; and Eduqas, which is the English brand for the Welsh Joint Examinations Council (WJEC). WJEC provides for the Welsh context (which differs at GCSE); CCEA (the Council for the Curriculum, Examinations & Assessment – a non-departmental public body) covers Northern Irish qualifications. In Scotland, the Scottish Qualifications Authority (SQA) runs examinations, which differ structurally from the rest of the UK.

12 www.aqa.org.uk/subjects/english/as-and-a-level/english-literature-a-7711-7712/subject-content-a-level/independent-critical-study-texts-across-time

13 Conveniently, these three articles formed the 'sample content' for this issue and are therefore available free to access to those who are not members of NATE, here: www.nate.org.uk/wp-content/uploads/2020/05/Changing-the-narrative.pdf

6

PINNING DOWN POETRY
Facts, emotion and attitudes

This chapter will consider what it means to have knowledge about poetry, particularly in a high-stakes assessment system. It draws on research data from student
teachers to suggest that a conception of poetry as primarily emotive is undergoing a
resurgence. It is contextualised with the reified object that is the GCSE poetry
anthology, as well as considering the teaching of more complex poetry which relies
on extensive contextual knowledge. I use the case of poetry to explore the question of knowledge in the case of multiple interpretations and literary ambiguity,
although it will also be noted that these are not exclusive to the genre of poetry. I
also explore the difference between knowledge of *a poem* and knowledge of *poetry*.

In their introduction to *Making Poetry Matter*, Dymoke, Lambirth and Wilson
(2013) suggest that there is some evidence that 'poetry is the least well-taught part
of English curricula in the United Kingdom' (p. 1), despite its prominence in
examinations. In his introduction to the report on poetry and young people published by the Booktrust, then Poet Laureate Andrew Motion noted:

> [P]oetry in schools is often seen as 'a problem' by many teachers, and as a bore
> by many pupils; outside schools it is often regarded as being on a par with
> clog-dancing.
>
> *(Booktrust, 2010, p. 4)*

Poetry seems to some extent to be the poor relation of the novel and the play in
terms of English literature as part of wider culture and as a part of teaching. Teachers report being scared of teaching poetry (e.g. Weaven & Clark, 2013); it was
not uncommon in the early years of my work as a PGCE tutor to hear new
English trainees declare they had 'managed' to get through an English degree
without studying any poetry (which in itself seems almost inexplicable). The poem
is unique in other ways – it is a type of literature where the form is inextricable

from the content. The medium is the message: to consider one in isolation from the other is to lose some part of what makes the poem.

One of the issues with the enjoyment of poetry in secondary schools in particular, and therefore teachers' enjoyment of teaching it, and perhaps the long-term attitudes to poetry generated in students, is its close association with high-stakes testing at GCSE. As Gary Snapper suggests:

> [I]t is the end-point of the teaching – the examination – as well as the intense time and performance pressures under which teachers and students work to prepare for that examination, which to a great extent determine the pedagogy.
>
> *(Snapper, 2013, p. 36)*

There is rarely an opportunity in the crammed English curriculum to enjoy poetry as part of 'reading for pleasure'; the pleasurable aspect of the class reader reflected on in Chapter 3 does not come up with poetry – the read of the poem is always in the close context of getting to grips with analysis, and the notation of bullet-point knowledge if the poem happens to be a set text. I was very lucky during my own teaching years to have had the flexibility allowed me that meant, about twice a year, I simply distributed books of poetry and various printed-out poems around the classroom, for all year groups, and allowed a sort of free-for-all for students to discover poems, choose and share their favourites, and talk about them in terms of pleasure and personal response, as opposed to carefully noting down their metre, rhyme scheme and images. Which is not to say that the answer to the question 'And why did you pick this one?' was not, on a fairly regular basis, an image, the rhyme, the bounce of the metre. These poetry lessons sustained me and were some of the few times that I felt students engaged with the possibilities of how poetry could matter to a person, and hence why we attached such importance to it in the English curriculum.

If there is one poem that has come to express some of the anxieties of poetry teaching in schools in the 21st century, it is Billy Collins' 'Introduction to Poetry', in which the students 'tie the poem to a chair with rope' and 'begin beating it with a hose to find out what it really means'.[1] In this chapter, I want to explore what it means to have knowledge about poetry, both in the context of the ways English is currently assessed and more broadly in terms of what poetry *is* and how we think about it inside and outside the secondary classroom.

When beginning to consider what it means to have knowledge about poetry, I focused on my own knowledge in the context of two poems. One is Kipling's 'If', and the other is Imtiaz Dharker's 'Blessing'. 'If' was voted Britain's favourite poem in two polls (2005 and 2009) of BBC television viewers (Bury, 2013); I encountered 'Blessing' as an NQT in AQA's anthology of 'Poems from Other Cultures' and loved it. Taking the specific examples, I then moved to the abstraction of what kind of knowledge each represented (Table 6.3).

What I cannot do is give you a list of examples of language, form, imagery or structure off the top of my head without looking at the poems. If I were preparing for a closed-book examination, then I would undoubtedly have created a list of those sorts of things to learn off by heart, including examples of its rhyme, imagery and so on. But that would be, for me, secondary to knowing the poem. I know these poems now; revising for an exam on them would be a separate endeavour. This in itself points to one of the difficulties of relying on high-stakes examinations to enforce curricular provision: what can be tested is not necessarily what is valuable.

The third column also raises the question of the nature of knowledge about poetry, or indeed the nature of poetry itself. Is an affective response knowledge? Is an aesthetic appreciation knowledge? Appreciation itself does not equal knowledge – I can appreciate a piece of music on Classic FM without knowing what it is. I do not have the aesthetic knowledge about classical music to know what I am listening to or why it is eliciting the embodied response it is. But aesthetic knowledge is a form of knowledge in its own right, as is embodied knowledge, which encompasses affective reactions. Affect is the physical component of emotion, in its simplest form: it's the raising of hairs on your forearm, or the sensation of joy in your chest. These two are closely linked together: aesthetic judgement and affect reactions are intertwined in the human (hence the 'sublime'). Interestingly, some research shows that sad poems are more likely to be judged highly in aesthetic terms than joyful ones are (Kraxenberger & Menninghaus, 2017).

Three types of knowledge: cognitive, aesthetic, affective?

There is a strong sense in the research literature on poetry teaching that students regard poems as a technical puzzle, or as something from which they must uncover the buried meaning, something that can be unlocked if they find or are given the right key (Xerri, 2017; Snapper, 2013). Pasquin (2010) recounts the surprise of student teachers on being instructed not to analyse a poem they had been given: 'they had struggled with the meaning of poetry all through their high school years and now a poem presented itself as a problem to be solved, in a fashion that must please the teacher and the examiner' (p. 256). It is this sense that is to be found in the Billy Collins poem 'Introduction to Poetry' in which students torture a poem to extract its meaning 'rather than [to] respond with sensitivity to its aesthetic effects' (Snapper, 2013, p. 31). This sense that a poem is a cryptic crossword puzzle, with a meaning to be uncovered through application of the right tool, suggests two locations for the ownership of meaning: the poet or the teacher (discussed in the next section). The former because it is presumably they who have locked up the meaning, and the latter because it is they who will supply the key for its uncovering. This construction of poetry is for me a cognitive one: poems are an intellectual challenge, not an aesthetic or emotive experience.

This construction has been squarely laid at the door of the assessment of poetry: what Sue Dymoke (2002) categorised as the 'Dead Hand of the Exam'. The recent switch to closed-book rather than open-book examinations in England has had further deadening effects, according to the limited research that has been done. Teachers interviewed by Marsh (2017) on the effects of the change suggested that

TABLE 6.1 From 'If' and 'Blessing' to types of knowledge about poetry

Knowledge that I have about 'If'	Knowledge that I have about 'Blessing'	Types of knowledge you can have about poetry
I know it as a cultural artefact (knowing 'of' it) which is frequently referenced even by people who do not read a lot of poetry.	I know it as a 'poem from other cultures'.	Knowing about the poem as an artefact in time.
I can recite a snippet of it.		Knowing a poem 'by heart'.
I know it's a good poem to rewrite into parody.		Knowing it as a sound, shape and rhythm.
I know a little about Kipling and Empire, and how this poem is a particular example of British jingoism.	I know a little about the standpipe system and also about drought, although not in so intense a way. I have some knowledge of India gained from television and reading.	Knowing about the context of a poem and making an analysis of it in a socio-historical context/informed by theory.
I can elicit the metre and rhyme scheme when looking at it, as well as the effect of the repeated syntax.	I can comment on the imagery, structure and form when looking at the poem.	Knowing about the possibilities of form, metre, rhyme, syntax, imagery. Knowing that these can have an effect on the reader (an aesthetic or affective effect).
I know it was voted Britain's favourite poem in a poll run by the BBC in 2005 and 2009 (Bury, 2013).	I know I am fond of it because of the place it represents in my teaching history, because I think it is beautiful, and because it reminds me of childhood playing with water and brings tears to my eyes.	Knowing poetry enough to have a 'favourite', which can be an affective or an aesthetic response to the poem or to your personal history with it.
	I understand what the 'blessing' is in the poem.	Knowing the answer to the 'puzzle' of any given poem.

teaching had become more exam-focused and less fun; they distinguished between the potential benefits of learning whole poems 'by heart' and the deadening effect of having to learn quotations for examination 'by rote'. Specifically, knowledge of poetry was reduced even more to being knowledge of *a* poem: 'instead of saying what onomatopoeia looks like... [we would say this poem] has got three examples of onomatopoeia' (Marsh, 2017, p. 282).

When I interviewed some student teachers a few years ago about teaching poetry, their responses suggested that, in principle, poetry was an affective experience.[2] When responding to the question 'Does it matter what students think about a poem?' five out of the six understood it in emotive terms, of feelings about poetry in general or about specific poems, rather than in terms of interpretation of meaning or aesthetic judgement. One student teacher, for example, framed the question of an interpretation in terms of 'feeling': 'if there's something else you feel about a text, then that's your feeling, and it's really hard to overcome that – but it might just be that I'm really emotional! [laughs].' Another espoused the importance of exploring students' interpretations because 'it can bring out different emotions in different people… I think poetry is so much about emotions and empathy and experience.' She elaborated on this in relation to GCSE poetry as being about the nature of the poems that were anthologised: 'it's usually meant to be quite thoughtful or pensive or dark or sad or nostalgic – there's all these sorts of complicated emotions.'

More recently, I undertook a brief online study to see how people conceptualised poetry when they were not being asked directly whether it was aesthetic, affective or cognitive (or intellectual) in nature. Via an online survey with a call-out through Twitter, I asked members of the public to give a metaphor beginning 'Poetry is…' and received 78 responses. Unsurprisingly, given the nature of my Twitter feed, the largest single group were teachers of literature or creative writing (27) and a further ten were either people with a degree in literature or creative writing or current students; the other 41 were not involved with the teaching or learning of literature. Thirty of the participants reported writing poetry for fun, and 65 said that they read poetry for fun. (All but one of the 13 who did not read poetry for fun also did not write poetry.)

I categorised the metaphors according to whether they had a primarily aesthetic, affective or cognitive view of poetry; these categories were read over and agreed by a student of English Literature who is not a teacher. We counted as cognitive any that refer to poetry as a way of reporting experience straightforwardly, or which indicated that poetry is about difficulty looking at something; anything where regulation was the primary metaphor; and any that prioritised meaning over other features.

Examples include:

- Life concentrated and controlled.
- Poetry is putting an aspect of life on the table to admire it, analyse it, decry it; to draw attention to and hold it for a while.
- Poetry is hard work!
- A palimpsest of ideas.

In addition, two of the three non-metaphors were cognitive.

Aesthetic included anything which referred to a sensual comparator such as music, painting, taste; water, or a non-straightforward comparison to a physical object (e.g. winged elephant; frogs). One of the non-metaphors (exactly the right words in exactly the right order) was categorised as an aesthetic judgement.

Examples include:

- Poetry is thought singing.
- Poetry is a mixing desk with infinite channels and a special effect called cosmic resonance.

- Cooking with language.
- Poetry is a multicoloured canvas.
- Poetry is starlight.
- Poetry is painting with words.
- The quiet heat just before a desert rainstorm
- Poetry is frogs.

Affective metaphors were ones that referred to emotions; to thoughts, where thoughts appeared to be uncontrolled and spontaneous rather than regulated; to comfort; or to soul or spirituality.

Examples include:

- Poetry is a pressure cooker of emotions and feelings, the more structured a poem is, the higher the pressure.
- A light shining through a dark tangled forest showing me the way. My spaghetti tangle of thoughts and feelings separated out. A comforting presence by my side, reminding me where I am and how I feel is beautiful and perfect.
- Poetry is the whirlwind-tamer of my thoughts.
- Poetry is a hypodermic needle of humanity.
- Poetry is anecdotal evidence of the heart.

Almost half the metaphors for the nature of poetry emphasised its aesthetic nature (37); a third focused on the affective (24); and the final fifth suggested it was cognitive in nature (17). The only difference between groups that was large enough to be interesting was between the writers and the non-writers: very few of those who wrote poetry used cognitive metaphors, whereas a third of those who did not write poetry conceptualised it as cognitive.

This exercise suggests that although we treat poetry largely as a cognitive, intellectual exercise in the secondary classroom, often reducing each poem to an easily memorised list of bullet points, neither teachers nor the public at large think that this is the knowledge about poetry that counts, or its most significant aspect. Aesthetic and affective conceptualisations are the main ways in which we think about poetry on a personal level, returning to the Romantic concept of the sublime, which in many ways combines the two kinds of response and which was hugely influential on British poets from the 19th century, and therefore on their successors. From the time of the Romantics, Eagleton suggests, the word 'Literature'

> was a signal that the virtues of all writing were epitomised in one, peculiarly privileged species of it: poetry. Poetry was the condition to which all the most authentic kinds of writing aspired. 'Literature' was a matter of feeling rather than fact, of the transcendent rather than the mundane, of the unique and original rather than the socially conventional.
>
> *(Eagleton, 2007, p. 12)*

To return to my earlier point, this may mean that the key aspects of poetry and why it matters to people are being omitted in the classroom, because poetry teaching at secondary level is largely associated with high-stakes examination. Poetry writing is mostly confined to extra-curricular contexts. 'Knowledge about poetry' is knowledge about reading poetry, not writing it (although in this poetry is certainly not unique in the discipline of English Literature). Most recently Kate Clanchy's work with Oxford Spires Academy has demonstrated the value that can be generated by working with young people to write poetry, and particularly with young people who are suffering trauma such as refugees (Clanchy, 2018, 2019). It is arguable that of all the forms of literature, poetry is one where experience of writing poems gives an insight into reading and analysing the poems of others. We might find similar insights gained by writing novels or plays, but the length of these forms prohibits doing so enough (in the context of the classroom) to gain the benefits.

What is essential knowledge about poetry?

In the clearly and optimistically named *Poetry: The Basics*, Jeffrey Wainwright (2004) exemplifies the essential knowledge in relation to poetry: metre, rhyme, free verse, stanza, image, metaphor and concrete poems, among others. These are 'know what x is' types of knowledge, which also suggests the ability to identify them in action. In terms of form, I would suspect that most teachers would add sonnet (usually limited to being a '14 line poem', perhaps with the addition of the Shakespearean rhyme scheme and rarely with the addition of the Petrarchan), haiku and possibly ballad. Most students will have experienced the acrostic poem, but more as a matter of standard early creative writing than as an essential form. At an advanced level, we might add villanelle, but are unlikely to consider sestina as essential knowledge because one would be too long to set as an unseen poem in an examination. This may be a cynical view, but it is also a realistic one about how our teaching of poetry has been shaped and constrained by assessment for many years.

Not all that long ago, essential knowledge for poetry for students would have included the ability to scan the metre of a poem: to identify and label the trochee and the dactyl and all that lay between. I suspect the move away from scansion has been a natural result of both students and teachers beginning to fear poetry as difficult, and a cycle of reassurance taking place that it does not have to include these complex terms and difficult-to-hear rhythms. Scansion is one of the few places in English Literature where there is a definite 'right' answer as well as a definite wrong one, and the fear of wrongness inculcated by the assessment system may well have moved us away from it in the UK context. However, I feel some sympathy for the arguments of Barbara Mather Cobb, an American English teacher:

> I teach scansion as a code system, presenting it as a language not unlike a
> computer language or the specialized discourses of mathematics or science or

even the language of phonics that students learned in elementary school, whose symbols it shares. All of these are familiar and tangible to students. Scansion is a code that we use to talk to each other about rhythm. I usually introduce the unit by demonstrating that students need to join me in using this code so that I don't have to stand in front of them and say, 'This poem's rhythm is "da-dump, da-dump, da-dump, da-dump," in four-line sets, with "dump-da" variations in the first two syllables of the first and third lines.' Typically, students are laughing at this point, and I turn to them again and say, 'Do you want to have to talk to me saying "da-dump, da-dump, da-dump" all class?'

(Cobb, 2006, p. 57)

She identifies the six basic feet as sufficient for understanding poetic rhythm: iamb, trochee, anapest, dactyl, spondee, pyrrhic. These have the additional virtue of being useful for Shakespeare, which is in fact the only area of study where students might regularly encounter the idea of a 'weak' or 'strong' syllable in current practice. However, if scansion simply becomes another 'fact' to learn about a poem, rather than being used as a tool to understand and talk about the rhythms of the words and lines – that is, being part of the aesthetic understanding of a poem – then it cannot be counted as knowledge rather than information. To be able to tell me that Keats uses spondees regularly in 'Ode on a Grecian Urn' is not to have valuable knowledge about the poem. To be able to identify them and think about their potential effect, or why they have been placed where they have, would be valuable knowledge. This brings us back to a key question: Is every fact we store 'knowledge' or is there something more to knowing than being able to list attributes?

For me, knowing about poetry is to have some understanding of the tools that we can use to approach individual poems. This is separate from knowing a poem, which has more of a resonance relating to the individual contexts and experiences of a poem, as per my exploration of 'If' and 'Blessing' above. Essential knowledge about poetry or about a poem also incorporates its uniqueness among literature: the fact that the form is inextricable from the content and the meaning of the poem.

> There is a widespread misconception about form, as the poet Elizabeth Jennings once pointed out: it is not a jelly mould into which one pours content. Rather, the two things are co-eval. Forms will arise to express content, and the established forms (sonnets, novels, collage) are those that, like an evolutionarily convergent body shape, have by long trial shown themselves to be optimally expressive.
>
> *(Eaves, 2016, p. 10)*

This is another aspect of knowledge that can be obscured by the cognitive 'solve the puzzle' approach to poetry, which tends to focus on content, utilising form as a clue, rather than an object of attention in itself.

What does a poem mean?

If form is inseparable from content, it suggests that part of the meaning of a poem is not intellectual – that there is not a solution to the puzzle. John Carey uses T. S. Eliot as an example:

> There is no agreement about what *The Waste Land* as a whole means, and for some sections of it no explanation has been found that seems even remotely satisfactory. The idea that the poem has a solution, like a crossword puzzle, would, in any case, be treated with disdain by its admirers. However, if it has no correct solution then its 'difficulty' is quite distinct from the difficulty of soluble tasks. Our normal word for things which cannot be understood is 'unintelligible', and in descriptions of high art, particularly high modernist art, this might be more accurate than 'difficult.'
>
> *(Carey, 2005, p. 47)*

So, for some poems there may not be a meaning to find, and the example of 'The Waste Land' shows that can be true of poems taught at sixth-form level at least. We tend to be keen, however, in poetry as in Shakespeare, to be able to 'know' what the meaning of a poem is. Few students (or teachers) are happy to sit with ambiguity, as is explored later in this chapter. Terry Eagleton suggests that there are limits to questions of meaning:

> Tone, mood and the like may be matters of interpretation over which critics can conflict; but this is not the same as their being purely sub-jective... we can conflict over meaning as well. But there are usually limits to such contentions.
>
> *(Eagleton, 2007, p. 105)*

I think, in regard to this, Eagleton is returning us to justified argument as discussed in Chapter 2 – there are limits to how we can interpret poems, but that does not mean that there is a single meaning.

Robert Eaglestone suggests that one of the prime ways that students engage with poetry in the classroom can lead to a misconception about poetry. On metaphor-spotting, he says: 'for students of literary studies, this process leads to the very mistaken idea that poetry is a kind of basic message to which floral decoration is added, and that their job is simply to classify the flowers' (2019, p. 40). The analogy, I feel, applies much more widely. Ultimately, much of the way that assessment drives poetry pedagogy is towards the classification of the flowers in relation to metre, rhyme, imagery and lexis. This has its dis-advantages: pinning down a poem can be a little like pinning down a butterfly; by the time you have taken it apart to find out how it works, it no longer flies, and the joy has vanished.

Eagleton, following the formalist critic Lotman, challenges the inseparability of form and content. He tells us that:

> each system in a poem is semi-autonomous of the others; and this is a point which many critics have damagingly overlooked. Instead, they have sought for a theory of the work which sees each of its aspects as harmoniously integrated with the rest. Prominent in this kind of approach has been what we might call the 'incarnational fallacy'. On this view, form and content in poetry are entirely at one because the poem's language somehow 'incarnates' its meaning.
>
> (Eagleton, 2007, p. 59)

He quotes as an example F. R. Leavis on Keats's 'To Autumn': including the line 'It is not fanciful, I think, to find that (the sense being what it is) the pronouncing of "cottage-trees" suggests, too, the crisp bite and the flow of juice as the teeth close in the ripe apple' (Leavis, 1962, p. 16). I think most would disagree with Leavis; this sounds to me like the furthest stretch of a GCSE student attempting to find a point to make to the examiner. It strikes me as potentially comforting to think that when we see students doing this in our classroom, they are simply acting as the heirs of Leavis.[3] Yet, within the bounds of reader response, such a consideration of the 'meaning' of a poem would be reasonable. In the light of this, and in relation to the question of form, Eagleton goes on to say:

> There is an argument against the close analysis of literary form that goes something like this. Establishing what a poem literally says, or what metre it may use, or whether it rhymes, are objective matters on which critics can concur... But talk of tone, mood, pace, dramatic gesture and the like is purely subjective. What I hear as rancorous, you may hear as jubilant. You read as garrulous what strikes me as eloquent. Tone in a poem is not a matter of F major or B minor. Ironically only a few features of form – metre and rhyme, for example – can actually be formalised. Form in poetry is mostly unformalisable. There can be no consensus on these questions, so it would be better to drop such fanciful talk altogether and concentrate on what we can be sure of.
>
> (Eagleton, 2007, p. 102)

Such lofty ideals may be within the remit of the literary critic, but are simply not practicable for secondary teachers in the light of assessment objectives. However, Eagleton's list of the 'purely subjective' is reassuring in another way in that it incorporates the aspects of poetry – and indeed literature more widely – which are most challenging to pin down for students and operationalise. They are indeed the aspects in which personal response may be the most appropriate approach and the justification for the argument may be the affective or aesthetic echo that arises in each of us.

Ultimately, for many critics who write most deeply about poetry, the meaning of the poem remains aloof in many ways. Unsurprisingly, many turn to metaphor to express what poetry is, and therefore what it can mean:

> [P]oetry is compressed meaning, yes, but it is also the meaning that leaks inadvertently effected by compression, the uncontainable heat that leaks out of usage
>
> *(Eaves, 2016, p. 11)*

Or they invoke the unknown ways of the human brain:

> Poetry works with ideas, but also within the subjective mystery of our consciousness, with the *qualia* of the mind when is operating other than in its consecutive series.
>
> *(Wainwright, 2004, p. 180)*

Who owns the meaning of a poem?

Poems are one of the main sites in secondary English in which we may come across, in principle if not in name, Barthes' proclamation that the author is dead (1967), despite assessment criteria which frequently ask students to consider the intentions of the author in terms of creating effect and meaning. Louise Rosenblatt's transactional or 'reader response' theory has had a lasting effect on the conceptualisation of poetry. She wrote:

> The poem must be thought of as an event in time. It is not an object or an ideal entity. A poem happens during a coming together ... of a reader and a text. The reader brings to the text his past experience and present personality. Under the magnetism of the ordered symbols of the text, he marshals his resources and crystallises out from the stuff of memory, thought, and feeling a new order, a new experience, which he sees as the poem. This becomes part of the ongoing stream of his life experience, to be reflected on from any angle important to him as a human being.
>
> *(Rosenblatt, 1978: 12)*

The centrality of the text/reader relationship has been challenged in recent years, not only by the 'instrumental approaches' which have often characterised poetry teaching and the place of poetry in the curriculum (Lambirth, 2014. p. 43) but also the comparative element introduced into GCSE examinations which emphasises instead the relationship between text and text (McGuinn, 2005).

The meaning of a poem may not be entirely between text and reader, however. Stead had this to say about poetry:

> A poem may be said to exist in a triangle, the points of which are, first, the poet, second, the audience, and, third, the areas of experience which we call variously 'Reality', 'Truth', or 'Nature'. Between these points run lines of

tension, and depending on the time, the place, the poet, and the audience, these lines will lengthen or shorten ... There are infinite variations, but ... the finest poems are likely to be those which exist in an equilateral triangle, each point pulling equally in a moment of perfect tension.

(Stead, 1964, p. 11)

To return, for example, to the poem 'Storm on the Island' by Seamus Heaney. The reading of this poem can vary widely depending on the contextual knowledge the reader brings to it, or the importance they attach to the author. For many teachers and students, the poem is simply a description of a storm, beautifully and aesthetically captured. However, taking the first eight letters of the title gives a clue to a different, more allegorical meaning: the poem is about Stormont, the Northern Ireland Assembly, and the difficulties of moving towards self-government. A reader from Northern Ireland might see that easily; a reader giving due care to Seamus Heaney's concerns might also see it. Or, in contrast, Ted Hughes' poem 'The Hawk' which many see as being about dictators – yet Hughes himself stated it was simply about a hawk.

One definition of poetry which I enjoy, from a rather left-field source, comes from Nick Harkaway's novel *Gnomon* and puts the focus squarely on the intention of the author:

Poetry is a shotgun aimed at our shared experience, hoping to hit enough of the target that we all infer a great bulk of information conveyed as implication and metaphor in an approximately similar way.

(Harkaway, 2018, p. 288)

But we can certainly say that the meaning of a poem does not belong solely to the poet. Between them, teachers and anthologies act as substantial gatekeepers (Xerri, 2017) to the world of poetry for students: 'it can sometimes be easier to keep gates closed, sharing only a limited, and consequently limiting, range of poems', notes Steele (2014, p. 24), because when students are hungry for 'the answer' and teachers are only confident with a limited range of poems (Cremin et al., 2008), exploration within the classroom can sometimes seem to be too risky. That limited range is often dictated by anthologies, whether prepared by the exam boards or for use with younger years, and as a result 'the poetry [students] do encounter tends to belong to the same narrow categories – usually a short lyric on the themes of love, death, relationship and the landscape' (McGuinn, 2014, p. 10). The 'cluster' approach to poems which has been adopted for GCSE poetry in recent years not only dictates the poems that can be chosen, but also to a certain extent dictates the interpretations that can be placed upon them, by framing them in particular ways, as discussed in the previous chapter (Rogers, 2015).

The interpretation of anthology poems is further limited by the vast range of supportive resources that are produced both freely and commercially for teachers and students of GCSE English. In a very real way, the meaning of a poem might be said to belong to BBC Bitesize for many students and teachers, both of whom use the site and other similar resources either to ensure that they have not missed an important meaning or to accelerate their preparation processes. Poetry is perceived as difficult by both teachers and students (Xerri, 2017). Nevertheless, the majority of Xerri's teacher participants regarded the poem as experience, or a personal conversation, although he reflects that he did not see this reflected in the majority of the lessons that he observed.

Rosenblatt (1978) argued that 'no-one can read a poem for you' (p. 14). Yet all too often that is exactly what is happening in GCSE classrooms. McGuinn (2014) quotes from an exercise with his first-year English and Education BA students in which one student reflected:

> The notes I wrote in my school copy of the poems were not my own thoughts and feelings but rather they're what my English teacher told us to write. They were his notes that would make us look clever and give us an *A*. I didn't even understand half the things I'd written down.
>
> *(McGuinn, 2014, p. 12)*

Naylor and Wood (2012) note that in Rosenblatt's *efferent* reading – in which the aim is to 'carry away' information – 'the work could actually be done by someone else for you, if they present you with a summary of a text' (p. 17). This is exactly the experience described by McGuinn's student above, which could hardly be said to be a satisfactory one, no matter what your views on the aims of the inclusion of poetry in the curriculum. It is also, arguably, an experience that is familiar to readers of, for example, any commercially produced student resources on the anthology such as those produced by CGP. It can also be the experience of the student in the GCSE classroom as they annotate their anthology, reifying the reading conveyed to them by their teacher. However, as Lambirth (2014) argues, 'paraphrasing a poem cannot hope to communicate the meaning of the poem, the meaning is wrapped up and indistinguishable from the way it is articulated in a poem' (p. 44).

In contrast to these experiences, the position promoted in the pedagogical and professional literature is one in which reader response plays a key role. Steele (2014) warns that 'letting poetry be poetry … means not substituting other aims that are about poetry for the experience of poetry' (p. 18). Even Ofsted's (2007) report on the teaching of poetry urged more routine reading and enjoyment of poetry with students, without the need for academic responses or written imitation. Naylor and Wood's vision of the poetry lesson is of 'a classroom that is exploratory, that values the voice of pupil, and promotes a joy in reading, discussing and writing poetry' (2012, p. 14). McGuinn (2014) also notes the genuine pleasure expressed in examiners' reports at 'inventive interpretations' of poems given by candidates (p. 9): allowing students their head in exploratory interpretation does not have to mean rejecting examination success. In transactional theory, 'the reader interacting with the text undertakes a creative role in keeping a poem alive' (Stevenson, 2017, p. 37) (a far contrast from the 'dead hand of the exam' (Dymoke, 2002)).

A few years ago, I interviewed seven of our English PGCE interns (labelled as P1–P7 below) about their understandings of the teaching of poetry based on their initial experiences in school and their reflections on their own experiences of having been taught poetry. Their responses form the basis of discussion for the remainder of this chapter.

There was a clear link established by some of them between being given own-ership of the meaning of a poem and their enjoyment of being taught poetry: 'I remember, especially through GCSE, being taught in a way that the teacher told us her interpretation and we wrote it down.' But at A level 'that's when I started enjoying it a bit more, when I had my own freedom to interpret it' (P2). The variety of interpretations was 'part of the joy of English – that that creativity is always there, there's always that potential to have more interpretations so I wouldn't want to crush that by telling my students that there is a set way of looking at this' (P3). Yet there was an acknowledgement that some interpretations were more important than others:

> I think that when teaching poetry you should make sure that students know that what they say isn't wrong, and that everyone's opinion is valid, but at the same time especially with GCSE and A level, there's an element of guiding them in – the right way – as horrible as that sounds, because certain inter-pretations are seen to be right by examiners.
>
> *(P2)*

Thus, there is a sense that the 'owner' of a poem is ultimately the examiner who will be assessing your essay. Only one of the seven interviewees (P5) suggested that students' understanding of poems should be the 'main focus' of teaching rather than 'what you need to write in an exam' or 'this is what good analysis is'.

The sense of the authoritative answer to the 'question' of the poem was widely noted by the interviewees, both as being unexpected ('it came as quite a surprise to me when I came to look at how poetry is taught around – the idea that there is one right answer wasn't an experience that I had at school' (P1)) but also as being extremely attractive for students and, at times, teachers.

In terms of the attraction for students, the interviewees reported having to counter the expectation of there being a singular 'meaning' to any given poem, and that the teacher was the one who held it and was able to dispense it:

- Maybe in KS3 there's more of a tendency to go 'yeah but what's the right answer miss?' and that's difficult because you're sort of saying 'well there is no right answer' (P1).
- I might say that there's a *common* way of looking at this but I wouldn't say it's the only way (P3).
- Students are 'always' looking for that 'right answer' but it's possible if you're 'patient enough to kind of wait and train them out of asking for a right

answer … I had some really needy classes that just learned that I wasn't going to bother answering those questions so they just kind of stopped asking' (P4).

This expectation continued even into the more advanced classes. One interviewee reported the difficulty of explaining the underlying ambiguity to sixth-form students:

> [Y]ou're not supposed to understand everything in poetry, some things are ambiguous, and getting them to understand that is quite difficult because they are always wanting to know the answer, and they're always wanting a really concrete answer and that's not always what you can give them, obviously.
>
> *(P3)*

Despite these understandings of poetry as ambiguous, and that there was not a single authoritative answer to give, most of the beginning teachers also noted the attraction of that possibility, with most of them recognising the inherent tension in that. Their answers were informed by a sense that they wanted to provide what their students deserved, and that checking their work via the internet was the way to attain that:

> I would read it and get my first impression of it … and then see what the internet has to say about it, see what approaches people would have, make sure that I know the context and any language features that I should be picking out and making the children aware of.
>
> *(P2)*

For several of them, the ultimate source of the authoritative answer seemed to be the poet themselves. P1 told me that 'I do like before I teach a poem to search out what the "received interpretation" is [quotation marks indicated with fingers] so that I know I've not just had a very niche interpretation of a poem' (P1), while at the same time asserting:

> I definitely don't like this idea of authorial intent being some sort of authority over the text. I think that the author has a valid interpretation of their text, but I don't necessarily see there's any reason to say that that interpretation of what they have written is any more or less valid than my interpretation or my students' interpretation.
>
> *(P1)*

This was supported by P4, but she acknowledged a tension in this:

> I lean massively towards authorial intent in terms of my own experience of literature [but] I think that your own experience and understanding of a poem can be damaged or completely eradicated once you have that sort of extra

info – I don't think that a poet can ever truly tell you what their poem means, because of reader response theory. However, once they've had a go it's kind of 'okay, well then…'

(P4)

This counter argument is also suggested by P5, who drew on her own experiences in writing: 'all writing is communication and it's trying to get an idea across' but it would be wrong to assume that you knew what the author had intended 'unless you can go and ask the author and they say yes! [laughs].'

Beyond the author's interpretation of a poem, a number of the interviewees suggested that they would draw on contextual knowledge, or seek out contextual knowledge, to validate the interpretation they were putting on the poem. For some, the cluster in which the poem appeared provided the framing for the 'right' answer to a poem, helping the students to understand any given poem by providing the major theme; this framing can be powerful but also ultimately can narrow the possible interpretations suggested to students, as in the case of the schemas provided by pre-reading activities or the teacher discussed in Chapter 3.

The poet's life was an important contributing textual factor which two interviewees noted they would conduct research on before they taught a poem. Another, however, saw the poet's life as a distraction from responding to a poem: 'If you know everything about them [authors] before you read it's much harder to just let it sit with you and just put your own thoughts on something' (P4). The biographical fallacy is particularly hard to escape in relation to poetry: few students remember to separate the narrator's voice from that of the poet, and societal mythification around particular figures makes it especially hard to resist. The classic examples in British literature are Ted Hughes and Sylvia Plath whose lives and relationship have tended to overshadow and drive interpretation of their poetry, or even the 'mad, bad and dangerous to know' Lord Byron.

Knowing the poet and the poet's context is not just about the biography of that individual, however: one intern saw the overall body of work of a poet as an important framework for interpreting their poetry, so that, for example:

> I think it's good that Carol Ann Duffy appears so much because by the time you get to GCSE you're pretty confident with Carol Ann Duffy and you've experienced her literature, it's part of your arsenal of experiences – it makes the rest of the anthology much easier to access because you can get at it relative to the one poem you feel confident with.

(P1)

Other than the poet, contextual information was considered to be important, particularly if it seemed as if the poem was written in another cultural context. That information would be shared with the students, usually beforehand: 'with GCSE I always share some [context] because obviously they're scored on their ability to incorporate that in their writing, but I think sometimes it's nice to just get that raw response without any of the extra stuff at play' (P4). This context might be the difference between an indifferent response and an enthusiastic one: 'With the GCSE poems, for example, you know "Storm on the Island", they didn't really like the poem – they didn't care about nature, whereas once I made it about building tension in Northern Ireland at the time, they just cared so much more' (P4). P5 agreed that she would rather hold back the context until after students had given their initial ideas, exemplifying through the poem 'Blessing' in which knowing the geographical context would stimulate the production of 'stereotype' by the students (as argued by Rogers (2015)).

Stereotype does not only apply to 'other cultures', however. Only a few weeks into my NQT year, I experienced my first full-blown Ofsted inspection, with the English inspector observing me teach Denise Levertov's 'What Were They Like?' The inspector took issue with our reading of the poem: she told me we should have taken into account the context of rural farming life, such as she experienced in the village in which she lived, telling a romanticised tale of the rhythms of nature and the innocence of peasants (!) who farmed. The school in which I worked was in a town in North Yorkshire and bussed in students from the surrounding rural villages daily – many of the students had parents who farmed or worked in related industries. I am the daughter of two vets. If I had tried to sell the romanticised view of farming to my students, they would rightly have reminded me that farming is largely about sex, death and manure. Far more cogent to the poem, I know now, was the context of the poet herself – a white American writer whose romanticised view of the Vietnamese peoples she thought she was honouring has been significantly challenged by critics. If we were composing an anthology today to consider different cultures, I hope the poem would be entirely excluded, despite its intriguing form.

Contextual information undoubtedly shifts our understanding of a text; it can entirely change the interpretation of an individual poem. In dealing with 19th-century poems in the secondary classroom, particularly at sixth-form level, we can often fall foul of the range of classical references which poets had at their disposal from their 'classical education', before much of anything else was taught at university. These references are somewhat easier to deal with: the 'known unknowns' are obvious, whereas with contemporary poetry it can be possible to miss significant contextual information and reference without prior framing (as the example of 'Storm on the Island' demonstrates). John Yandell makes this point in relation to 'Poetry from Other Cultures':

> Did it matter that Tatamkhulu Afrika's 'Nothing's Changed' was written in the immediate aftermath of the end of apartheid in South Africa? Or that Achebe's 'Vultures' moves from the lived experience of the Nigerian Civil War to pose a more universal question about the ethical status of 'kindred love'?
>
> *(Yandell, 2008, p. 31)*

Does it matter, indeed? A fuller contextual framing may indeed enable a deeper interpretation or one that it is closer to the author's original intention; it is, in the terms of the framing of this chapter, knowledge about a poem, rather than knowledge about poetry.

To return to Seamus Heaney for exemplification: I remember arguing strongly with the lecturer in an adult education creative writing class a few years ago over the poem 'Digging'. I argued that there was a metaphorical reference to the Northern Ireland Troubles in the poem: the pen is 'snug as a gun', and, I argued, Heaney would never use such a simile unintentionally given the context in which he was writing. The lecturer was adamant that there was no such reference being made; she also implied that there was only one right answer (which in this case there might be – Heaney either was or was not referencing the Troubles – but that interpretation of the poem could be valid either way). For me, used to being the final arbiter of a poem's meaning in the classroom, the experience was an infuriating one, which also drove home the difficulties of abdicating ownership of the meaning of a poem in a classroom context, in order to allow for varying interpretations.

Conclusion

Poetry is a high-stakes topic in terms of English Literature and school examinations. As a result, it can suffer more than other forms from knowledge about individual texts being reified and conveyed in efferent readings to the students, rather than their being encouraged to develop their own interpretations. The 'meaning' of a poem is often seen as a set thing, in the possession of the author or the teacher, to be transmitted. The nebulous existence of an authoritative answer is tempting for both students and teachers, and ties into cognitive conceptions of poetry as a form, despite the importance of affective and aesthetic knowledge in relation to this particular form. Knowledge of poetry is wider than knowledge of any individual poem, and can draw on the challenge of scansion as well as the simpler identification of metaphor or simile.

Notes

1 www.poetryfoundation.org/poems/46712/introduction-to-poetry
2 This study and the one described below that asked people to generate metaphors both gained ethical clearance through the Oxford University ethics review process. Neither has been reported elsewhere.
3 If you are interested in further discussion, I recommend Eagleton's comparison of Heaney's 'Digging' and Rupert Brooke's 'The Soldier' (2007, pp. 16–17).

7

CULTURAL LITERACY IN A UK CONTEXT

This chapter explores some interrelated terms: cultural capital, cultural literacy and cultural hegemony, and how they map on to the knowledge-based curriculum. It then moves on to consider how these approaches can conspire to create a deficit model of education, putting responsibility squarely on the shoulders of those with the least power and telling them that if they do not succeed, it is their own fault for not acquiring the requisite cultural capital. It ends by exploring how we might take the most positive aspects of both progressive and traditional approaches to the concept of knowledge in English Literature and combine them to make a powerful inclusive and egalitarian educational experience, while warning of the risks on both sides.

Cultural capital

The knowledge turn in the curriculum has been widely linked to the need to develop cultural capital as a means of levelling the playing field between rich and poor. Beginning in the rhetoric around curriculum reform, its place has now been firmly cemented in the accountability framework in England:

> As part of making the judgement about quality of education, inspectors will consider the extent to which schools are equipping pupils with the knowledge and cultural capital they need to succeed in life. Ofsted's understanding of this knowledge and cultural capital matches the understanding set out in the aims of the national curriculum. It is the essential knowledge that pupils need to be educated citizens, introducing them to the best that has been thought and said, and helping to engender an appreciation of human creativity and achievement.
>
> *(Ofsted, 2019b, p. 10)*

'The best that has been thought and said' is a direct quotation from Michael Gove, who is quoting Matthew Arnold in his turn. Once again, we ask 'according to whom?' However, the term under consideration in this section is 'cultural capital'. Cultural capital is a term taken from Bourdieu, a French sociologist. The 'capital' part is transactional: he is seeking to account for the items other than actual capital (i.e. money) that affect the ways in which people move through life. Unlike the ways in which the phrase is used in the British educational discourse, cultural capital can come in a range of forms, and be applicable to a range of cultures (principally class cultures): the 'culture' referred to is not necessarily high culture.

The *Social Theory Re-Wired* website published by Routledge has an excellent summary of Bourdieu's cultural capital:

> Bourdieu's concept of cultural capital refers to the collection of symbolic elements such as skills, tastes, posture, clothing, mannerisms, material belongings, credentials, etc. that one acquires through being part of a particular social class. Sharing similar forms of cultural capital with others – the same taste in movies, for example, or a degree from an Ivy League School – creates a sense of collective identity and group position ('people like us'). But Bourdieu also points out that cultural capital is a major source of social inequality. Certain forms of cultural capital are valued over others, and can help or hinder one's social mobility just as much as income or wealth.
>
> According to Bourdieu, cultural capital comes in three forms – embodied, objectified, and institutionalized. One's accent or dialect is an example of embodied cultural capital, while a luxury car or record collection are examples of cultural capital in its objectified state. In its institutionalized form, cultural capital refers to credentials and qualifications such as degrees or titles that symbolize cultural competence and authority.[1]

There is no clear link between this, original, definition of cultural capital and the ways in which it is used in the educational discourse today, aside from the fact that both are acknowledged to be related to social inequality. An important aspect is the symbolic nature of cultural capital, to create in-groups and out-groups. To a certain extent, cultural capital is like the common image of the iceberg, nine-tenths of it invisible below the waterline. What can be seen above the waterline is what can be taught (or faked) with cultural capital, but it is the invisible portion which brings the societal advantage (or otherwise). When the visible portion is no longer an adequate signal to the invisible portion, the signals will change, but the cultural capital in terms of the advantage will not. In reference to the widening attainment gap during the era of school reform in the USA, Warner (2018) points out: 'When achievement is framed as a competition and places at the top appear scarce, inevitably those with more resources will do better' (p. 61). Without structural reform, teaching the signals of cultural capital will not help.

In the BBC Radio 4 sitcom *Hut 33*,[2] based on Bletchley Park cryptographers, there is a running joke that Charles, a Professor at Oxford, rejected Archie, the

Geordie mathematician who is now his colleague in the Hut, from the University, because he didn't know how to use a fish knife. This is a perfect example of cultural capital at work. It is different from social capital: that is based in the networks of people with whom you are connected, and is the kind of capital that Toby Young's father drew on to get him into Oxford when he rang up the master of Brasenose College and got his son accepted despite the fact that he had missed his grades (Booth, 2018).

Cultural capital, moreover, although some forms are more advantageous than others, is not wholly devoted to social climbing. It is the factor than enables belonging or otherwise in a number of different groups. This is exemplified for me by the subtle differences between the worlds of my two sets of grandparents: on one side, an oral surgeon who was a university graduate and his wife, fitting into the upper side of the middle middle classes; on the other, a pair of primary teachers who attended teaching training college (rather than university) and who moved themselves from working to lower middle class. In theory, both were middle class, therefore, but looking back there are some subtle differences that exemplify the ways in which cultural capital works. Being able to code-switch between these different cultures was the gift of having two such sets of grandparents. For one set, there was a literal front room (that is, a room for 'best' at the front of the house); the other would never have dreamed of referring to anything except the sitting room. One side found Aunt Bessie's Yorkshire Puddings an acceptable addition to the Sunday dinner table, while the other could only contemplate the freshly cooked sort. One grandmother invited the bin men and the Ringtons man in for tea,[3] whereas the other one bought her Broken Orange Pekoe (loose) exclusively from Betty's.[4] Note that these are not universals; they are a set of symbolic elements that combine to make a general cultural rule. They are complicated by differences in England between north and south as well as between different classes. On the whole, those with more cultural, social and financial capital are more able to flout the unwritten rules. In Chapter 4, I suggested Shakespeare was a shibboleth in terms of cultural capital; importantly, however, those with cultural capital to spare can afford to critique Shakespeare, to declare, for example, that they do not enjoy Shakespeare's comedies.

Food provides a vast array of opportunities for cultural capital to declare itself: when I was five and visiting an Indian friend, I was completely nonplussed by dinner until her father, Dr Yadav, took some mildly spiced potato and wrapped it in a chapati for me.[5] Similarly, I remember encountering fajitas for the first time in my early twenties and having to be taught how to eat them. These are the less socially fraught equivalent of the fish knife or knowing which glass is used for each drink at a formal dinner, and the fact that they *are* less socially fraught is an indication of the differing value placed by society (or, specifically, by the powerful) on the cultural capital that belongs to different groups. These distinctions appeared in the discourse of the Coalition government in the UK around food in schools, in a number of government documents that suggested tablecloths and cutlery as essentials to school dinners in preparing students for future success, a theme which a colleague and I described as 'Manners Maketh Man' (Elliott & Hore, 2016). 'Because eating together, talking together, using that knife and fork, learning how to be civilised, learning how to be courteous, learning how to be polite sets them on a course for success later in life' (Gove, 2013b).

Fundamentally these distinctions are not important: it is the reactions to them and their usage to create in-group and out-group and the consequent inequalities that arise which are important. In contrast, I would argue that the kinds of knowledge that are currently being advocated for teaching in the name of cultural capital are both important and not relevant to cultural capital. It is actually a matter of cultural literacy, which is explored in the next section.

Cultural literacy

The cultural literacy model draws from the work of E. D. Hirsch and is a very different thing from cultural capital. To be culturally literate is to have the level of background knowledge that enables you to partake in the national social discourse; defined by Hirsch as

> the background information, stored in [readers'] minds, that enables them to take up a newspaper and read it with an adequate level of comprehension, getting the point, grasping the implications, relating what they read to the unstated context which alone gives meaning to what they read.
>
> *(Hirsch, 1987, p. 2)*

The principal requirement is being able to understand metaphorical phrases and allusions to a wide range of reference points. The required knowledge to be culturally literate alters from country to country – Hirsch includes in his list the date 1066, which would also be important in a UK context. On the other hand, Mount Vernon, which also appears in his list, is less essential outside the USA (Mount Vernon was George Washington's plantation home, and the only context in which I have ever encountered it was the film *National Treasure 2: Book of Secrets*). In the UK, the equivalent might be to know what Chequers is, but again it is not a piece of knowledge that is necessary for cultural literacy in other English-speaking countries. In Australia, knowing of Uluru would be essential; most other English-speaking countries would provide a gloss when referring to it, or use the name Ayers Rock.

Hirsch used as his benchmark the editorial of *The New York Times*. In order to parallel this, and to give an example, I went seeking *The Times* leader column (the 'editorial' columns which are not credited to individual writers). These tend to focus on the major news stories of the day, usually with two serious and one less serious each day. Picking the first leader column from 5 February 2014, I encountered an article about the Labour Party changing their leadership election rules. It is notable, in fact, for the lack of cultural literacy needed to understand it, as opposed to plain literacy. The exceptions are the phrases 'not with a bang, but with a whimper' and 'navel-gazing' (The Times, 2014, p. 26). However, it is not necessary to know that 'not with a bang, but with a whimper' is a quotation from T. S. Eliot's 1925 poem 'The Hollow Men' ('this is the way the world ends/ Not with a bang but with a whimper') but only to know its meaning – which has entered everyday discourse. Navel-gazing again is an idiom which merely needs to be understood, rather than its origin fully known (although in writing this I was delighted to discover that the practice was originally an aid to meditation, rather than a reference to self-absorption). Interestingly, a phrase later in the article – 'one member, one vote' – does draw on an item that Hirsch includes in his list of 'What Literate Americans Know' – 'one man, one vote'. However, it seems likely that he is referring to its relevance to a Supreme Court judgement in the US in the 1960s which led to congressional voting districts being redrawn so that they were roughly equal in population, a reference that is not relevant in a non-US context. Its origins in trade union pamphlets of the 1800s might be more relevant to this particular article but are not particularly drawn on by the author.

On the other hand, there is a leader column on the same day that requires a large amount of background knowledge to understand, or rather to appreciate: it is a short, jocular column on the final episode of *Who Wants To Be A Millionaire?* which draws on various famous moments from the television series, and is structured around a series of questions in the format of the programme, including 'phone a friend'. The opening paragraph is rather a definition of cultural literacy:

> So, for £3500 in this last, final-ever episode of *Who Wants To Be A Million-aire?* when did the phrase 'do you want to phone a friend?' pass into common usage? Think carefully. 1998, you say? And is that your final answer?
>
> Quite right. For this was the year that this show began. For £1000, when did the term 'your final answer' gain common currency? Indeed, the same year.
>
> *(The Times, 2014, p. 26)*

These terms are not high culture, nor particularly difficult, but they are markers of a common cultural reference point. As Barbara Bleiman points out: 'As adults, we can make our way in the world through our popular cultural interests as much as our high culture one, by sharing a passion for the same football team or by our obsession with *Strictly Come Dancing*' (Bleiman, 2020, p. 75). The same applies to the national discourses in which we all share. However, it is also notable that what we have here are the cultural references related to the powerful (the name of the country house of the Prime Minister, for example) and also to mainstream white and largely middle-class popular culture. They are the examples that spring most easily to my mind, which is a signal of my own limitations and biases. We need as much to know about the Brixton riots, Stephen Lawrence's murder and Canal Street in Manchester, to name but a few, to enter into the national discourse.

Some of cultural literacy, the part that is of direct relevance to English teachers, draws on the literary heritage which is considered to be common knowledge.

Take, for example, the play *Romeo and Juliet*, which appears in Hirsch's list of necessary content in the following guises:

- Parting is such sweet sorrow
- Romeo and Juliet (title)
- Romeo, Romeo, wherefore art thou Romeo?
- Star-crossed lovers
- What's in a name? (text)

(Hirsch, 1987, passim)

It did not include 'Capulets and Montagues', which surprised me, as I would say this is another reference to the play likely to have wide applicability in terms of talking about two groups entrenched in long-term enmity. I might also have included 'a plague on both your houses', but that may well have become more entrenched in the public imagination since the Baz Luhrmann film of the play, some time after 1987. However, to deal with Hirsch's list, it includes three short quotations and one passage from the play, indicated by '(text)'. This is the 'rose by any other name' speech from Juliet. Hirsch may intend the full 11 lines, but two might suffice to provide the majority of the cultural literacy from this text:

What's in a name? That which we call a rose
By any other word would smell as sweet.

(2.2.43–44)

It is instantly clear that to obtain the necessary level of cultural literacy about *Romeo and Juliet* it is completely unnecessary to study the entire play. Cultural literacy is a thin veneer of knowledge that enables understanding references in the wider discourse without requiring in-depth knowledge. This is why it cannot be the be-all and end-all of English teaching. The meanings and purpose of the study of literature go far beyond this thin gruel that leaves us asking, 'Please sir, can I have some more?'[6] Robert Eaglestone in his excellent book *Literature: Why It Matters* suggests: 'Cultural literacy is educational fast food: easy to make and cheap to offer, not really nutritious and often regurgitated or excreted without digestion' (Eaglestone, 2019, p. 38).

Cultural literacy is important in some ways, however. Hirsch's point is that it is key to understanding texts more broadly, and in this respect it is a concern of English teachers because we teach reading. It cannot, however, be only the concern of English teachers, nor their be-all and end-all. In 2019, the Education Endowment Foundation released their *Guidance on Secondary Literacy* which incorporated strong recommendations about the development of disciplinary literacy such as vocabulary and ways of writing in that subject. In addition to this, however, there are parts of each subject that form part of cultural literacy. Hirsch includes, for example, 'mean' (as in averages), a variety of political terminology, song names, computer terminology, a variety of geographical locations inside and outside the United States, and a number of historical figures, from Saint Augustine to Machiavelli to Leonardo da Vinci. Our list today, more than 30 years later, and in various locations across the world might well look different.

Which returns us to the thorny question that animates challenges to many of the choices examined in this book: Who arbitrates the list of essential knowledge? Hirsch designed his list by generating a list with a historian and a physicist, and then consulting 100 others on their provisional list. To his credit, despite the use to which his terminology and ideas have been put, he does note that:

> No such compilation can be definitive. Some proposed items were omitted because they seemed to us known by both literate and illiterate persons, too rare, or too transitory. Moreover, different literate Americans have slightly different conceptions of our shared knowledge. The authors see the list as a changing entity, partly because core knowledge changes, partly because inappropriate omissions and inclusions are bound to occur in a first attempt … [Readers] should bear in mind that we do not seek to create a complete catalogue of American knowledge but to establish guideposts that can be of practical use to teachers, students, and all others who need to know our literate culture.
>
> *(Hirsch, 1987, p. 146)*

Note here that the terms 'core knowledge' and 'shared knowledge' are used, rather than cultural literacy (and elsewhere the term 'background knowledge'). This takes the emphasis off 'culture', which has been the prime reason for the confusion with cultural capital in the UK and elsewhere. The list, however hedged, was generated by a small selection of white men, and from a small number of subjects. As Hirsch himself says, a different set of authors would have created a different list; there is inherent bias in anyone's choice of list, dependent on their own background knowledge. A more equitable approach might be to utilise an analysis of texts from each nation, to examine what is actually in use, as opposed to perceived to be in use. This could be done systematically, or it could be done on an ad hoc basis, perhaps by explaining the references in each text as it was read in the classroom. I am not unaware that this represents the majority of traditional engagement with texts in the English classroom. One might then choose to ensure that this background knowledge was thoroughly committed to memory through the use of retrieval practice as described in Chapter 2: the difference being that by identifying this knowledge as it becomes relevant, the student can both see why it is useful to know this and, by having an existing mental schema to draw on, has another aid to memory. (I am glad to say that this is indeed the way that I have seen retrieval practice implemented in many schools.)

So far, I have concentrated on the cultural literacy or background knowledge required to take part in the national discourse, in terms of reading national papers and understanding references made by speech makers. For teachers of English Literature, there is a further need for cultural literacy (perhaps in its more truly cultural sense) in terms of the intertextuality of literature and helping students to understand and engage with complex literary texts. When I was teaching 'Love through the Ages' in an inner-city Bradford school in my PGCE year, there was a significant challenge to teaching our multicultural class in terms of the concept of chivalry, courtly and platonic love. I lacked the cultural knowledge to draw on Islamic heritage concepts to widen the class's understanding, and indeed many of the white working-class students were also unfamiliar with the concepts. We had to go back to basics and teach the ideas from scratch, including reference to King Arthur and his round table. Of great relevance in the context of the revival of the 19th-century novel as a subject of study in schools is the knowledge of biblical stories which might have been taken for granted in the early part of the 20th century but which has been diminishing along with church attendance.

Some call for this knowledge to be pre-taught, but as Barbara Bleiman (2020) points out, this also raises questions. Which biblical stories would you teach as a basis? Which Roman and Greek myths? Hirsch, naturally, has a few suggestions for particular biblical figures. However, the issue for the English teacher is that whatever you choose to teach *a priori*, there will always be further allusions and references to be developed, and those will depend entirely on the specific texts that you are teaching. One of the skills of English Literature is to identify what is a necessary and interesting allusion to follow up (or read the note on) and how you can pursue that. I would also say that this is one of the joys of studying English. While I enjoy a random fact as much as the next person, to come across it in relation to something of interest to me, even of only passing interest, makes it a greater joy. I refer you back to Mount Vernon and the *National Treasure* film. I will almost certainly remember what Mount Vernon is now (having learned about it yesterday and recalled it today, and linked it to an existing schema in my mind of American historical locations, admittedly largely drawn around two Nicolas Cage films) in a way that I would not without relevance. I would not even have noticed it in Hirsch's list had I not had a pre-existing knowledge of the name. Which brings me to the idea of cultural literacy in relation to unfamiliar cultures and unfamiliar literatures, of particular interest to the English teacher.

> We were at our somewhere when they came.
>
> *(Parkes, 2010, p. 2)*

I read Nii Ayikwei Parkes's *Tail of the Blue Bird* in the summer of 2019. It's a beautiful short novel set in a village in the Ghanaian hinterland, which pitches science against traditional beliefs. I enjoyed it thoroughly. But I also found it challenging to read in places. The quotation above features the phrase 'we were at our somewhere', which is repeated throughout the novel; it feels like a ritual storytelling phrase, a 'once upon a time' phrase. In writing about the novel, I have tried googling it and found nothing. I do not know if it is a Yoruba phrase translated, or something that Parkes originated. Individually, I understand each word; pragmatically, I can only clutch at the meaning they have here together.[7]

When I read 'The smallest catch I have ever brought home is adanko. (Ndanko are not hard to catch ...)' (p. 1) I was able to infer that ndanko are a sort of animal, and also that the native language of the narrator has a prefix which denotes singular (a-) or plural (n-). It threw me a little, but not for long. I don't need to know what sort of animal it is. I don't need to know what 'banku' is, apart from food, although that one I did look up at the time. (It is a white dough made from fermented corn and cassava, cooked in hot water.) Many of the referents in the story were unfamiliar: the types of tree, the dishes, the layout of the houses and the village. This is the meaning of cultural literacy; to be literate in the culture in which we find ourselves, or in the culture of the texts that we read. However, this is full of unknown unknowns: I may be missing particular thematic significance in the form of the ndanko, for example. Reading even a handful of texts from the same culture does not convey cultural competence in that culture and it is perilous to suppose that it does.

I deliberately sought out this experience of a challenging (for me) read. Some of the things I did not know I allowed to wash over me; others I had to work at. I am an experienced reader, in many genres. I do not have much experience of African-set or -written fiction; it's the area I have been working on over the last couple of years. Reading something that is outside your comfort zone, and specifically outside your cultural reference points, is more tiring than reading within it, and it is something we are asking many students to do in every English lesson. We, often unthinkingly, gloss aspects of vocabulary, background knowledge, geography, history, culture, industry, citizenship, society every time we read a text with students. The turnpike house that Pip and Mr Wopsle come across on their way home from Pumblechook's in *Great Expectations*, for example, or the explanation that 'sable warder' (Dickens, 1860–1861/1985, p. 298) means 'black guard' and the man is one of the undertakers. But the books we pick are ones where we tend to know the referents; or to bluff when we do not. Our students, though, have different sets of knowledge, different referents to draw on, and it is often the most vulnerable who have the least cultural literacy in the texts that are set for study, while the richest students are able to draw on a great deal already.

Cultural hegemony

This leads us to the concept of cultural hegemony. 'Hegemony' is a term taken from the work of Antonio Gramsci, an Italian social theorist who was imprisoned by the Fascist regime in Italy for much of his adult life: his primary writings are called *The Prison Diaries*. He developed the term from its original place in the writings of Russian communists into a fully fledged social theory. Effectively, hegemony is the inculcation of the ruling class's norms and values to such an extent into the lives and minds of those who are ruled that they come to be accepted as universal norms (Jones, 2006). In terms of culture, therefore, cultural hegemony is the inculcation of a particular set of cultural values into the population so that the culture that is valued by a subset of the population is regarded as 'high culture', which supersedes all other culture. One example might be the ways in which the practices and curriculums of elite public schools in the UK are held up as ideal educational practices, allegedly because their 'medieval cloisters connect seamlessly to the corridors of power' (Gove, 2013a; ironically, where he cites Gramsci's work), rather than understanding that the pipeline here is not due to the education but to the surrounding social capital, the 'old boys' network' and so on. (The lionisation of public schools is also a link back to the height of the British Empire, when they were used as the model of British education across the globe (Kenway et al., 2017).)

Cultural hegemony means that resistant forms of culture, such as the sub-cultures of hip-hop and rap can be subverted and adopted into safe forms of the dominant culture: what we now tend to call cultural appropriation – for example, when forms of Black culture are taken on and subsequently sanitised when practised by white people, but remain potentially dangerous or critiqued when seen in the originating groups. The social capital of the white middle class enables them to adopt 'sub-culture' practices while still drawing on their privileged societal position to protect them. A connected example is the wearing of non-medical face masks during the coronavirus pandemic; on African Americans, this is coded as dangerous and threatening (and therefore rather more dangerous and threatening to the individual wearing it), whereas on white Americans the range of facial coverings was merely seen as adhering to new social norms (Taylor, 2020).

The concept of cultural hegemony helps us to understand why the cultural capital approach to schooling works to prevent social mobility on the large scale and to uphold the status quo, rather than undermining it. As Anne Neumann (1999) argues, the emancipatory power of literary heritage texts is limited, because 'a dominant culture uses its authors to oppress those who are not dominant at any one time' (p. 6). In the context of English in Britain in particular, the emphasis on Victorian texts, or 'the canon', harks back to a time of more rigid social order but one that is still largely reflected in the make-up of the halls of power today.[8] By emphasising the inclusion of more modern texts and ones which undermine the hegemonic power of capitalism such as *The Cheviot, The Stag and the Black, Black Oil* (McGrath, 1974/2015), the Scottish texts of the syllabus in Scotland reflect their changing social order, and a political process that seeks to disrupt one of the traditional hegemonies in Scotland, the ownership of 70 per cent of the land by a relatively small number of landowners, most of whom come from outside the country (see, for example, Carrell, 2019).

By valuing one particular set of cultural objects, we advantage the same group of people over time, instead of recognising the value of what other groups may bring to bear. At this time, we have the potential for the English curriculum in England to be a colonising project of both the working classes and the non-white students, promoting a white middle-class set of valued knowledge as the ultimate arbitration of 'what is worth learning', bringing us full circle to the concept of 'powerful knowledge'.

The deficit model promoted by 'cultural capital' et al.

Whether we term it cultural capital or cultural literacy, or indeed 'powerful knowledge', the knowledge turn in the curriculum is presented as a social justice move. Those who object to it are challenged for the 'soft bigotry of low expectations' (a phrase attributed to Michael Gerson, George W. Bush's speechwriter), and accused of not wanting to do the best for their students. There are two problems with this line of argument, one of which is the cultural hegemony quandary raised above, and the other of which is the deficit model that it creates. If success in life is dependent on a certain set of knowledge, whatever we call it, then if it is provided in school, the responsibility for the lack of success is implicitly on the shoulders of the child who becomes the adult, rather than the entrenched inequalities in society, or indeed the real social and cultural capital that is used for the reproduction of class and advantage. It is the social and class equivalent of being told to 'lean in' (Sandberg, 2013). I am not alone in my concerns about this model. Odelia Younge, writing about her experience of discussing Michael Young's 'powerful knowledge' in a graduate seminar, says:

> I voiced concern that he was using old 'blame the victim' tactics. He was suggesting that if disadvantaged students were to learn the skills he believed were the only ones worth learning, they would be as powerful as others in society. This, without any regard to external factors or structural barriers.
>
> *(Younge, 2019, p. 167)*

She describes this work as 'slightly sinister in its deepest notions' (p. 167), which I do not regard as being an exaggeration. It feels right, but cannot be: how can there be merely a set of knowledge that will free the poor and the non-white from the systemic entrenched disadvantage created by decades if not centuries of colonialism, imperialism and classism?

Structural disadvantage is the inequality inherent in society and the effect it has on outcomes of all sorts, including educational outcomes, life expectancy, quality of life and others. It was brought into sharp view by the lockdown for the coronavirus pandemic in 2020: we can see it in the people who could work from home because of the types of jobs they hold, and those who could not; the people who had access to private outdoor space so could gain the health and mental health advantages associated with that; those who did not have to rely on public transport; those who could not continue to work because of a lack of child care.[9] To claim that the teaching of a specific set of knowledge in school would conquer all these kinds of disadvantage is to ignore the finite number of professional jobs, and the fact that we continuously undervalue the work of those engaged in essential work like social care and food picking. Or perhaps if we all enjoyed listening to opera and reading Hardy novels, our mental satisfaction would overcome the cognitive and physical challenges imbued by scarcity (Mullainathan & Shafir, 2014).

There is a further notion of deficit built into the model of cultural capital as social justice; it promotes a belief that there are some students whose homes are 'less' than those of others. If a child does not have access to the Classics of English Literature at home, they are therefore behind those who do: there is a deficit to be made up in school. This attitude is deeply ingrained in English teaching: John Seeley, in a speech given in 1867 and later printed, worried that teaching the same curriculum to the working classes that had previously been taught to the ruling classes would not have the same result: 'For them the schoolmaster must do more because the parents and the home have done much less. To them he must become a kind of priest or missionary of culture' (Seeley, 1870, p. 219). The fervour of the 'missionary' is not absent from educational discourses today.

While we may individually claim to care and value the cultural backgrounds of each child, and what Moll et al. (1992) termed the 'funds of knowledge' that they bring with them, the system does not value those funds of knowledge, and does not acknowledge them as being knowledge at all, to some extent. Yet I know that I taught students who went to Islamic school on Saturdays and learned Arabic and read Middle Eastern poetry – that's not something I can do. I know that I taught students who could strip down and mend car engines while still in Key Stage 3. How can that not be valuable knowledge? I know I taught students who had spent every summer or even years of their lives in other countries, visiting family, and had better international experience and understanding than I ever could have. I had students whose lives as young carers enabled them to empathise and connect with others in literature in a real and vibrant way. Not considering these other forms of knowledge encourages teachers to 'develop and maintain a deficit view of students' (Emdin, 2016, p. 42). This truly is the 'soft bigotry of low expectations' because we know that teacher beliefs about student potential have the very real ability to influence those student incomes. Teacher beliefs about students influence what set they are put in, which can limit attainment: for example, Black students are two and half times more likely to be wrongly allocated to lower sets in mathematics than the general rate and girls are one and half times (Connolly et al., 2019). Being in a lower set can have a limiting effect on attainment because of the range of material that is taught (Elwood & Murphy, 2002; Gillborn & Youdell, 2000). This is just one way in which we can see the impact of teacher beliefs about students.

There is another powerful perception of deficit that comes into play in this cultural capital model too, and that is the students' own perceptions of their homes and their families, or of the way in which they are valued by their teachers and schoolmates. To return to Cabrera et al. (2014), bringing the cultural heritage of all students into the classroom and valuing it as real knowledge is incredibly powerful in raising attainment of all students. Students are acutely aware of the identities that are projected on to them in schools, and the ways that these clash with their own personal identities, and which can form part of the risk of disengagement (Elliott & Dingwall, 2017). Individuals have multiple identities, including the 'Discourse identity' imposed by the way they are framed by the discourses around them (Gee, 2001). Think of the acute awareness of students around assessments, for example, and the way that a grade can be embodied into the student: 'I'll be a nothing', as one Key Stage 2 child said of themselves in relation to national assessment (Reay & Wiliam, 1999). Think also of the ways in which Traveller children are framed by the national and local discourses about their communities, and how they are framed in particular by the ways in which their attendance, behaviour and attainment are talked about in schools.

It is important, therefore, for social justice reasons, those very reasons espoused by proponents of so-called cultural capital, that we also value the cultures and home knowledge of all students, including those who do not have exposure to 'high' culture at home. It is true that having a theatre-going family who made you read George Eliot at 12 and took you to museums gives you an edge academically; refusing to value anything but those kinds of experiences exponentially increases that edge. Educators 'are conditioned to perceive anything outside their own ways of knowing and being as not having value' (Emdin, 2016, p. 11). However, that is not to say that we do not need to pursue the valuable knowledge in the classroom too, and to give students experiences of a wide range of cultural phenomena and literature from a wide range of contexts, as I argued in Chapter 5. To only value home knowledge is to make the same mistake as to only value high cultural knowledge, and it is, in the words of Christopher Emdin, 'irresponsible':

> [S]tudents must be taught to become code switchers, social chameleons, and instigators/catalysts of the new norms in the world through the development of new and powerful hybridized identities. To validate the codes of young people in the classroom and then fail to arm them with the tools they need to be successful across social fields is irresponsible; students must use what emerges from the enactment of their culture in schools to help navigate worlds beyond the classroom that have traditionally excluded [them].
>
> *(Emdin, 2016, p. 176)*

Reading Christopher Emdin's *For White Folks Who Teach in the Hood* (2016), I was also struck by the flipside of social and cultural capital. We (as teachers and education professionals) spend a lot of time agonising over the social and cultural capital that our students don't have, but need to gain, in order to achieve what is a largely white and largely middle-class version of success. But all too often, we are lacking in social capital too. We don't have the social capital to engage with them on their terms, to make them see why they should trust us, to make the classroom a place where we can communicate profitably for both sides. We are so sure that the way forward is to make sure everyone plays on our terms, because that is the lesson that must be learned, that we don't stop to think about whether we have a deficit and if sorting ourselves out might be a valuable bridge between the two gaps. The theory of social capital helps to explain why various approaches work: the gently humorous teacher whom the class finds funny and therefore gets on with; why PE teachers who spend their time in a non-classroom context often make excellent pastoral leaders because their relationship with students has a different dynamic; why going on a school trip with students can revolutionise the way they respond in the classroom; why some zero-tolerance schools with eye tracking, for example, also work, because they have got everyone to buy into a model of education together with the trust that they are there to work for the betterment of the students.

What do we teach when we teach English Literature?

The second question that has animated this book, alongside 'Who chooses?' is 'What are we teaching anyway?' English Literature has become a proposed lever for social advancement in the last few years, explicitly, and implicitly a potential nationalising and homogenising force. But teaching knowledge alone, even the kinds of knowledge that are unique to English Literature as described in Chapter 2, has never been the only purpose of engaging in teaching English. Literature is studied by virtually every student in the UK up to the age of 16, and is similarly widely taught across the globe, and has been fundamentally entangled with what is called 'English Language Arts' in the USA, or 'literacy', or just plain 'English'. As a result of that, it is easy to forget that we too, like all subjects, are engaged in preparing students for the next phase of studying our subject, for the group who will go on to A level, and for the group who will go on to university study, who will go on to teach English in schools, and potentially become the academics of the future. The gruel of thin facts about literature, even if they were the socially mobilising force it has been claimed, would not be sufficient for this group, nor indeed enticing them to continue in the hope of a more nourishing textual soup later on.

For me, teaching English is very much teaching about what it is to be human, and literature is the basis of that. Morgan (1990) makes the claim that English studies is mainly about the process that Michel Foucault called 'subjectification': the discourses by which we turn ourselves into 'subject' rather than object. We know that reading fiction increases empathy (Djikic et al., 2013); we need to ensure that empathy encompasses all walks of life, backgrounds, heritages and colours of skin. To read fiction is to walk a mile in another person's shoes: how dull if those shoes are always the same make, colour and design (I am tempted to make a joke about *Hobson's Choice* here…). We have a responsibility to all children to help them populate their mental territory with both people who look like them and people who do not: to make sure we do not have Black children telling each other that stories have to be about white people (Chetty, 2016), and to enable white people to 'police their imaginations' (Rankine, 2014, p. 132).

Conclusion

These are times in which the polarisation of education debate has become pronounced, aided by the ways in which Twitter as a medium of communication discourages nuance and promotes the pile-on. Neither the traditionalists nor the progressives recognise themselves in the caricatures drawn by the other side, and each considers themselves to have the best interests of their students at heart and that the other side is therefore the 'enemy of promise'. For me, this polarisation is itself the enemy of promise. We all have things to learn from each other. The very embodiment of the progressive, the originator of critical pedagogy, Paulo Freire himself, suggests the value in learning to utilise the discourse (and the requisite knowledge therefore) of the powerful:

> A call for situating any debate about what constitutes meaningful knowledge in relationship to considerations that expand rather than limit the potentialities that various students have to be literate not only in the language of their community, but also in the languages of the state and the larger world.
>
> *(Freire & Faundez, 1989, p. xi)*

There are things that we can point to and say 'this works', but the message of education research is always that working is contingent, context-dependent. If it were simple, we would hand out a sheet with the answers on how to teach on the first day of PGCE and everyone would gain the same results with every group. Education is a place where some of the wrongs of society can be mended, but it cannot mend them alone. We can improve examination results for students, and that is helpful in terms of 'life chances', but it is not the only outcome of education that matters, not even in 'life chances'. What I have tried to do in this book is to link the two sides of the debate and to inject some nuance into the consideration of knowledge in this subject which is so close to my heart.

We do not have infinite space in the English curriculum, even if we also mandate 100 books for our students to read in their spare time in Key Stage 3. We must make choices. The choices we make represent what we value and what we allow our children to understand we value. A model that requires us all to teach the same texts gives additional advantage to those who already have high levels of cultural capital and cultural literacy, particularly if it *only* values those texts. The national discourse and therefore the necessary background knowledge for cultural literacy so that students can participate are both changing. By demonstrating that there is knowledge that middle-class white students do not already have, and requiring them to acquire some of those broader cultural references and, in the context of English, study diverse texts from backgrounds not their own, we are both levelling the playing field for educational attainment and generating a broader cultural literacy for all our students. The choices we make in designing an English Literature curriculum, therefore, help us to provide essential cultural literacy but also to sustain and enhance our students' inner lives, and to help them take their place in our society. They provide the footing for further advanced study of English Literature, and they provide some of the common reference points for the whole of our adult lives.

Notes

1 http://routledgesoc.com/category/profile-tags/cultural-capital
2 Here is a signal of my own cultural capital: I listen to Radio 4 sitcoms. It is, however, cultural literacy that enables me to understand the context and references within it.
3 I am not sure how universal this reference is – the Ringtons man came round in a van and sold Ringtons' products such as tea and biscuits door to door. My primary memory is that he was the source of Tunnock's Caramel Wafers. Or presumably, Ringtons' Caramel Wafers. It may be a purely Yorkshire phenomenon.
4 Another cultural footnote: Betty's is a Yorkshire institution consisting of a handful of shops each with a tearoom and selling loose tea out of caddies along with a selection of eye-wateringly expensive cakes. Their staff all dress in Victorian uniforms. They are both unutterably middle-class and a major tourist attraction in York, Harrogate and Ilkley.
5 Here, in another example of how cultural capital operates, I made this friendship because Dr Yadav and my mother were both PhD students in the same group at the University of Liverpool at the time (vets from India being granted the honorific 'Dr'), a group which was highly international and made for a more multicultural upbringing than I might otherwise have expected. It also meant that as far as I was concerned it was entirely normal to do a doctorate and from the age of about 4 I grew up expecting to do so.
6 Apparently, only Shakespeare quotations are part of cultural literacy. 'Oliver Twist (title)' appears in Hirsch's list but nothing more.
7 Sometime after writing this, I connected with Parkes on Twitter, who explained that 'we were at our somewhere' is a translation from Twi, one of Ghana's major languages. 'It embodies a state of normalcy/ rest … that's why it's often the first phrase used when a big change is being described' (Parkes, 2020).
8 To take one example, in July 2019 members of the Cabinet in the British government were nine times more likely to have attended independent schools than the general population. Forty-five per cent of them were Oxbridge-educated, which is more than double the proportion of MPs more widely (Walker, 2019). Only 1 per cent of the UK population attend Oxford or Cambridge Universities.
9 For an excellent book on the nature of structural inequality in society, see *The Spirit Level* (Wilkinson & Pickett, 2009).

REFERENCES

Adichie, C. N. (2009). The danger of a single story. TED talk. Available from: www. ted.com/talks/chimamanda_ngozi_adichie_the_danger_of_a_single_story?language= en (accessed 12 August 2020).

Agbabi, P. (2015). *Telling Tales*. (Edinburgh: Canongate).

Akala (2019). *Natives: Race and Class in the Ruins of Empire*. (London: Two Roads).

Ariail, M. and Albright, L. K. (2005), A survey of teachers' read-aloud practices in middle schools. *Literacy Research and Instruction*, 45(2), 69–89.

Arnold, M. (2006). *Culture and Anarchy* (ed. J. Garnett). (Oxford: Oxford University Press).

Atherton, C. (2010). Coming of age in Shakespeare: A levels to university. *English Drama Media*, 16, 56–57.

Ayer, A. J. (1956/1990). *The Problem of Knowledge*. (London: Penguin).

Bell, S. (1994). New Zealand or Aotearoa? The battle for nationhood in the English curriculum. *Curriculum Studies*, 2(2), 171–188.

Barthes, R. (1967). The Death of the Author. *Aspen: The Magazine in a Box*, 1(5–6).

Bhatia, N. (1998). Shakespeare and the Codes of Empire in India. *Alif: Journal of Comparative Poetics*, 18, 96–126.

Bleiman, B. (2020). *What Matters in English Teaching*. (London: English and Media Centre).

Booktrust (2010). *The Motion Report: Poetry and Young People*. (London: Booktrust).

Booth, R. (2018). Toby Young: Social media self-obsessive still battling with father's shadow. *The Guardian*, 5 January 2018. Available from: www.theguardian.com/media/ 2018/jan/05/why-impulsive-vain-toby-young-wants-us-to-take-him-seriously (accessed 28 May 2020).

Brewer, C. (2013). Shakespeare, word-coining, and the OED. *Shakespeare Survey*, 65, 345–357.

Brooks, M. D. and Frankel, K. K. (2018). Oral reading: Practices and purposes in secondary classrooms. *English Teaching: Practice & Critique*, 17(4), 328–341.

Burgess, S. and Greaves, E. (2013). Test scores, subjective assessment, and stereotyping of ethnic minorities. *Journal of Labor Economics*, 31(3), 535–576.

Bury, L. (2013). Robert Frost's snowy walk tops Radio 4 count of nation's favourite poem. *The Guardian*, 26 September 2013. Available from: www.theguardian.com/books/2013/sep/26/robert-frost-radio-4-favourite-poem (accessed 23 April 2020).

Butler, I. (2015). Why is Othello black? Slate, 11 November 2015. Available from: https://slate.com/culture/2015/11/why-is-othello-black-understanding-why-shakespeare-made-his-hero-a-moor.html (accessed 12 August 2020).

Cabrera, N. L., Milem, J. F., Jaquette, O. and Marx, R. W. (2014). Missing the (student achievement) forest for all the (political) trees empiricism and the Mexican American Studies controversy in Tucson. *American Educational Research Journal*, 51(6), 1084–1118.

Calvino, I. (1999). *Why Read the Classics?* (London: Jonathan Cape).

Candido, J. (2019). Seeing the Elizabethan Playhouse in Richard II. In S. Homan (ed.), *How and Why We Teach Shakespeare*. (New York: Routledge), pp. 51–61.

Carey, J. (2005). *What Good Are the Arts?* (London: Faber and Faber).

Carrell, S. (2019). Report calls for reform of 'unhealthy' land ownership in Scotland. *The Guardian*, 20 March 2019. Available from: www.theguardian.com/uk-news/2019/mar/20/report-calls-for-reform-of-unhealthy-land-ownership-in-scotland (accessed 22 May 2020).

Carter, S. P. (2007). 'Reading all that white crazy stuff': Black young women unpacking whiteness in a high school British Literature classroom. *Journal of Classroom Interaction*, 41 (1), 42–54.

Chetty, D. (2016). 'You can't say that! Stories have to be about white people'. In N. Shukla (ed.), *The Good Immigrant*. (London: Unbound), pp. 96–107.

Cheung, K. (2019). *Beautiful Wastelands: Teachers Talk Texts in 'Bog Standard' Schools*. Unpublished PhD thesis, Macquarie University.

Clanchy, K. (2018). *England: Poems from a School*. (London: Picador).

Clanchy, K. (2019). *Some Kids I Taught and What They Taught Me*. (London: Pan Macmillan).

Cobb, B. (2006). Playing with poetry's rhythm: Taking the intimidation out of scansion. *The English Journal*, 96(1), 56–61.

Colley, L. (2002). *Britons: Forging the Nation 1707–1837* (2nd ed.). (London: Pimlico).

Collins, F. M. (2005). 'She's sort of dragging me into the story!' Student teachers' experiences of reading aloud in Key Stage 2 classes. *Literacy*, 39(1), 10–17.

Connolly, P., Taylor, B., Francis, B., Archer, L., Hodgen, J., Mazenod, A. and Tereshchenko, A. (2019). The misallocation of students to academic sets in maths: A study of secondary schools in England. *British Educational Research Journal*, 45(4), 873–897.

Cremin, T., Mottram, M., Bearne, E. and Goodwin, P. (2008). Exploring teachers' knowledge of children's literature. *Cambridge Journal of Education*, 38(4), 449–464.

Daly, C. (2000). Gender difference in achievement in English: A sign of the times? In J. Davison and J. Moss (eds), *Issues in English Teaching* (London: Routledge), pp. 224–242.

Davis, J. (2018). 'Something real to carry home when day is done: The reader in future'. In R. Eaglestone and G. Marshall (eds), *English: Shared Futures Essays and Studies 2018*. (Cambridge: D. S. Brewer), pp. 210–216.

Day, T. (2018). In praise of slow learning in literary studies. In A. Goodwyn, C. Durrant, L. Reid and L. Scherff (eds), *International Perspectives on the Teaching of Literature in Schools: Global Principles and Practices*. (London: Routledge/NATE), pp. 125–132.

Deem, R. (1978). *Women and Schooling*. (London: Routledge).

Denholm, A. (2012). Pupils told they must study Scots literature. *The Herald*. Available from: www.heraldscotland.com/news/13045596.pupils-told-they-must-study-scots-literature (accessed 20 August 2020).

Dentith, S. (2017). Teaching Historically: Some Limits to Historicist Teaching. In B. Knights (ed.), *Teaching Literature: Text and Dialogue in the English Classroom*. (London: Palgrave McMillan), pp. 173–188.

DfE (2013). *English Literature: GCSE subject content and assessment objectives*. (London: HMSO). Available from: https://assets.publishing.service.gov.uk/government/uploads/system/uploads/attachment_data/file/254498/GCSE_English_literature.pdf (accessed 23 May 2020).

Dickens, C. (1860–1861/1985). *Great Expectations*. (London: Penguin Classics).

Dickens, C. (1854/2000). *Hard Times*. (London: Penguin Classics).

Di Stasio, V. and Heath, A. (2019). Are employers in Britain discriminating against ethnic minorities? Briefing note summarising the GEMM project findings. (Oxford: Centre for Social Investigation). Available from: http://csi.nuff.ox.ac.uk/wp-content/uploads/2019/01/Are-employers-in-Britain-discriminating-against-ethnic-minorities_final.pdf (accessed 20 August 2020).

Djikic, M., Oatley, K. and Moldoveanu, M. C. (2013). Reading other minds: Effects of literature on empathy. *Scientific Study of Literature*, 3(1), 28–47.

Dymoke, S. (2002). The Dead Hand of the Exam: The impact of the NEAB anthology on poetry teaching at GCSE. *Changing English*, 9(1), 85–93.

Dymoke, S., Lambirth, A. and Wilson, A. (eds). (2013). *Making Poetry Matter: International Research on Poetry Pedagogy*. (London: Bloomsbury).

Eaglestone, R. (2017). Transition into the Profession: Accuracy, Sincerity and 'Disciplinary Consciousness'. In B. Knights (ed.), *Teaching Literature: Text and Dialogue in the English Classroom*. (London: Palgrave McMillan), pp. 67–80.

Eaglestone, R. (2019). *Literature: Why It Matters*. (Cambridge: Polity).

Eagleton, T. (2007). *How to Read a Poem*. (Oxford: Blackwell).

Eaves, W. (2016). *The Inevitable Gift Shop*. (London: CB Editions).

Eddo-Lodge, R. (2017). *Why I'm No Longer Talking to White People About Race*. (London: Bloomsbury).

Elliott, V. (2014). The treasure house of a nation? Literary heritage, curriculum and devolution in Scotland and England in the twenty-first century. *Curriculum Journal*, 25(2), 282–300.

Elliott, V. (2016). 'Study What You Most Affect': Beginning Teachers' Preparedness to Teach Shakespeare. *CEA Critic*, 78(2), 199–212.

Elliott, V. (2017). Gender and the contemporary educational canon in the UK. *International Journal of English Studies*, 17(2), 45–62.

Elliott, V. (2019). Detecting the Dane: Recreating Shakespearian Genre in a Level Literature. *English: Journal of the English Association*, 68(262), 283–304.

Elliott, V. (2020). Black and Brilliant. *Teaching English*, 23, 37–38.

Elliott, V. and Dingwall, N. (2017). Roles as a route to being 'other': Drama-based interventions with at-risk students. *Emotional and Behavioural Difficulties*, 22(1), 66–78.

Elliott, V. and Hore, B. (2016). 'Right nutrition, right values': The construction of food, youth and morality in the UK government 2010–2014. *Cambridge Journal of Education*, 46 (2), 177–193.

Elliott, V. and Olive, S. (2018). *State of the Nation: Shakespeare Teaching Today*. Full session at British Shakespeare Association Conference, Queen's University Belfast, 16 June 2018.

Elliott, V. and Olive, S. (2019). Secondary Shakespeare in the UK: What gets taught and why? *English in Education*. Online. doi:10.1080/04250494.2019.1690952.

Elwood, J. and Murphy, P. (2002). Tests, tiers and achievement: Gender and performance at 16 and 14 in England. *European Journal of Education*, 37(4), 395–416.

Emdin, C. (2016). *For White Folks Who Teach in the Hood … and the Rest of Y'All Too*. (Boston, MA: Beacon Press).

Fernie, E. (2017). *Shakespeare for Freedom*. (Cambridge: Cambridge University Press).

Fiedler, L. A. (ed.). (1981). *English Literature: Opening Up the Canon. Selected Papers from the English Institute, 1979* (vol. 4). (Baltimore, MD: Johns Hopkins University Press).

Frager, A. (2010). Enter the villain: Against oral reading in secondary schools. *American Secondary Education*, 38(3), 28–39.

Freadman, A. (1988). Untitled: (On Genre). *Cultural Studies*, 21(1), 67–99.

Freedgood, E. (2010). Souvenirs of Sadism: Mahogany Furniture, Deforestation, and Slavery in Jane Eyre. *The Ideas in Things: Fugitive Meaning in the Victorian Novel* (Chicago, IL: University of Chicago Press), pp. 30–54.

Freire, P. and Faundez, A. (1989). *Learning to Question: A Pedagogy of Liberation* (trans. T. Coates). (New York: Continuum).

Frow, J. (2015). *Genre*. (Abingdon/New York: Routledge).

Gee, J. P. (2001). Identity as an Analytic Lens for Research in Education. In W. G. Secada (ed.), *Review of Research in Education*, Vol. 25. (Washington, DC: American Educational Research Association), pp. 99–126.

Gerzina, G. H. (2017). Contrasts: Teaching English in British and American Universities. In B. Knights (ed.), *Teaching Literature: Text and Dialogue in the English Classroom*. (London: Palgrave McMillan), pp. 17–30.

Gibson, J. (2017). Beyond the Essay? Assessment and English Literature. In B. Knights (ed.), *Teaching Literature: Text and Dialogue in the English Classroom*. (London: Palgrave McMillan), pp.99–114.

Gibson, R. (2016). *Teaching Shakespeare* (2nd ed.). (Cambridge: Cambridge University Press).

Gibson, S. (2008). Reading Aloud: A Useful Learning Tool? *ELT Journal*, 62, 29–36.

Gill, J. (2014). Written on the Face: Race and Expression in Kazuo Ishiguro's *Never Let Me Go*. *Modern Fiction Studies*, 60(4), 844–862.

Gillborn, D. and Youdell, D. (2000). *Rationing Education: Policy, Practice, Reform and Equity*. (Buckingham: Open University Press).

Giovanelli, M. and Mason, J. (2015). 'Well I don't feel that': Schemas, worlds and authentic reading in the classroom. *English in Education*, 49(1), 41–55.

Gladwell, M. (2005). *Blink*. (New York: Little, Brown & Company).

Goodwyn, A. (2016). Still growing after all these years? The resilience of the 'Personal Growth model of English' in England and also internationally. *English Teaching: Practice & Critique*, 15(1), 7–21.

Goodwyn, A., Durrant, C., Reid, L. and Scherff, L. (eds). (2017). *International Perspectives on the Teaching of Literature in Schools: Global Principles and Practices*. (London/New York: Routledge).

Gove, M. (2010, October). *All pupils will learn our island's story*. Speech presented at Conservative Party Conference, Birmingham. Available from: https://conservative-speeches.sayit.mysociety.org/speech/601441 (accessed 20 August 2020.)

Gove, M. (2011, November). *A liberal education*. Speech presented at Cambridge University, Cambridge. Available from: www.education.gov.uk/inthenews/speeches/a00200373/michael-gove-to-cambridge-university (accessed 20 August 2020).

Gove, M. (2013a, February). *The Progressive Betrayal*. Speech presented at the Social Market Foundation. Available from: www.smf.co.uk/michael-gove-speaks-at-the-smf (accessed 20 May 2020).

Gove, M. (2013b, October). Speech to the Conservative Party Conference. Available from: www.youtube.com/watch?v=uIljoF3P9l4 (accessed 24 August 2020).

Gramsci, A. (1971). *Selection from the Prison Notebooks* (ed. and trans. Q. Hoare and G. N. Smith). (London: Lawrence and Wishart).

Green, B. (2018). *Engaging Curriculum: Bridging the Curriculum Theory and English Education Divide.* (Abingdon: Routledge).

Green, B. and Cormack, P. (2008). Curriculum history, 'English' and the new education; Or, installing the empire of English? *Pedagogy, Culture & Society,* 16(3), 253–267.

Greene, M. (1995). *Releasing the Imagination: Essays on Education, the Arts, and Social Change.* (San Francisco, CA: Jossey-Bass).

Grumet, M. (2014). Imago, Imago, Imago. *Journal of the Canadian Association for Curriculum Studies,* 12(1), 82–89.

Guillory, J. (1993). *Cultural Capital: The Problem of Literary Canon Formation.* (Chicago, IL: University of Chicago Press).

Harkaway, N. (2018). *Gnomon.* (London: Heinemann).

Hartley, A. J. (2019). Theatricality and the resistance of thesis. In S. Homan (ed.), *How and Why We Teach Shakespeare.* (New York: Routledge), pp. 19–29.

Hawkes, T. (2002). *Shakespeare in the Present.* (London: Routledge).

Henderson, M., Sullivan, A., Anders, J. and Moulton, V. (2018). Social class, gender and ethnic differences in subjects taken at age 14. *The Curriculum Journal,* 29(3), 298–318.

Hirsch, A. (2018). *Brit(ish): On Race, Identity and Belonging.* (London: Jonathan Cape).

Hirsch, E. D. (1987). *Cultural Literacy: What Every American Needs to Know.* (Boston, MA: Houghton Mifflin).

Hopkins, L. (2016a). *Shakespearean Allusion in Crime Fiction: DCI Shakespeare.* (London: Palgrave Macmillan).

Hopkins, L. (2016b). Shakespearean allusion and the detective fiction of Georgette Heyer. *Palgrave Communications,* 2(1), 1–7.

Ingram, J. and Elliott, V. (2016). A critical analysis of the role of wait time in classroom interactions and the effects on student and teacher interactional behaviours. *Cambridge Journal of Education,* 46(1), 37–53.

Jackson, R. (2019). 'Performing *Hamlet*': Repeated Visits to Elsinore. In S. Homan (ed.), *How and Why We Teach Shakespeare.* (New York: Routledge), pp. 75–82.

Jones, S. (2006). *Antonio Gramsci.* (Abingdon: Routledge).

Jones, T. (2019). Her Own Best Thing. In G. Edim (ed.), *Well-Read Black Girl.* (London: Trapeze), pp. 23–30.

Justice, D. H. (2018). *Why Indigenous Literatures Matter.* (Ontario: Wilfrid Laurier University Press).

Kamal, S. (2019). *Unmarriageable.* (London: Allison & Busby).

Kara, B. (2017). Colouring in the curriculum. *Schools Week.* Available from: https://schoolsweek.co.uk/colouring-in-the-curriculum (accessed 20 May 2020).

Kaufmann, M. (2017). *Black Tudors: The Untold Story.* (London: Simon and Schuster).

Kemmis, S. and Fitzclarence, L. (1986). *Curriculum Theorising: Beyond Reproduction Theory.* (Geelong, Victoria: Deakin University).

Kendi, I. X. (2017). *Stamped from the Beginning: The Definitive History of Racist Ideas in America.* (London: Random House).

Kendi, I. X. (2019). *How to Be an Anti-Racist.* (London: Bodley Head).

Kenway, J., Fahey, J., Epstein, D., Koh, A., McCarthy, C. and Rizvi, F. (2017). *Class Choreographies: Elite Schools and Globalization.* (London: Springer).

Knights, B. (2017). Introduction: Teaching? Literature? In B. Knights (ed.), *Teaching Literature: Text and Dialogue in the English Classroom.* (London: Palgrave McMillan), pp. 1–16.

Knights, B. (2018). Pedagogic Criticism: An Introduction. In R. Eagleston and G. Marshall (eds), *English: Shared Futures Essays and Studies 2018* (Cambridge: D. S. Brewer), pp. 40–50.

Kraxenberger, M. and Menninghaus, W. (2017). Affinity for poetry and aesthetic appreciation of joyful and sad poems. *Frontiers in Psychology,* 7, 2051.

Lambert, D. (2011). Reviewing the case for geography, and the 'knowledge turn' in the English National Curriculum. *Curriculum Journal*, 22(2), 243–264.

Lambirth, A. (2014). Commentary and practical implications: Righting the 'wrong kind of orientation'. In S. Dymoke, M. Barrs, A. Lambirth and A. Wilson (eds), *Making Poetry Happen*. (London: Bloomsbury), pp. 43–47.

Lauder, H., Young, M., Daniels, H., Balarin, M. and Lowe, J. (eds). (2012). *Educating for the Knowledge Economy? Critical Perspectives*. (Abingdon/New York: Routledge).

Leavis, F. R. (1948). *The Great Tradition*. (London: Chatto & Windus).

Leavis, F. R. (1962). *The Common Pursuit*. (Harmondsworth: Penguin).

Lessing, D. (1964/2014). *The Golden Notebook*. (London: Fourth Estate).

Lobban, G. (1975). Sex-roles in reading schemes. *Educational Review*, 27, 202–210.

London, N. A. (2002). Curriculum and pedagogy in the development of colonial imagination: A case study. *Pedagogy, Culture & Society*, 10(1), 95–121.

London, N. A. (2003). Ideology and politics in English-language education in Trinidad and Tobago: The colonial experience and a postcolonial critique. *Comparative Education Review*, 47(3), 287–320.

MacLachlan, M. (2004). *Embodiment: Clinical, Critical and Cultural Perspectives on Health and Illness*. (Berkshire: Open University Press/McGraw-Hill).

Marsh, C. (2017). Poetry and assessment: An investigation into teachers' perceptions of the impact of closed book examinations on teaching and learning at GCSE. *English in Education*, 51(3), 275–293.

Mason, J. (2014). Narrative. In P. Stockwell and S. Whiteley (eds), *The Cambridge Handbook of Stylistics*. (Cambridge: Cambridge University Press), pp. 179–195.

Mason, J. (2016). Narrative Interrelation, Intertextuality, and Teachers' Knowledge about Students' Reading. In M. Giovanelli and D. Clayton (eds), *Knowing about Language: Linguistics and the Secondary English Classroom*. (London: Routledge), pp. 162–172.

Mason, J. [DrofletJess]. (2020a, 27 March). Another clear pattern in relation to lying about books we haven't read is a distinction being made between active and passive forms of lying! Many participants wouldn't 'outright' lie, but would let people assume, not correct them, and allow people to think they've read something [Tweet]. Available at https://twitter.com/DrofletJess/status/1243522008312406016 (accessed 20 August 2020).

Mason, J. [DrofletJess]. (2020b, 31 March). If you're an English teacher out there who feels like you should have read more of the classics, don't worry. I can confirm that LOTS AND LOTS AND LOTS of your colleagues secretly feel the same! #TeamEnglish [Tweet]. Available at https://twitter.com/DrofletJess/status/1246097156508975107 (accessed 20 August 2020).

Mason, J. and Giovanelli, M. (2017). 'What do you think?' Let me tell you: Discourse about texts and the literature classroom. *Changing English*, 24(3), 318–329.

McGrath, J. (1974/2015). *The Cheviot, The Stag and the Black, Black Oil*. (London: Bloomsbury).

McGuinn, N. (2005). Living in contradiction without shame: The challenge of intertextual response in GCSE poetry. *Changing English*, 12(2), 243–252.

McGuinn, N. (2014). The challenges and opportunities for engaging with poetry. In S. Dymoke, M. Barrs, A. Lambirth and A. Wilson (eds), *Making Poetry Happen*. (London: Bloomsbury), pp. 7–15.

Mercer, N. (2008). Three types of talk. Faculty of Education, University of Cambridge. Available from: https://thinkingtogether.educ.cam.ac.uk/resources/5_examples_of_talk_in_groups.pdf (accessed 20 August 2020).

Meyer, J. and Land, R. (2003). *Threshold Concepts and Troublesome Knowledge: Linkages to Ways of Thinking and Practising Within the Disciplines.* (Edinburgh: University of Edinburgh).

Meyer, J. H. and Land, R. (2005). Threshold concepts and troublesome knowledge (2): Epistemological considerations and a conceptual framework for teaching and learning. *Higher Education,* 49(3), 373–388.

Miernik, M. (2015). A vicious circle: How canon continues to reinforce sex segregation in literature in the 21st century. *Acta Philologica,* 47, 85–96.

Mohamed, N. [thesailorsgirl]. (2020, 4 June). It was rarely open aggression or contempt shown by peers or tutors at university but more a dislocating feeling that you, your history, your thoughts, your experiences don't matter and a resultant fatigue. What do black students feel now? What do they want now? We need to know. [Tweet]. Available at https://twitter.com/thesailorsgirl/status/1268522031697604608 (accessed 20 August 2020).

Moll, L. C., Amanti, C., Neff, D. and Gonzalez, N. (1992). Funds of Knowledge for Teaching: Using a Qualitative Approach to Connect Homes and Classrooms. *Theory into Practice,* 31(2), 132–141.

Morgan, R. (1990). The 'Englishness' of English teaching. In I. Goodson and P. Medway (eds), *Bringing English to Order: The History and Politics of a School Subject.* (London: Falmer Press), pp. 197–241.

Mullainathan, S. and Shafir, E. (2014). *Scarcity: The True Cost of Not Having Enough.* (London: Penguin Books).

Naylor, A. and Wood, A. B. (2012). *Teaching Poetry: Reading and Responding to Poetry in the Secondary Classroom.* (London: Routledge).

Neelands, J. and O'Hanlon, J. (2011). There is some soul of good: An action-centred approach to teaching Shakespeare in schools. *Shakespeare Survey,* 64, 240–250.

Nelson-Addy, L. (2020). A journey of discovery. *Teaching English,* 23, 35–36.

Neumann, A. W. (1999). *Should You Read Shakespeare?* (Sydney: University of New South Wales Press).

Nicklin, L. L. (2020). *An Ethnographic Exploration of Participant and Practitioner Perceptions of a Shakespeare-focussed Prison Education Programme.* PhD thesis. University of York.

Norris, C. (1988). Editor's Foreword. In M. Bell, *F.R. Leavis.* (Abingdon: Routledge), pp. vii–xv.

O'Connor, R. (2019). The 20 books Brits lie about reading the most, from War and Peace to 1984. *The Independent,* 7 October 2019. Available from: www.independent.co.uk/arts-entertainment/books/newtis/best-books-most-read-uk-war-peace-lie-1984-a9145946.html.

OECD (2002). *Reading For Change Performance And Engagement Across Countries - Results From PISA 2000.* Available from: www.oecd-ilibrary.org/education/reading-for-change-performance-and-engagement-across-countries_9789264099289-en (accessed 20 August 2020).

Ofsted(2007). *Poetry in schools: A survey of practice, 2006/07.* Available from:https://webarchive.nationalarchives.gov.uk/20141106091137/https://www.ofsted.gov.uk/sites/default/files/documents/surveys-and-good-practice/p/Poetry%20in%20schools%20%28PDF%20format%29.pdf (accessed 24 August 2020).

Ofsted (2019a). *Inspecting the curriculum: Revising inspection methodology to support the education inspection framework* (London: HMSO). Available from: https://assets.publishing.service.gov.uk/government/uploads/system/uploads/attachment_data/file/814685/Inspecting_the_curriculum.pdf (accessed 8 June 2020).

Ofsted (2019b). *Schools' inspection update: January 2019 – Special edition.* (London: HMSO). Available from: https://assets.publishing.service.gov.uk/government/uploads/system/up

loads/attachment_data/file/772056/School_inspection_update_-_January_2019_Special_ Edition_180119.pdf (accessed 28 May 2020).

Ogunbiyi, O. (2019). #AcademiaSoWhite. In C. Kwakye and O. Ogunbiyi (eds), *Taking Up Space: The Black Girl's Manifesto for Change.* (London: Merky Books), pp. 55–103.

Olive, S. (2015). *Shakespeare Valued: Education, Policy and Pedagogy.* (Bristol: Intellect).

Olua, I. (2019). *So You Want To Talk About Race.* (New York: Hachette).

Olufemi, L. (2019). Academic and Unbearable Whiteness. In O. Younge (ed.), *A Fly Girl's Guide to University.* (Birmingham: Verve Words), pp. 56–58.

Olufemi, L. (2020). *Feminism, Interrupted: Disrupting Power.* (London: Pluto Press).

Parkes, N. A. (2010). *Tail of the Blue Bird.* (London: Vintage).

Parkes, N. A. [BlueBirdTail]. (2020, 13 August). Congrats on the book! I hope you do get to include it. Apart from being a beautiful phrase it embodies a philosophy about one's state of normalcy/rest: it's the way we were/are – it's our somewhere. That's why it's often the first phrase used when a big change is being described [Tweet]. Available at : https://twitter.com/ BlueBirdTail/status/1293980104188735488 (accessed 24 August 2020).

Pasquin, L. (2010). Poetry as breath: Teaching student teachers to breathe-out poetry. *LEARNing Landscapes,* 4(1), 255–263.

Perkins, D. (1999). The Many Faces of Constructivism. *Educational Leadership,* 57(3), 6–11.

Petersen, L. B. (2010). *Shakespeare's Errant Texts: Textual Form and Linguistic Style in Shakespearean 'Bad' Quartos and Co-authored Plays.* (Cambridge: Cambridge University Press).

Radio Times (2015). Selma star David Oyelowo: 'I had to leave Britain to have an acting career'. *Radio Times,* 7–13 February 2015.

Raffles, T. S. (1819). Minute on the Establishment of a Malay College at Singapore. Available from: https://eresources.nlb.gov.sg/printheritage/detail/ec629c60-58e9-40c6-847e-43d191da da47.aspx (accessed 20 August 2020).

Rankine, C. (2014). *Citizen: An American Lyric.* (London: Penguin).

Rawnsley, A. (2019). Like Macbeth, Johnson is too steeped in blood to turn back. What next? *The Guardian,* 8 September 2019. Available from: www.theguardian.com/comm entisfree/2019/sep/08/like-macbeth-johnson-too-steeped-in-blood-to-turn-back-what-next (accessed 20 May 2020).

Reay, D. and Wiliam, D. (1999). 'I'll be a nothing': Structure, agency and the construction of identity through assessment. *British Educational Research Journal,* 25(3), 343–354.

Rich, A. (1994). *Blood, Bread and Poetry.* (London: Norton).

Richards, I. A. (1929). *Practical Criticism.* (London: Kegan Paul Trench Trubner & Co.).

Riddell, S. L. (1992). *Gender and the Politics of the Curriculum.* (London: Routledge).

Rogers, A. (2015). Crossing 'other cultures'? Reading Tatamkhulu Afrika's 'Nothing's Changed' in the NEAB. *English in Education,* 49(1), 80–93.

Rosenblatt, L. (1978). *The Reader, The Text, The Poem: The Transactional Theory of Literary Work.* (Carbondale, IL: Southern Illinois University Press).

Rowland, C. A. (2014). The effect of testing versus restudy on retention: A meta-analytic review of the testing effect. *Psychological Bulletin,* 140(6), 1432–1463.

Royal Shakespeare Company. (2011). *The RSC Shakespeare Toolkit for Teachers: An Active Approach to Bringing Shakespeare's Plays Alive in the Classroom.* (London: A&C Black).

Saadawi, A. (2018). *Frankenstein in Baghdad: A Novel.* (London: Penguin).

Sandberg, S. (2013). *Lean In.* (New York: W. H. Allen).

Seeley, J.R. (1870). *Lectures and Essays.* (London: Macmillan).

Singh, J. (1989). Different Shakespeares: The Bard in Colonial/Postcolonial India. *Theatre Journal,* 41(4), 445–458.

Smith, E (2020). *This Is Shakespeare.* (London: Penguin).

Snapper, G. (2013). Exploring Resistance to Poetry in Advanced English Studies. In S. Dymoke, A. Lambirth and A. Wilson (eds), *Making Poetry Matter*. (London: Bloomsbury), pp. 31–41.

Snapper, G. (2018). Devolving English Literature in Schools: 'Non-Standard' Approaches to the Literature Curriculum. In A. Goodwyn, C. Durrant, L. Reid and L. Scherff (eds), *International Perspectives on the Teaching of Literature in Schools: Global Principles and Practices*. (London: Routledge/NATE), pp. 209–219.

Snapper, G. (2020). Why is my curriculum white? *Teaching English*, 23, 39–40.

Stead, C. K. (1964). *The New Poetic: Yeats to Eliot*. (London: Hutchinson).

Steele, S. (2014). Lifting Poetry off the Page. In S. Dymoke, M. Barrs, A. Lambirth and A. Wilson (eds), *Making Poetry Happen*. (London: Bloomsbury), pp. 17–27.

Stevens, J. (2018). From A level to HE: working towards a Shared Future? In R. Eagleston and G. Marshall (eds), *English: Shared Futures Essays and Studies 2018*. (Cambridge: D. S. Brewer), pp. 16–24.

Stevenson, A. (2017). *About Poems and How Poems Are Not About*. (Newcastle: Bloodaxe Books).

Stockwell, P. (2009). *Texture: A Cognitive Aesthetics of Reading*. (Edinburgh: Edinburgh University Press).

Stokes, L., Rolfe, H., Hudson-Sharp, N. and Stevens, S. (2015). *A Compendium of Evidence on Ethnic Minority Resilience to the Effects of Deprivation on Attainment*. (London: Department of Education).

Stredder, J. (2009). *The North Face of Shakespeare: Activities for Teaching the Plays*. (Cambridge: Cambridge University Press).

Taylor, C. (1994). The politics of recognition. In A. Gutmann (ed.). *Multiculturalism: Examining the Politics of Recognition*. (Princeton, NJ: Princeton University Press).

Taylor, D. B. (2020). For Black Men, Fear That Masks Will Invite Racial Profiling. *New York Times*, 14 April 2020. Available from: www.nytimes.com/2020/04/14/us/corona virus-masks-racism-african-americans.html (accessed 22 May 2020).

Teifouri, S. (2018). English Literature and Discursive Changes in Iran after the Islamic Revolution (1979). In A. Goodwyn, C. Durrant, L. Reid and L. Scherff (eds), *International Perspectives on the Teaching of Literature in Schools: Global Principles and Practices*. (London: Routledge/NATE), pp. 164–173.

Thein, A. H. (2018). Beyond the Personal and the Individual: Reconsidering the Role of Emotion in Literature Learning. In A. Goodwyn, C. Durrant, L. Reid and L. Scherff (eds), *International Perspectives on the Teaching of Literature in Schools: Global Principles and Practices*. (London: Routledge/NATE), pp. 55–67.

The Times (2014). Leader column. *The Times*, 5 February 2014, p. 26.

Thomas, K. (2006). 'Please can we have a man?': Male trainee English teachers entering predominantly female English departments. *Changing English*, 13(1), 137–150.

Thompson, G. and Bailes, S. (1926). The reliability of essay marks. *Forum of Education*, 4, 85–91.

Trouillot, M.-R. (1995/2015). *Silencing the Past: Power and the Production of History*. (Boston, MA: Beacon Press).

University of Cambridge Local Examinations Syndicate (UCLES) (1966). English Advanced Level Paper 2 (Shakespeare). (Cambridge: UCLES).

Vallance, E. (1974). Hiding the hidden curriculum: An interpretation of the language of justification in nineteenth-century educational reform. *Curriculum Theory Network*, 4(1), 5–22.

Viswanathan, G. (1998). *Masks of Conquest: Literary Study and British Rule in India*. (Delhi: Oxford University Press).

Wainwright, J. (2004). *Poetry: The Basics*. (London/New York: Routledge).

Walker, A. (2019). Two-thirds of Boris Johnson's cabinet went to private schools. *The Guardian*, 25 July 2019. Available from: www.theguardian.com/education/2019/jul/25/two-thirds-of-boris-johnsons-cabinet-went-to-private-schools (accessed 22 May 2020).

Warner. J. (2018). *Why They Can't Write*. (Baltimore, MA: Johns Hopkins Press).

Warner, L., Crolla, C., Goodwyn, A., Hyder, E. and Richards, B. (2016). Reading aloud in high schools: Students and teachers across the curriculum. *Educational Review*, 68(2), 222–238.

Weaven, M. and Clark, T. (2013). 'I guess it scares us'–Teachers discuss the teaching of poetry in senior secondary English. *English in Education*, 47(3), 197–212.

Westbrook, J., Sutherland, J., Oakhill, J. and Sullivan, S. (2019). 'Just reading': Increasing pace and volume of reading whole narratives on the comprehension of poorer adolescent readers in English classrooms. *Literacy*, 53(2). 60–68.

Wilkinson, R. and Pickett, K. (2010). *The Spirit Level: Why Equality Is Better for Everyone*. (London: Penguin).

Winston, J. (2015). *Transforming the Teaching of Shakespeare with the Royal Shakespeare Company*. (London: Bloomsbury).

Wyatt-Smith, C. and Murphy, J. (2001). What English counts as writing assessment? An Australian move to mainstream critical literacy. *English in Education*, 35(1), 12–31.

Yandell, J. (2008). Exploring multicultural literature: The text, the classroom and the world outside. *Changing English*, 15(1), 25–40.

Yandell, J. (2013). The social construction of meaning: Reading *Animal Farm* in the classroom. *Literacy*, 47(1), 50–55.

Young, M. (2009). Education, globalisation and the 'voice of knowledge'. *Journal of Education and Work*, 22(3), 193–204.

Young, M. (2014). Powerful knowledge as a curriculum principle. In M. Young, D. Lambert, C. Roberts and M. Roberts (eds), *Knowledge and the Future School: Curriculum and Social Justice*. (London: Bloomsbury), pp. 65–88.

Younge, O. (2019). From Overwhelmed to Empowered. In O. Younge (ed.), *A Fly Girl's Guide to University*. (Birmingham: Verve Words), pp. 163–172.

Xerri, D. (2017). Teachers' beliefs and literature teaching: The case of poetry. In B. Schaff, J. Schlegel and C. Surkamp (eds), *The Institution of English Literature: Formation and Mediation*. (Göttingen: V&R unipress), pp. 207–229.

INDEX

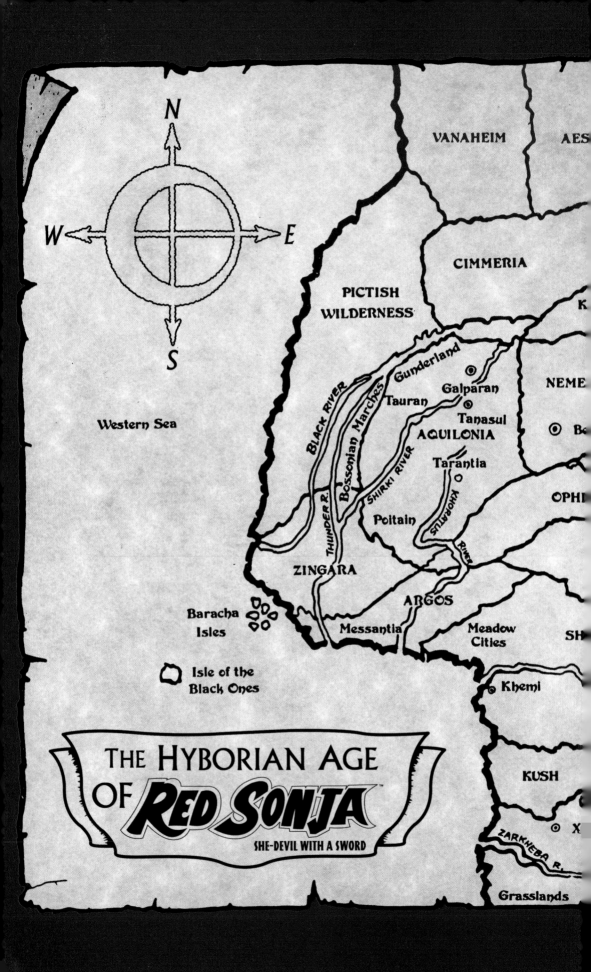

N

W   E

S

VANAHEIM

AES

CIMMERIA

K

PICTISH
WILDERNESS

NEME

Western Sea

Gunderland

Galparan

Tauran

Tanasul

AQUILONIA

Bo

Black River

Bossonian Marches

Shirki River

Tarantia

OPHI

Khoralus

Thunder R.

Poitain

River

ZINGARA

ARGOS

Baracha
Isles

Messantia

Meadow
Cities

SH

Isle of the
Black Ones

Khemi

THE HYBORIAN AGE
OF RED SONJA
SHE-DEVIL WITH A SWORD

KUSH

ZARKHEBA

X

R.

Grasslands

Dynamite Entertainment Presents

RED SONJA

SHE-DEVIL WITH A SWORD

Volume I

Dedicated to **Robert E. Howard**

- **WRITERS**
  MICHAEL AVON OEMING
  MIKE CAREY

- **ART**
  MEL RUBI

- **COLOR**
  CAESAR RODRIGUEZ (ISSUES 0-6)
  RICHARD ISANOVE (ISSUES 0-6)
  IMAGINARY FRIENDS STUDIOS (ISSUE 3)
  MICHAEL KELLEHER (ISSUE 4)
  BRIAN BUCCELLATO (ISSUE 5)
  BLONDE (ISUE 6)

- **LETTERING**
  RICHARD STARKINGS
  AND COMICRAFT

THIS VOLUME COLLECTS ISSUES ZERO THROUGH SIX OF RED SONJA: SHE-DEVIL WITH A SWORD.

BASED ON THE HEROINE CREATED BY
ROBERT E. HOWARD

EDITORIAL CONSULTANT
LUKE LIEBERMAN

SPECIAL THANKS TO ARTHUR LIEBERMAN
AT RED SONJA CORPORATION

DYNAMITE ENTERTAINMENT
NICK BARRUCCI   PRESIDENT
JUAN COLLADO   CHIEF OPERATING OFFICER
JOSEPH RYBANDT   DIRECTOR OF MARKETING
JOSH JOHNSON   CREATIVE DIRECTOR
JASON ULLMEYER   GRAPHIC DESIGNER

First Edition
Softcover ISBN-10: 1-933305-11-8 ISBN-13: 9-781933-305110
Hardcover ISBN-10: 1-933305-36-3 ISBN-13: 9-781933-305363
10 9 8 7 6 5 4 3 2 1

To find a comic shop in your area, call the comic shop locator service toll-free **1-888-266-4226**

WHOA! STEADY, THORNE. STEADY NOW.

HOO...OOOOO

WERE YOU FRIGHTENED BY AN OWL, SWIFT ONE?

OR WAS IT SOMETHING ELSE THAT STARTLED YOU?

AAAAAAGGH!

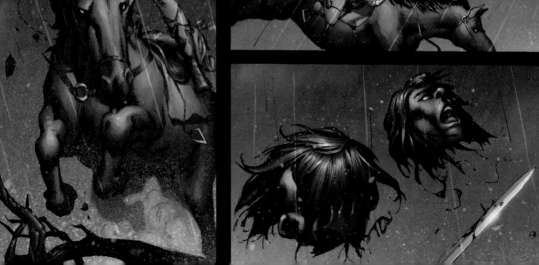

CAREFUL NEAR THE *WATER*, RED-HAIR... STRANGE BEASTS ONCE DWELLED THERE. NOBODY KNOWS IF THEY'RE GONE OR JUST *ASLEEP*.

GATHIA WAS LONG SINCE *CLEANSED* OF SUCH CARRION, BY OUR LORD --

DOES THIS *LORD* OF YOURS HAVE A NAME?

MY LIPS WOULD *PROFANE* HIS HOLY NAME! HE IS OUR SAVIOR!

HE *REBUILT* THE LAND AFTER THE FAMINE AND THE PESTILENCE. HE *PURIFIED* US -- GAVE US THIS PARADISE TO *DWELL* IN.

RAISED US *ABOVE* THE ZEDDAS AND THE *OTHER* BEASTS OF THE FIELD.

AND HOW DOES THIS *PARADISE* KEEP ITS PRIVACY? NO ENEMIES, NO THREATS FROM BEAST OR MAN. IS IT JUST THAT YOU'RE AS FAR FROM *CIVILIZATION* AS STYGIA IS FROM *HEAVEN?*

OUTSIDERS WOULD *DILUTE* OUR PURITY.

OUR LORD *CHOSE* US, THE BEST OF ALL THE TRIBES OF THE WORLD, LIFTED US FROM THE MUD AND GAVE US NEW LIFE. HE COMMANDS US TO GUARD...

ONLY THE FACT THAT YOU *SAVED* ME ACCORDS YOU A WELCOME.

AND STILL YOU *REEK* WITH THE SINS OF THE WORLD. YOU'LL HAVE TO BE *PURIFIED*....

...UNLESS YOU *DANCE* AS WELL AS YOU FIGHT.

GULP

GULP

NO!

AUUUGGH!

RRRRRA--

SHLKK

THOSE STRINGS
WILL LOSE THEIR
TENSION IF YOU
HOLD THEM TAUT
FOR TOO LONG.

NOW MIGHT
BE A GOOD TIME
TO LET THEM
REST.

I'VE HEARD
STORIES OF A
LONE FEMALE
WARRIOR... WITH
RED HAIR.

HER
REPUTATION
HAS BEEN A
BURDEN
TO ME.

YOUR
MESSENGER
WAS ATTACKED. I...
INTERVENED.

BUT THEN
HE SUCCUMBED IN
THIS LAND TO A
DARK MAGIC. SOME
THING FROM
THE WATER.

SO I BRING
HIM *HOME* TO
HIS REST.

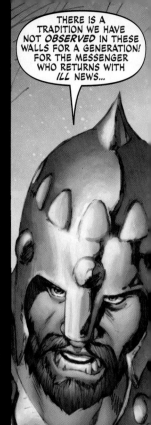

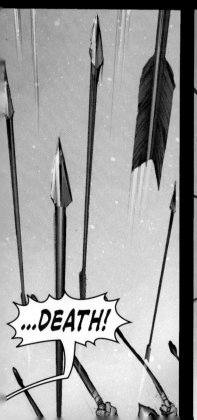

EYAAHHH!

KREEEE

FIRE.

ALL THESE YEARS, I'VE SEARCHED THE STARS FOR THE SIGNS, AND THEY HAVE FORETOLD HER COMING...

...BUT NOW I DOUBT MY READINGS...

...FOR NO ONE SURVIVES THE PIT.

TARIM'S BLOOD! THEY'VE THROWN ME DOWN LIKE A SCRAP FOR THE DOGS BENEATH THE TABLE.

BUT ANYTHING THAT BITES ON ME WILL WORK FOR ITS SUPPER.

AND YOU... USELESS AS ANY MAN I'VE MET...

RRRRR...

RRRRRRRGH...

ON SECOND THOUGHT...

PEACE TO YOUR SPIRIT, FRIEND -- BUT I NEED THIS MORE THAN YOU!

IT IS A FACT. A GIVEN.

LIKE THE FAITHLESSNESS OF WOMAN AND THE PULL OF FATE.

RRRGH... SNEF SNEFF... GUPH...

NO ONE SURVIVES THE PIT.

WHAT IS SHE DOING WITH THOSE ROPES?

PERHAPS SHE IS GOING TO HANG HERSELF.

I WOULD.

RAAAGH!

THOOM

FOOOM

BE STILL, DEMON-THING. AND I'LL PUT YOU OUT OF BOTH OF OUR MISERIES.

I BELIEVED NO MAN COULD SURVIVE THE PIT...

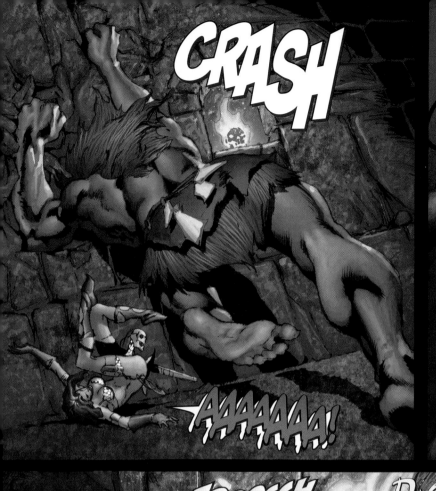

CRASH

AAAAAAA!

FOOOSSH

RAGHGHAHR!

ROOOOGH

AGH! CURSE IT!

RRRAAAH!

IT SEEMS MY FAITH IS TO BE TRIED IN THIS FIRE.

PERHAPS IN MORE WAYS THAN ONE.

URCHCH!

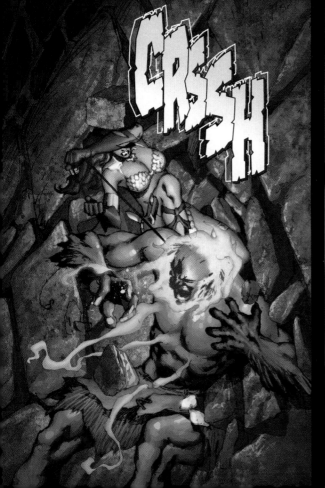

GRSSH

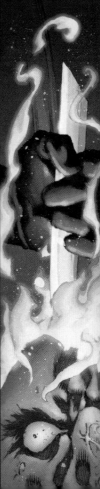

NO MAN...

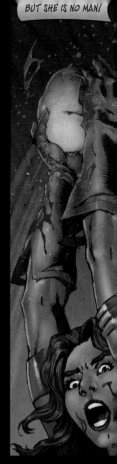

ONLY THE GREATEST WARRIOR WHO EVER SET FOOT
UPON THIS LAND COULD DO WHAT SHE HAS DONE.

TRULY, SHE IS THE ONE FROM MY VISION,
THE NAME WRITTEN IN THE STARS...

AND I NEED HER.

AAA...

WHICH PRESENTS ME WITH SOMETHING OF A DILEMMA.

I KNOW NOT HOW TO ANSWER YOU, CELESTIAL ONE. SHE IS EXCEPTIONAL.

HER DEEDS... HER SPIRIT...

COME, FA. ANY BERSERKER MIGHT WIN AGAINST ABSURD ODDS.

MASTER, THAT IS TRUE. AS ALL YOUR WORDS ARE TRUTH'S DISTILLED ESSENCE.

BUT TO DEFEAT THE OGRE, AND EMERGE FROM THE PIT UNSCATHED... THAT SPEAKS OF GREATER TALENTS.

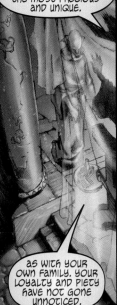

YOU PLEASE ME, FA AND YOUR WORDS REMIND ME THAT THOSE BROUGHT TO ME IN SACRIFICE ARE THE MOST PRECIOUS AND UNIQUE.

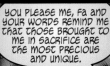

AS WITH YOUR OWN FAMILY. YOUR LOYALTY AND PIETY HAVE NOT GONE UNNOTICED.

TO SERVE YOU IS JOY BEYOND MEASURE, CELESTIAL ONE.

BUT... IT SEEMS UNLIKELY SHE IS A VIRGIN. AND IF MEN HAVE KNOWN HER, THEN PERHAPS SHE IS NOT FIT TO DIE FOR YOU AFTER ALL.

I SEE. OR IS IT THAT IF MEN HAVE KNOWN HER, FA MIGHT KNOW HER.

NOW I AM... DISAPPOINTED.

GUUUH!

CELESTIAL ONE, I--I AM SORRY TO HAVE DISPLEASED YOU.

IF I CANNOT ATONE, THEN LET ME BE SACRIFICED TOO, THAT I MAY AT LEAST --

NO, NO. THERE'S NO NEED FOR THAT.

I CHIDE YOU AS A FATHER CHIDES HIS SON, BUT LIKE A FATHER I LOVE YOU STILL.

AS FOR THE WOMAN -- WHY, THE TOUCH OF MY ALTAR WILL SANCTIFY HER. YOU UNDERSTAND?

...AH... OF COURSE.

NOW MASTER, THE ZEDDA REJECTED YOUR INVITATION TO SURRENDER, AND KILLED YOUR MESSENGER.

SHOULD I ASSEMBLE A RAIDING PARTY?

NO, FA. BUILD A DAM, TO BLOCK THE RIVER AT BROKEN STEP.

WHY SHOULD MY PEOPLE DIE IN BATTLE AGAINST THOSE DOGS? THE FLOODWATERS WILL KILL THEM JUST AS SURELY.

NOW GO, AND LET ME MEDITATE.

YOU MUST BE CLEANSED. SACRIFICE IS A WONDERFUL THING. YOU ARE BLESSED, I MUST AWAIT MY DAY.

GET... GET *AWAY* FROM ME, GIRL.

I'M SORRY, WOULD YOU PREFER A BOY?

NO ONE TENDS TO ME.

AND NO ONE *BOWS* TO ME. EVER. NOR SHOULD ONE BE FORCED TO BOW TO OTHERS.

SHE HOARDS HER SCREAMS AS A MISER DOES HIS COINS. SHE DENIES THE CROWD THE SPECTACLE OF HER SUFFERING.

BUT SHE CANNOT DENY ME.

SHE WILL BE MINE --

CRCK

-- EVEN IN DEATH.

SHE MUST HAVE WONDERED IF THIS WAS DEATH.

ROTTING FLESH. COLD SKIN... WET...

NO, NOT DEATH... OR AT LEAST, NOT HER OWN...

IT WAS SOMETHING ELSE THAT STOPPED HER BREATH.

UHHHH!

SOME LIVING HELL, VISITED ON HER BY HER PEOPLE'S UNFORGIVING GODS.

HHHHHHGHG!

LIVE BURIAL, THE FATE OF TRAITORS AND KIN-SLAYERS.

SHE COULD NOT REMEMBER BEING EITHER.

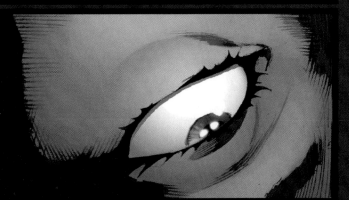

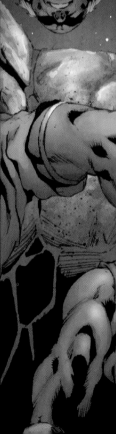

IS THAT HER?

YES.

BUT IS IT *HER?*

WE'LL KNOW THAT SOON ENOUGH.

LAY HER DOWN THERE, THEN LEAVE.

I'M SORRY I HAD TO LEAVE YOU IN THE PIT SO LONG.

WE HAD TO WAIT FOR THE RIGHT TIME FOR YOUR RECOVERY, AS THE CELESTIAL HAS MANY EYES.

EVEN NOW I FEAR HIS GAZE. NOTHING ESCAPES HIM.

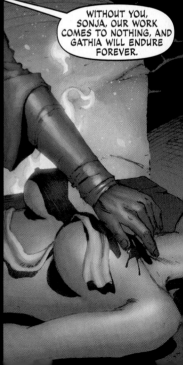

WITHOUT YOU, SONJA, OUR WORK COMES TO NOTHING, AND GATHIA WILL ENDURE FOREVER.

AHHH--

ASHA FALA ZHEZINZ

--WHERE?

SEINZ YIS...

...

...NOW YOU MUST RETURN TO US...

FLAMES?

ALL THAT NIGHT I SPOKE, HOPING SHE WOULD HEED MY WORDS.

I SPOKE OF HER DESTINY AND HER NEED TO FULFILL IT.

COME OUT NOW, SONJA.

YOU SEE? I SPOKE THE TRUTH. WE ARE IN DIRE NEED, AND ONLY YOU CAN HELP US.

I THOUGHT -- I FELT MYSELF DIE.

IT WAS I WHO BROUGHT YOU BACK FROM THE EDGE OF DEATH.

THE KNIFE I USED ON YOU IS THE BLADE OF THE VAVEN, THE ZEDDAS' GREAT IDOL. IT WAS A RUSE TO FEIGN YOUR DEATH.

IT IS ALL THAT KEEPS YOU ALIVE... FOR A WHILE, AT LEAST.

AND THEN?

IT WILL FALTER SOON, UNLESS RETURNED TO ITS PLACE UPON THE IDOL.

DONE QUICKLY, THE WOUND WILL HEAL. OTHERWISE --

OTHERWISE?

TRUE DEATH.

IF THIS IS YOUR WAY OF BUYING MY LOINS, YOU'D BEST KNOW THEY'RE NOT FOR SALE.

TOUCH ME, AND I'LL TAKE THIS KNIFE -- SACRED OR PROFANE -- AND HEW YOU INTO SLICES.

I'M A EUNUCH. I CAN SHOW YOU IF YOU LIKE.

I'LL LIVE WITHOUT IT.

IT'S TRUE THAT I HAVE USES FOR YOU -- BUT THEY'RE NAUGHT TO DO WITH RUTTING. YOUR COMING WAS SEEN IN THE STARS.

YOURS WILL BE THE HAND THAT ENDS THE CELESTIAL ONE.

RRRRRR

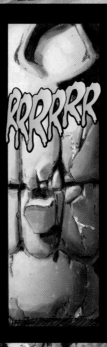

RRRRAAAAA

THESE BEASTS REJECT YOUR WORD, MASTER.

NOW IT IS TIME FOR THEM TO BE CLEANSED BY IT.

HOW MANY TIMES MUST I LEND OUT MY HAND IN PEACE, ONLY TO HAVE TO RAISE IT AGAIN IN DEATH? IF ONLY THEY WOULD HEED MY WORDS.

I COULD HAVE SAVED THOSE FILTHY THINGS.

FFFFFTT...
AH, WHAT?

ACK!!

AWAY FROM ME, YOU --

⸮ACK-HAKKK⸮, I SEE, ⸮HAKKK⸮, YOU'RE RECOVERED! ⸮COUGH⸮

YOU USED THE BLADE TO SAVE ME -- AND WASTED PRECIOUS SECONDS. FORTUNATELY IT WAS FOUR HEARTBEATS, NOT THREE.

BUT STILL YOU ALMOST DIED. I -- DRESSED THE WOUND AS BEST I COULD.

THANK... THANK YOU, OSIN. WHAT OF THE OTHERS?

DEAD. WE LOWERED OUR GUARD BECAUSE WE TRUSTED SOLATH. BUT THE LORD WORMS HIS WAY INTO MANY HEARTS.

I'LL MAKE MY OWN WAY INTO HIS... WITH COLD STEEL.

NOT WITHOUT ME, SONJA.

CRRACKA THROOM

GODS!
I CAN BARELY
SEE!

I'VE NOT
SEEN A DOWNPOUR
LIKE THIS SINCE I
WAS A CHILD!

DOGS
OF HELL...

WAIT, SONJA. BEST NOT TO DRAW UNTIL YOU KNOW WHAT WE ARE FIGHTING.

I'M GRATEFUL FOR YOUR SAFE RETURN, RED ONE. WE ALL ARE.

SAFE? SOLATH WAS A SPY FOR THE CELESTIAL! SHE KILLED MIKA AND KANG AND TRIED TO TAKE OUR HEADS.

I... I'M SORRY, SONJA. I KNEW HER FROM CHILDHOOD. I WOULD HAVE TRUSTED HER WITH MY LIFE.

AYE, BUT YOU TRUSTED HER WITH MINE.

HOW MANY MORE OF YOUR FRIENDS ARE EYES FOR THE CELESTIAL?

WHO CAN KNOW?

WHO CAN KNOW? THESE PEOPLE HAVE PLACED THEIR LIVES IN YOUR HANDS, FA.

LEARN TO KNOW. OR LET SOMEONE ELSE LEAD.

SONJA, THIS IS NOT THE TIME FOR US TO FIGHT AMONG OURSELVES.

THE HOLY ONE HAS BREACHED THE DAMS AND WASHED AWAY THE ZEDDA VILLAGES. THE SURVIVORS HAVE APPEALED TO US FOR HELP.

HELP? SINCE WHEN DO THE ZEDDAS SEEK HELP FROM MEN?

SINCE THE CELESTIAL DROWNED THEIR WOMEN AND CHILDREN. THEY'RE HUNGRY FOR REVENGE.

I'D ALREADY MADE OVERTURES — SUGGESTED AN ALLIANCE. NOW THEY SWEAR THEY'RE WITH US, SO LONG AS WE STRIKE AT ONCE.

THEN WE RUSH INTO DEATH. MOST LIKELY OUR OWN.

IS THAT A CHALLENGE?

PLEASE, WE HAVE ENEMIES ENOUGH WITHOUT --

FA, YOU WILL NOT HAVE US IF SHE BACKS DOWN FROM THIS CHALLENGE.

LEADERSHIP MUST BE WON, NOT GIVEN.

NO. FA IS RIGHT. WE'VE LOST ENOUGH MEN.

AYE. BUT ONE WOMAN IS A LOSS WE CAN STILL BEAR!

ARE YOU SATISFIED NOW? OR SHALL I KEEP ON CARVING?

HOW HIGH DO THE BODIES HAVE TO BE PILED BEFORE I EARN YOUR RESPECT?

GOOD THEN... BURY HIM.

MY MEN WILL ATTACK THE TOWER HEAD-ON, SUPPORTED BY ARCHERS TO RIGHT AND LEFT.

MEANWHILE SONJA AND OSIN WILL ENTER THROUGH THIS PASSAGE, HERE.

I WAS A SLAVE IN GATHIA FOR MANY YEARS. I ESCAPED MY DEATH BY USING THESE PATHS. I KNOW THE WAY.

YOU'LL SURFACE HERE, AND RISE THROUGH THE TOWER. IT WON'T BE EASY, THOUGH.

OUR ATTACK WILL DRAW OFF SOME OF THE GUARDS, BUT THE CELESTIAL SURROUNDS HIMSELF WITH DARK MAGICS AND FELL CREATURES.

SOUNDS LIKE FUN.

IT WILL BE MORE DANGEROUS THAN THE GATES. YOURS IS THE TRUE BATTLE.

TELL THAT TO YOUR TROOPS. I'M SURE THEIR DEATHS WILL FEEL REAL ENOUGH.

THEY GIVE THEIR LIVES WILLINGLY. FOR JUSTICE. FOR THE RECKONING SO LONG POSTPONED.

FA, YOU UNDERSTAND THE ZEDDAS ARE ONLY ALLIES AS LONG AS YOU HAVE A COMMON CAUSE. ONCE THE CELESTIAL IS GONE --

WAS IT NOT I WHO RETURNED YOU FROM THE DEAD? IF I CAN MOVE LIFE AND DEATH, THEN I CAN CONTROL THESE SAD CREATURES.

THEY'RE LIKE CHILDREN, AND THEY'LL RESPOND TO A FATHER'S CARE. I'VE READ THE SIGNS.

IF YOU'VE READ THEM *WRONG*, YOU'LL BLEED FOR IT. BUT AS YOU WILL.

SONJA --

YOU MAY FIND YOUR DEFINITION OF JUSTICE IS DIFFERENT FROM THEIRS.

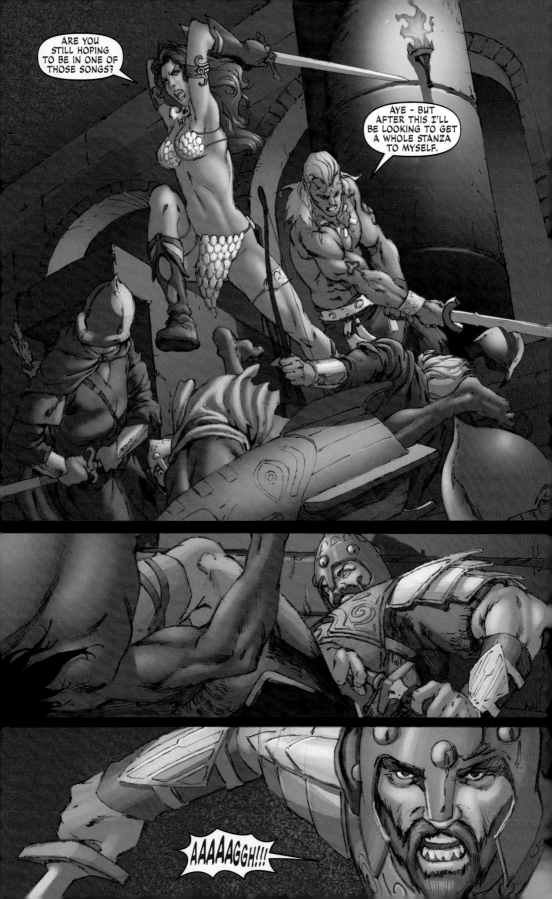

THUD

DONT LET THE DOOR SHUT, FOOL! WE'RE LOCKED IN!

PRETTY RED...

BLOOD... ...BLOOD FOR THE HOLY ONE.

SOME -- SOME ENCHANTMENT?

I KNOW NOT. BUT CHILDREN--! OSIN, I CAN'T--

AUCK!

THEN MITRA BE PRAISED. THIS IS BUTCHERS' WORK AFTER ALL!

BUT WHAT BLIGHTED WOMB BIRTHED THESE MONSTERS?

YOU SHOULD KNOW HIS EVIL BY NOW SONJA. THESE ARE THE FILTHY DROP OF THE CELESTIAL'S GOD, *THE BORAT-NA FORI!*

RRRAAAH!

I WISH HIS GOD HAD A THROAT TO BE SLIT!

LET'S MOVE.

WE'RE AT THE CENTER OF THE TOWER, HOW MUCH FURTHER DO WE CLMB?

AS FAR AS WE NEED TO. UNTIL WE REACH THE CELESTIAL, WE DON'T STOP.

GODS!... HEAT...

FA AND THE OTHERS MUST BE INSIDE THE CITY. AND NOW IT BURNS. THIS IS GOOD NEWS.

NOT FOR US. THIS OVEN MAY BROIL US IN OUR OWN JUICES.

AS LONG AS WE KILL THAT BASTARD, IT MATTERS NOT.

HUSH... DO YOU HEAR THAT?

I HATE IT WHEN YOU HEAR THINGS FIRST. SOMEHOW IT'S ALWAYS A PRELUDE TO DISASTER.

WHAT DO YOU HEAR? MUSIC? WINE BEING POURED?

HHHHHHHH

NOTHING SO SWEET....

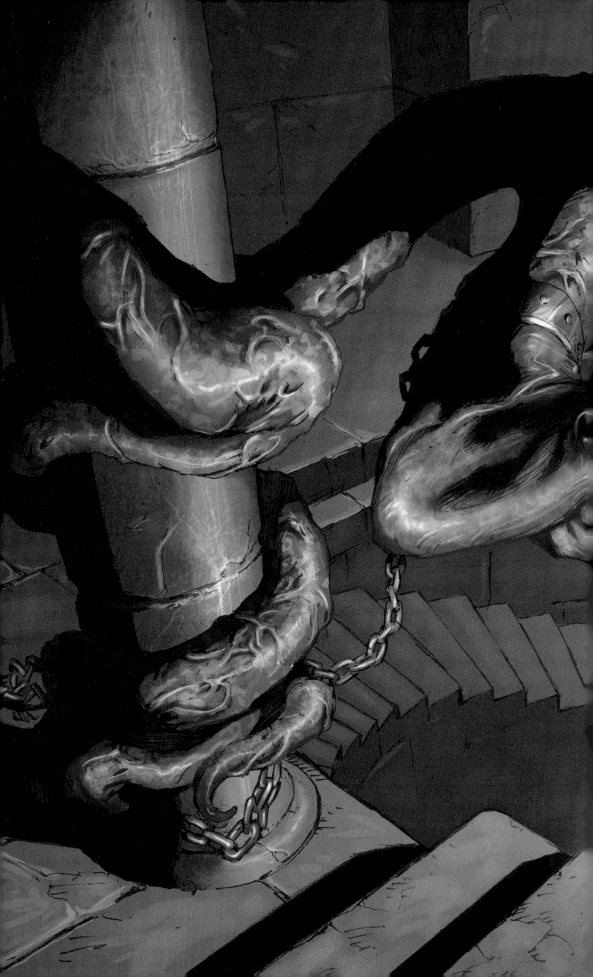

TING

SCALES ARE LIKE ARMOR! OSIN, GET BACK. THE DAMNED THING IS GOING TO --

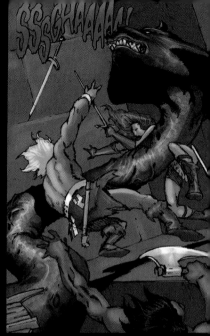

SSSCHAAAA!!

AAAAHHH!

SONJA! IT'S -- CRUSHING --

HHHH...

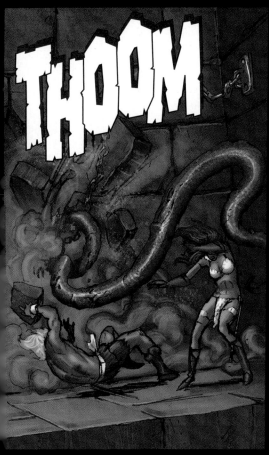

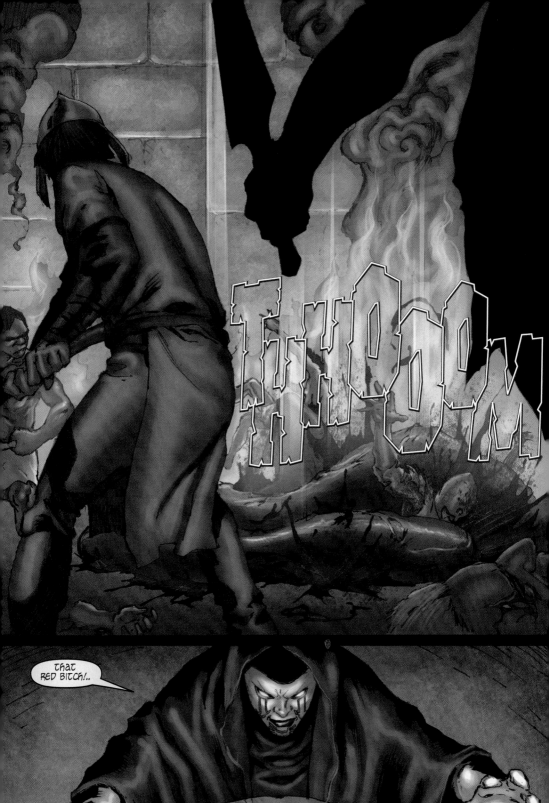

YOU... YOU GUIDED HIS BLOODLUST, SONJA... HE DIED SAVING US.

HIS IS A WARRIOR RACE. IT WAS THE DEATH HE WOULD HAVE CHOSEN.

WE CAN ONLY HOPE FA HAS DONE HIS PART WITHOUT LOOSING CONTROL OF THE ZEDDA...

LOOK BELOW, PAST THE FIRES.

IT'S EASIER TO LIGHT FIRES THAN TO PUT THEM OUT.

TRUE, BUT SOME THINGS HAVE TO BE BORN IN FLAMES. AND THIS BLOODBATH IS STILL BETTER THAN THE CELESTIAL'S "PEACE".

A GOOD PHILOSOPHY FOR A SWORDSMAN.

I'M MORE THAN THAT, SONJA.

AS I'M LEARNING.

AARRRR!

BLADES OF ERLIK! WHAT ELSE DOES HE HAVE TO THROW AT US?

CELESTIAL, I COME FOR YOU! FOR YOU!

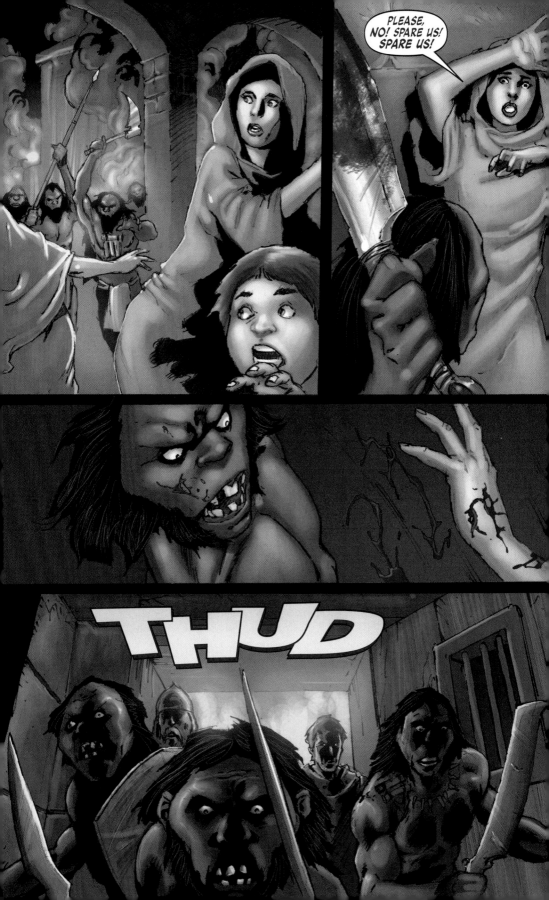

DEATH IS ALL YOU KNOW, SONJA. YOU RAISE YOUR SWORD FOR JUSTICE.

CHTING

THEY WILL BEGIN ANEW-- TO STAND OR FALL UNDER THEIR OWN WEIGHT, NOT HELD UP LIKE A PUPPET.

AND BRING THE TEMPLE DOWN ON YOUR HEAD. WHAT HAPPENS TO THE PEOPLE SONJA?

WHEN YOU CUT THE STRINGS, THE PUPPET COLLAPSES.

THCK

UGHF!

AND THE PEOPLE WILL BECOME ENTANGLED IN THE STRINGS OF WAR, FEAR, AND HATE.

I ENDED ALL THAT. HOW MANY CITIES HAVE YOU SEEN LIVING IN SUCH PEACE?

YOU MEAN TO DESTROY THESE PEOPLE, NOT SAVE THEM!

...MY FURY WAS ANSWERED BY A GODDESS, WHO BLESSED ME WITH THE POWER TO DESTROY THE SERVANTS OF EVIL, IF ONLY IT WERE THAT SIMPLE.

MERCY, PLEASE! MERCY!

WE SAW YOUR SLAVE PITS, WOMAN! IF YOU WANT TO BEG--

BEG FOR A SHARPER BLADE WOMAN!

NO, NO FOOLS-- COOL YOUR BLOOD! WE WILL NOT KILL THE INNOCENT!

BWWAAA-AAA!

THOOCKT

WAAA-KKT

AAAAA!

LONG HAVE BEEN CRUSHED UNDER A GATHIAN BOOT! WE WANT BLOOD NOW FA, WE WANT JUSTICE!

UGGHGH!

NEIGHBORING TOWNS HAVE COME HERE TO DEFEND GATHIA, I WILL FIND A PRIEST AND GIVE MYSELF TO SACRIFICE--

THESE FILTHY DOGS WILL NOT ROB ME OF THAT!

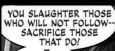

YOU SLAUGHTER THOSE WHO WILL NOT FOLLOW-- SACRIFICE THOSE THAT DO!

I KNOW YOUR EVIL!

I AM THE HOLY PROPHET OF BAROT-na FORI!

THE BLOOD OF A *THOUSAND* SACRIFICES FLOWS THROUGH ME...

AND IT IS MINE TO COMMAND!

SONJA!

FOOLISH WOMAN!

THE GOD YOU SEEK TO DESTROY IS NOT ONLY IN MY HEART, BUT THOSE OF MANY WIZARDS, WARRIORS AND KINGS!

DESTROY ME AND YOU WILL CHASE BAROT -NA FOR! IN CIRCLES!

YOU ARE BUT AN ANT AGAINST AN ARMY!

THAT'S TWO ANTS, ZEDDA!

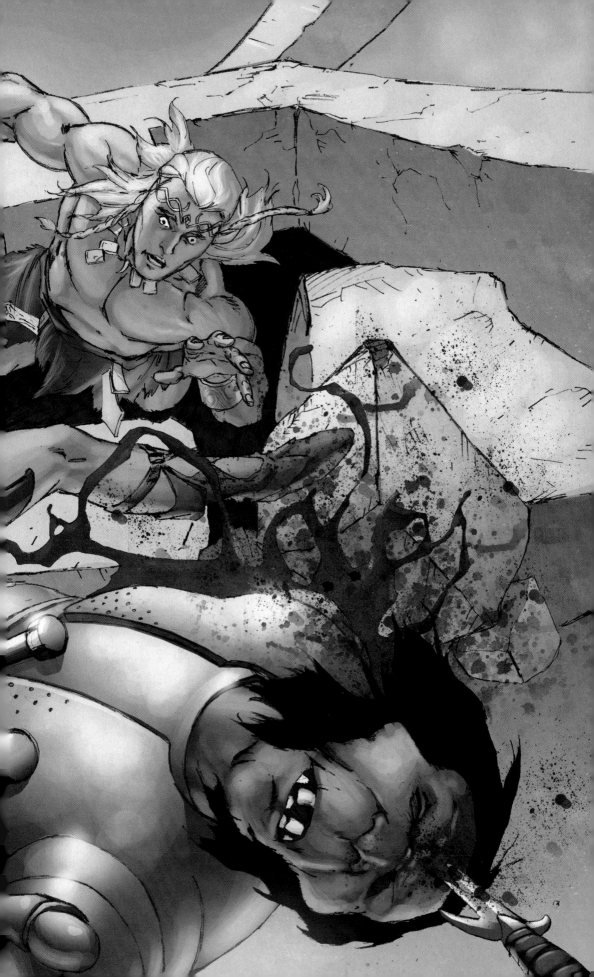

SPLOOSH

ᚦCUAHGHGᚦ
ᚦAHCKOUGH!ᚦ
OSIN!

YOUR WISH IS FULFILLED, FA.
GATHIA IS FALLEN.
THE CELESTIAL IS DEAD.

OSIN!

OSIN, YET ANOTHER BRAVE WARRIOR TO DIE AT MY SIDE.

THESE PEOPLE ARE NOW FREE TO BE THEMSELVES FOR GOOD OR ILL.

FA HAS RAISED THE ZEDDA BLOOD INTO A FIRE, AND I'M SURE IT HAS CONSUMED HIM...

...THAT LUST WILL QUELL IN TIME, BUT WHAT THEN?

RRAAAAA...

WHAT WILL BECOME OF THEM NOW?

WILL IT BE PEACE, OR WILL WAR BLOSSOM AGAIN AND AGAIN WITH EACH PASSING SEASON?

SSHTCK

WHAT HAVE I DONE HERE? REPLACED THE IRON GRIP OF "PEACE" WITH ANARCHY?

ONLY TIME WILL TELL.

OSIN?

I HOPE YOU PASS TO YOUR GODS IN PEACE AND THEY WELCOME YOUR NAME.

MY NAME HOWEVER... RED SONJA. I THOUGHT IT WAS FOR MY FIRE HAIR, BUT NOW I KNOW.

IT MEANS BLOOD... DEATH TO MY ENEMIES, AND MY FRIENDS...

I LEAVE A RED WAKE BEHIND ME. RED FOR DEATH. RED FOR ANGER. RED FOR BLOOD.

RED SONJA... I CURSE THAT NAME...

THAT GIRL... THAT SLAVE GIRL...

EVEN NOW, SHE SEARCHES FOR THE OTHER PRIESTS OF THE BORAT-NA FORI...

...STILL WILLING TO PAY IN BLOOD, FOR A LITTLE PEACE.

SHE CAN LEAD ME TO THEM, AND THEY TO THIS DARK GOD'S NEXT SERVANT OF POWER.

I WOULD HAVE TO AWAIT THE RIGHT MOMENT, BIDE MY TIME.

THE TOWN SHE SEEKS WAS DRAINED OF ITS MEN, DRAFTED FOR GATHIA'S ARMY...

IT WILL BE NEARLY EMPTY, BUT FOR THE PRIESTS, THOSE WHO CAN LEAD ME TO THE NEXT SERVANT OF THE DARK GOD...

There was a storm...

A storm with red winds. Fire and blades were in it.

It came to a forest and left one tree standing.

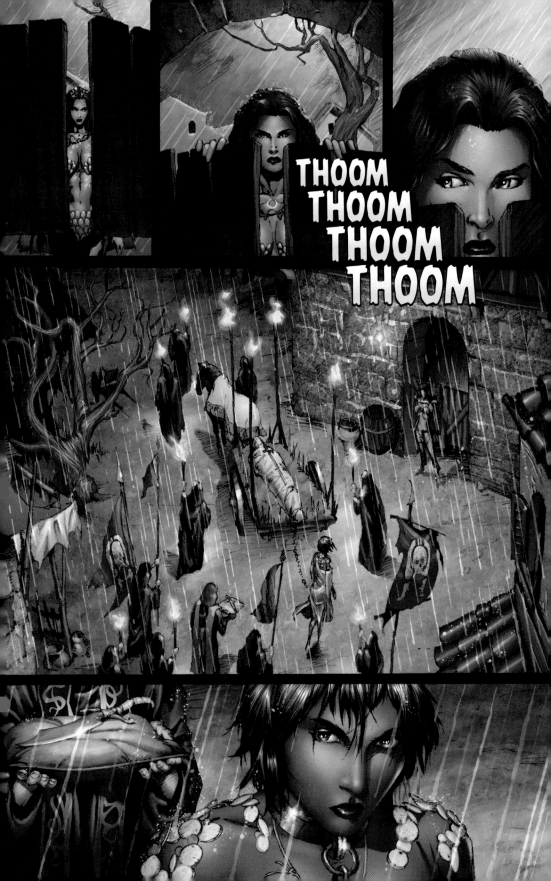

THOOM
THOOM
THOOM
THOOM

SHKT

SHUMP

She was white and red, like sand on fire.

The storm had blown in. If only I had known, I would have run... or poisoned her drink.

WE ONLY HAVE THE "ALL KINDS," DRIPS OF EVERYTHIN', BUT IT PACKS A PUNCH.

YOU PASSING THROUGH OR STAYING?

CLINK CLANK

THEN KEEP IT FLOWING.

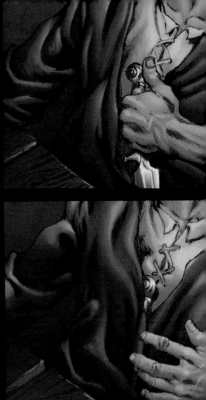

PASSING THROUGH. I CAN TELL.

SECOND SIGHT? OR JUST THE NORMAL KIND?

I *NOTICE* THINGS. COMES WITH THE JOB.

I don't know why I did it. They said they'd hurt me, if I didn't.

But men have hurt me before. That wasn't it.

I think -- part of me wanted it. The part of me that belongs here.

The part of me that prays to him and cheers on the sacrifice.

RRRAAAAAA!

...but the winds had shifted and the eye was gone!

UGH!

THUMP

THUMP THUMP

AIEEE

COVER GALLERY

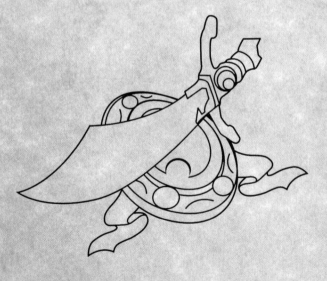

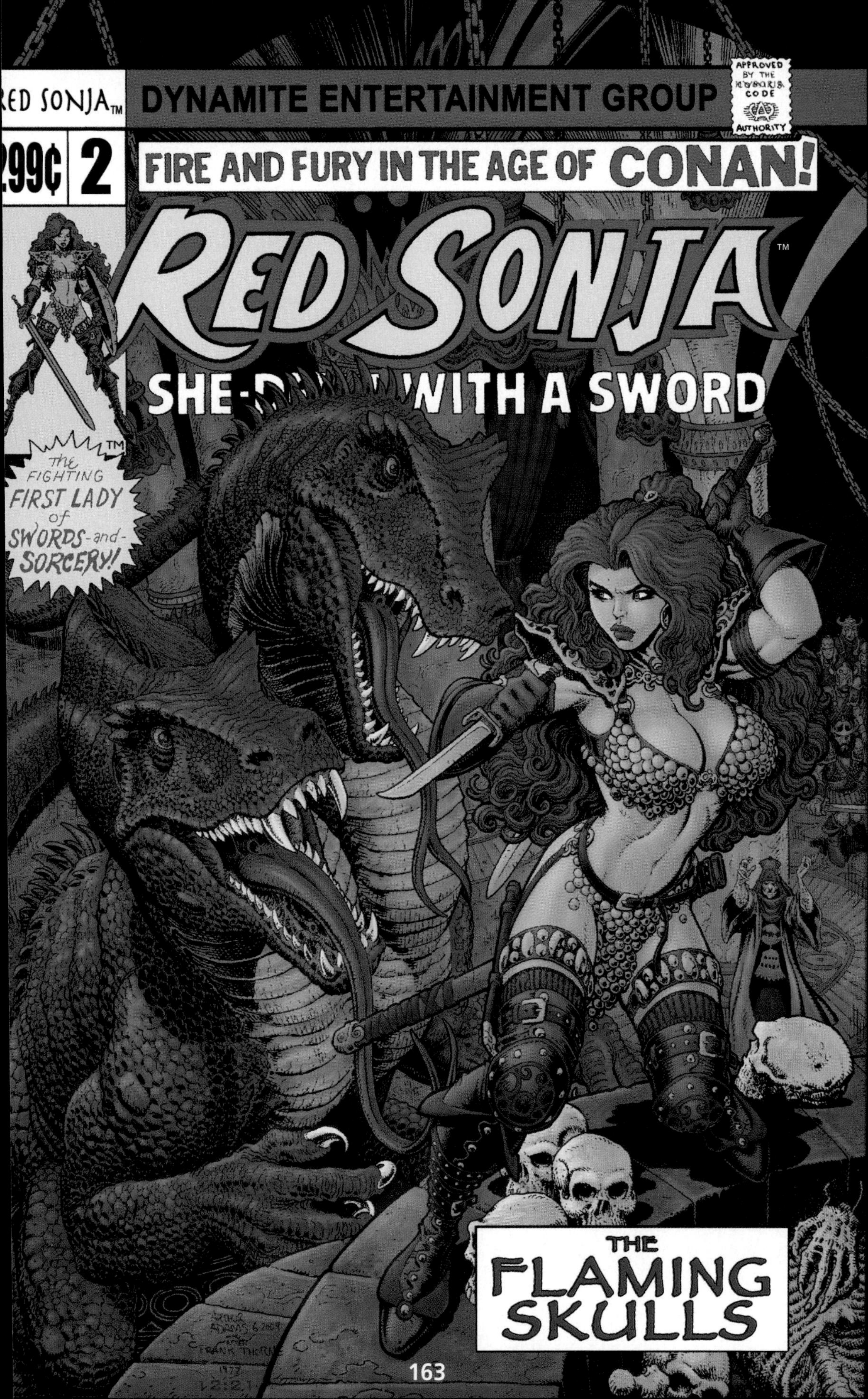
RED SONJA™
DYNAMITE ENTERTAINMENT GROUP
APPROVED BY THE
CODE
AUTHORITY
299¢
2
FIRE AND FURY IN THE AGE OF CONAN!
RED SONJA™
SHE-
WITH A SWORD
™
the FIGHTING FIRST LADY of SWORDS-and-SORCERY!
THE FLAMING SKULLS

© FRANK BRUNI '02
José Villarrub

RED SONJA BY THE NUMBERS FROM WRITERS MICHAEL AVON OEMING AND MIKE CAREY.

Oeming: Hey this is fun stuff, and quite self indulgent, which makes it even more fun. First, I'll attempt to tell you how much I enjoyed working with Mike Carey, but I know I'll fail miserably because I no longer have Carey reworking my dialogue to become poetry. I would guess if he were here, he'd change it to "…Carey reworking my dialogue into poetry…"

It was great talking to Carey long distance (though my phone bill would disagree) about Red Sonja, and even better working with Carey on the actual scripts. It was a pleasure Mike. I'm looking forward to our next "thingie" (place appropriate Mike Carey Correction here).

OEMING: This was scary. I felt like a cat falling out of a tree blindfolded, just hoping we would land on our feet. It's a "Zero" issue, an introductory issue with a limited number of pages to re-present to you a character you sort of know without being a cliché of things you've already encountered. PLUS, we decided this issue should tie in with issue 6, our final issue of the first arc- and yet we didn't have that story yet! Not completely anyway.

Not to mention everyone would be comparing Howard's "red-headed step-child" to Conan, who came out of the gate with an amazing issue #0.

CAREY: I admit to being conflicted about the ass-shot. On the one hand, it's a cinematic device that's stylishly used here to open the story out and feed the situation to the reader in intriguing chunks. On the other hand, it's an ASS-SHOT! And I'd been going round the forums saying how much more there was to Sonja than T&A. I'll get you for this some day, Mel...

OEMING: First thing's first -- Sonja has a reputation, the whole T&A aspect. I thought it would be best to address it right away as well as defusing it. I think that's all in Mel's art. There it is, right away, this really nice butt-shot, but at the same time, its not slutty, its not even sexual. That's what we needed to do. Sonja is sexy, but she doesn't pose, she's not a stripper or a slut. Well, maybe she poses for the covers a bit, but those are covers. We decided to treat her sexuality as a weapon in the series, and we'll even find ryme and reason for the seeming madness of wearing a chain mail bikini in later issues. Then we see the ruined town, and a hanged man at the gates

CAREY: But then here we are with the splash, and whatever you think of Sonja's bum (love it or loathe it) it's clear that this is a woman with a really commanding presence, who makes the workd meet her on her terms. Great rain effects. Perfect facial expression - cold, haughty, not giving a millionth of an inch.

OEMING: The smart thing do to was just forget about all the baggage. Just come up with a theme, and the story would come. Who is Sonja? What is she in this world?

Well, she's a force, someone nearly unstoppable, like a storm, once the idea of the storm came, the rest fell into place. Carey and I also knew we wanted to present Sonja as a morally ambiguous character- at least to the modern reader. Compared to everyone else in her world, she's the freakin' Madonna, and I'm not making a pop culture reference here. So we wanted to do something relatively horrible, defiantly questionable, and yet within the context of the story, completely acceptable.

CAREY: We played out Page 3 in silence, this is like a scene from a Sergio Leone movie. If you were that archer, wouldn't you have thought about your wife and kids and decided to clock off early for once?

CAREY (Page 4): still with the western influences, right up until the point where Sonja pushes open those hinged, saloon-style doors. But when she turns at the sound of the drum, we're in a whole other world, and it's a very dark one. Funeral processions in the driving rain: living sacrifices walking alongside dead warriors. It takes a lot to shake Sonja's cool, but the look that passes between her and the slave girl is an index to a lot of memories, a lot of associations.

CAREY (Page 5): The kiss. This isn't Sonja: the sacrifice embraces her own death, and Sonja changes her mind about a bloody intervention. You can't save people against their will. This was very much Mister Oeming's scene, and it speaks volumes to me about the cultural divide between Sonja and the place where she finds herself. I can't imagine there'd be many things she'd find more nauseating than a willing victim.

CAREY (Page 6): Our third female protagonist introduced - the barmaid, Jessa. She's also the narrator, but we don't realize that until we get to this point - the give-away being "or poisoned her drink". Jessa is as alien to Sonja as the sacrifice outside is - again, a product of her culture who's learned to survive by rolling with every blow. That's the central opposition of the story: survival through surrender set against survival by fighting until you drop.

CAREY (Page 9): And now the stage is set, more or less. But we haven't yet seen Sonja interacting with a man. Here we see her unromantic, coldly pragmatic view of battle as she picks up the toast of a sot who can barely stay upright. Terrific body language here, both on Sonja's part and on the drunk's. "Hail to the heroes..." Sonja's answer to that would probably be the same as Marshall Law's: "haven't found any yet."

CAREY (Page 10 and 11): As we built to the climax, we wanted to suggest a lot of time passing and open up the possibility that Sonja might actually be incapacitated by booze and unable to defend herself. The big panel at the top of page 11 is a terrific moment - the men staring down on Sonja's apparently sleeping form - but in some ways the hinge that the whole story turns on is that last panel: the detail of the dark god. Jenna kisses it, just as the woman walking in the funeral procession did. She accepts her fate instead of pushing against it, and it's here that she parts company from Sonja.

CAREY (Page 12 and 13): In a scene like this, choreography is everything. The two flights of arrows divide the pages and punctuate the action. Sonja reacts to both with whatever is readiest to hand. Necessity is the mother of invention, and Sonja is the meanest mother of all.

OEMING: I feel bad for the character from whom we are witnessing the events- Jessa. I wonder if we will ever see her again? I almost feel bad for the town itself, despite that they all try and kill Sonja. They town has been emptied for a war near by, a war sparked by Sonja. We'll learn more about this war in the next six issues and what lead up to the town's demise. This was the set up for issue Zero, Six issues later, we would come back to this exact same place and time, but how, we did not know yet. It would take a lot of planning.

CAREY (Page 7): We wanted the barmaid to be more than just a cypher. She's beaten down by her job and her life, but not beaten flat. Sonja is prepared - at least at first - to meet her as an equal. Look at that lovely facial expression in the final panel - coquettish, but with no real confidence behind it. Or is it just that she finds it hard to meet Sonja's gaze directly? Either way, her sidelong glance contrasts with Sonja's frank, direct one.

CAREY (Page 8): Again, it was important to get the interplay between the two women right, and Mel did a sweet job. Envy, fear, avid curiosity: you can see the way the barmaid's feelings about Sonja keep shifting, while Sonja's own reactions are momentarily dropped into the background.

CAREY (Page 14): Remember the end of High Plains Drifter? That's what's going on here. Ultimately, it's not just the killers who pay for what was done to Sonja, it's everyone who stood by and watched or assisted in an advisory capacity. When you take on the She-Devil, there are no sidelines.

CAREY (Page 15): What I loved about this was the sudden change in the palette - the chill of the morning after is right there on the page. That's the note we were aiming for: the ashes and the ruins and the naked realisation of your own inadequacy that comes after you've sold yourself for what turns out to be less than the market rate.

OEMING: Carey and I knew certain events would take place in the first six issues- there would be fighting, there would be a wizard, there would be a war. We wanted to give readers a Sonja story with all the traditional traps, but give everything a fresh twist. A villain who was beneficial in many ways, and a hero who would actually cause a lot of harm, that would be a good place to start, and the rest would follow that idea, flipping every cliché on its ear- or so we would hope.

By issue SIX, we were really pleased to have tied it in with issue Zero, like a great joke, a good story often ends best where it started...

Mel Rubi
SKETCHBOOK

"I wanted to give Sonja a new style with these sketches that we all haven't seen. Starting with her boots, I gave it a look that had some manga influence in it. Also I wanted it to extend with leather up to the mid thighs. Her armor is decorated with jewels which I thought looked kinda cool." -- Mel Rubi

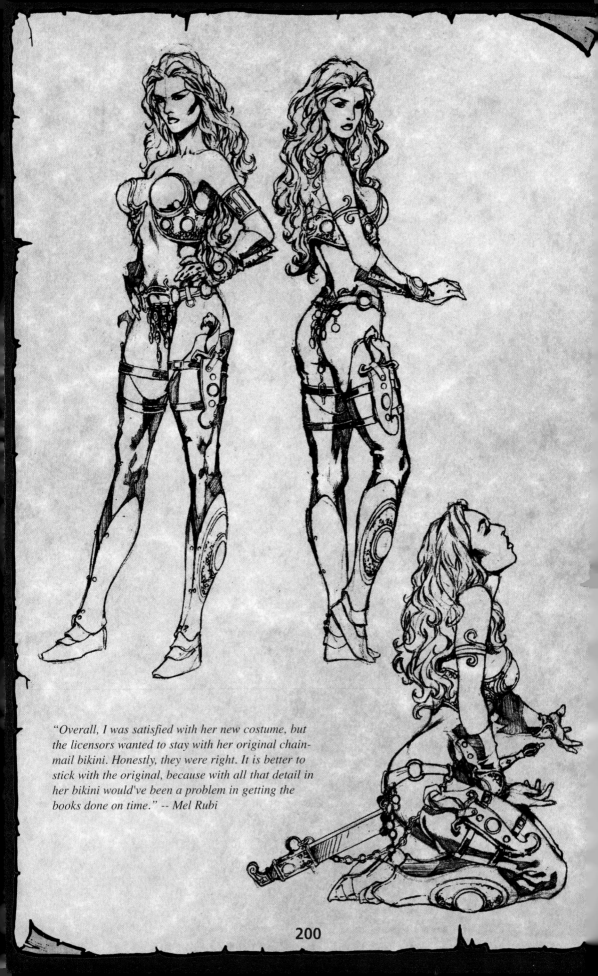

"Overall, I was satisfied with her new costume, but the licensors wanted to stay with her original chain-mail bikini. Honestly, they were right. It is better to stick with the original, because with all that detail in her bikini would've been a problem in getting the books done on time." -- Mel Rubi